PRAISE FOR RICHARD B. SCHWARTZ

Proof of Purchase

It's like this guy is just channeling Raymond Chandler on every page. . . . The ending . . . would make Mike Hammer proud.
— Jochem Steen, *Sons of Spade*

In this engaging hard-boiled mystery, one of three in Schwartz's Jack Grant series (Frozen Stare; The Last Voice You Hear), the seasoned California PI looks into the disappearance of an ex-girlfriend at the request of the woman's husband. When her mutilated body turns up in the woods, Grant makes it his mission to track down her murderer. With the assistance of Lt. Diana Craig, an attractive fast-riser in the San Bernardino police department, Grant follows leads that point to his client, as well as to a consortium of underworld bosses who are branching out into a mega-real estate project. The pair find time, between car chases and gun battles, to begin a relationship. . . . Fans of Robert Parker will enjoy encountering Grant . . . .
— *Publishers Weekly*

The Last Voice You Hear

It's not often that an author's second book is as good as the first, and even less frequent are the instances when an author . . . top[s] it with an extraordinary second . . . deliver[ing] a walloping good tale as well. Richard B. Schwartz has done just that. In *The Last Voice You Hear*, Mr. Schwartz places himself on par with our finest contemporary murder-mystery writers. This is a book you won't want to miss. . . .
— Alan Paul Curtis in *Who Dunnit*

The author . . . writes vividly, putting the reader right into the scene. Schwartz explores the meaning of right and wrong, crime and justice.
— Mary Helen Becker in *Mystery News*

The story rockets along . . . a fast-moving, well-told story with a surprising conclusion that blurs the line between crime and justice.
— Joseph Scarpato, Jr. in *Mystery Scene*

Jack Grant, the Vietnam vet and Pasadena-based PI who debuted in Frozen Stare (1989), returns in this engrossing sequel by Schwartz, author of several scholarly studies of Samuel Johnson. Schwartz knows his London, but surprisingly he evokes California with equal ease, mainly with vividly etched strokes. An apparently maniacal killer is on the loose in London, someone strong and very practiced at impalement. So far, so nasty. But when a victim is dispatched in similar fashion in Disneyland, of all places, Jack Grant is called in. He discovers the killer's identity, but there's a problem: there's a method to the killer's madness. Moreover, Grant has an ethical problem of his own: he's plagued by his conscience, since he understands and even sympathizes with the murderer's cause. The cinematic climax takes place high above the floor of the California desert, and Schwartz squeezes every last drop of suspense from his setting. . . . The result is a high-tension thriller awash in sanguinary detail. Paper towels, anyone?
— *Publishers Weekly*

Frozen Stare

I welcome Richard Schwartz to the club. It's been a long time since I've seen two more engaging characters entering the series scene.
— Sandra Scoppettone

Grant and White play nicely off each other and the switch-on-a-switch works well.
— *Kirkus Reviews*

This tale, in the California private eye tradition, has a rousing finish and is an enjoyable read.
— *Publishers Weekly*

A new author devoted to the hard-boiled tradition. . . . Schwartz has the hard-boiled formula down pat. . . . Schwartz does not break any rules in Frozen Stare. . . . He writes crisply. The narrative moves at a slam-bang pace as bodies pile up. . . . As a dedicated student of the hard-boiled school of detective fiction [Schwartz] has learned his lessons well.
— *The Washington Post Book World*

Gives a whole new meaning to the phrase 'cold-blooded murder'. . . . This is a quick read with plenty of action. Schwartz's first novel is a winner!
— *Sarasota, FL Herald Tribune*

This is a delightful tale, full of amusing touches, and the relationship between Grant and his good cop friend, black Frank White, is a joy. I hope that Schwartz can keep this standard up for a long time to come.
— *The Armchair Detective*

Nice and Noir: Contemporary American Crime Fiction

Opinionated but always fascinating, shrewd and smart, but always readable. . . .
— *The Thrilling Detective*

BOOKS BY RICHARD B. SCHWARTZ
FICTION

The Jack Grant Novels

Frozen Stare
The Last Voice You Hear
Proof of Purchase

The Tom Deaton Novels

Into the Dark
The Survivor's Song
Nightmare Man
Death Whispers
Poison Touch

CRITICISM

Samuel Johnson and the New Science
Samuel Johnson and the Problem of Evil
Boswell's Johnson: A Preface to the Life
Daily Life in Johnson's London
After the Death of Literature
Nice and Noir: Contemporary American Crime Fiction
The Wounds that Heal: Heroism and Human Development
(with Judith A. Schwartz)
ed. The Plays of Arthur Murphy, 4 vols.
ed. Theory and Tradition in Eighteenth-Century Studies

MEMOIRS

The Biggest City in America: A Fifties Boyhood in Ohio
Accidental Soldier: A Reserve Officer at West Point in the Vietnam Era
Postwar Higher Education in America: Just Yesterday

EBOOK

Is a College Education Still Worth the Price? A Dean's Sobering Perspective

A TOM DEATON NOVEL

POISON TOUCH

RICHARD B. SCHWARTZ

DARK
HARBOR
BOOKS

POISON TOUCH

Published by Dark Harbor Books
First Edition 2022

Cover design: Jana Rade

ISBN: 979-8-9855721-2-4 Paperback Edition
          979-8-9855721-3-1 Hardcover Edition
          979-8-9855721-4-8 Digital Edition

Library of Congress Control Number: 2022904071

Author services by Pedernales Publishing, LLC
www.pedernalespublishing.com

10 9 8 7 6 5 4 3 2 1

Printed in the United States of America

v9

For Vincent James, his mother, grandmother and great-grandmother.
Welcome to a world of strong women.

Alas, the love of women! it is known
To be a lovely and a fearful thing.

Byron

I

SADDLEBACK

ONE

Checking his watch, thinking to himself as he approached the emergency room lane, looking for the yellow line that guides you to the battered double doors ... *this is definitely not going anywhere good. Everything calm for a minute; then suddenly I pull up; they're all over me like health inspectors on a new restaurant and the rest of my day is shot. Three of them visible from here. Probably orderlies ... shooting the breeze, looking up at the sky, looking toward the highway, waiting for the next ambulance or the next family van with the husband with the hastily-wrapped hand and the wife screaming about all the blood ... none in sight yet; all they've got coming in is me ...*

Now two nurses taking a break, waiting for some action, standing around smoking; how can they do that? They see that thick, black goop in the lungs, hear those people hacking and gasping, maybe even smoking through one of those throat rings after they've had a tracheotomy or whatever it's called. It's those colored shirts that they wear now ... too informal, too laid-back; when they had the starched uniforms and those little folded cap things pinned in their hair, the rubber-soled shoes and the white hose ... they couldn't be holding a cigarette, not dressed like that. Oh well, shouldn't judge I guess, maybe they need it ... after the stuff that they see--the broken glass in peoples' eyes, the kitchen knife wounds, the addicted babies, the untreated skin cancers ... but still ...

Anyway, I have to do something. I can't leave him in the truck and I can't stick around for a sitdown with the admitting woman with the old computer with the pictures of her grandkids taped to the sides or the 'patients' advocate' with the clipboard and the endless list of prescribed questions. I'll pull up and three seconds later they'll all be on me, wanting to call the highway patrol or the local cops, making reports, asking more questions, making more reports, calling somebody from the local press corps …

*Maybe I shouldn't worry. It's not like **I've** committed any crime. I'm trying to play the good Samaritan here, the one who stopped to help, to do the right thing … but the company pays me to drive over the road, not to make stops and pick up the halt, the blind and the wounded. My quota is already short and I can't make up the time tomorrow. I've got to unload him and head back to Phoenix. The dispatcher doesn't hand out any attaboys for good citizenship; he just checks logs and certifies arrivals and departures. If you stay sober, protect the truck and deliver on time you might get an occasional nod.*

It doesn't look as if I can get in there with this rig anyway. I'll pull over to the edge of the lot, position myself so they can't see the plate numbers easily, and get them to focus on him rather than on me. Diversionary maneuver. Tell them that they should take care of him first. Then I'll be right back. Gotta call my dispatcher, tell him where I am and what's happened; then I'll be right with them … answer all their questions, fill out all their forms … do whatever they need me to do.

Wait a second … the orderly on the left is signaling to me. Have to signal back. Give him a thumb's up, then the index finger: 'I see you … it's cool … just gimme a minute … I'll be right with you.' Can't drive away fast … better give him the index finger again, along with a smile. OK, he's coming over with his buddy …

"Yes, he's in my truck, over there on the edge of the lot … he's in the bed behind the driver's seat where I sleep. I strapped him down so he'd be comfortable and not roll around. I'll show you how to get to him, even help get him out if you'd like me to."

"That won't be necessary, sir," the orderly said. A tall, black man, his nametag read **Calvin Tompkins**. "We'll get a gurney and meet you there. We'd appreciate it if you didn't touch him."

"I understand. Not a problem."

It took three orderlies to lower him onto the gurney. One of the nurses had felt around for neck injuries before they moved him. "Where did you find him, sir?" she asked.

"On the east edge of the 5, a few miles down the coast; I saw him just as the sun was coming up."

"Did you try to administer any aid, sir?"

"No, I just verified that he had a pulse, then checked my Garmin, found your hospital and drove straight here. He was breathing evenly and I didn't see any obvious wounds … I covered him with the blanket that you saw there …"

"He doesn't appear to have any neck injuries."

"He was just off the burn, lying facedown, his shoulder leaning against some brush. I was concerned about moving him, but I figured it was important to get him to a hospital."

"And you lifted him by yourself?"

"Another truck stopped. The driver helped me."

"We'll need you to help us complete a report …"

"I understand. Let me call my dispatcher, tell him I've lost an hour or so and that I'll be a few minutes late with my delivery."

"Where are you headed?"

"L.A., then over to Vegas."

"And your name, sir?"

"Jim Jeffers."

TWO

Still feel a little guilty about the 'Jim Jeffers' lie, but I couldn't give them my real name. Another hour there and I'd never get caught up again. Plenty of people want these jobs these days and if you've got one and need it you've got to hold onto it. I couldn't just leave him lying there in the dirt, but I couldn't devote the rest of my life to his recovery either. It wasn't really that big of a lie, more like a fib. I use that name all the time. If I'm talking to a realtor or any of those people that keep calling you back until either you or they die ... I'm Jim Jeffers. It sounds American enough. A little unique, not like Bill Brown or John Smith. And it's always Jim, not James. Easier when they're trying to bond with you. Makes them feel more comfortable. Never met anybody actually named Jeffers. There was a Jeffords back in Ashtabula. Ralph Jeffords. Mailman. Nice man. Don't know where the Jeffers came from. It always seems to work though.

Well, here we are in beautiful downtown City of Industry. Sky looks about the same as it did the last time, a soft light brown with pale yellow accents. I'll drop off the auto parts, pick up some valves and head back to Phoenix.

"My God, that's Dr. Barnes," the nurse said, her voice rising as she spoke his name. Her name tag read **Carol Draper, R.N., MSN**. She wore the starched white uniform that the trucker remembered fondly.

"Yes, Carol," the ER nurse answered. "We didn't notice at first, because of the dirty hair and the beard growth. We were focused on cleaning him up and determining what was wrong with him. I mean ...

we would never have expected to see *him* like this. He's always so meticulous about his appearance."

"Who brought him in?"

"A truck driver. He found him by the side of the road, down on the **5**."

"Where's the contact information?"

"I don't think they got any. The driver dropped him off and got back in his truck and drove away."

"You didn't even get a name?"

"Oh yes, we did get a name. I believe it was Jeffers."

"Has anyone called the police?"

"I believe that Dotty did."

Dotty Blaine was the admitting officer. She called Carol Draper 'Nurse Draper', who in turn called her 'Dorothy'.

"I'm told that the man who brought in Dr. Barnes left without leaving any contact information."

"That's true, Nurse Draper. He told Nurse Kinley that he needed to call his company dispatcher. He wanted to tell him that he'd be late with his delivery. The nurse and the orderlies brought Dr. Barnes to the ER. When the driver didn't return promptly, one of them checked on him. I believe it was Mr. Tompkins. He went outside and said that the truck had pulled away."

"And did anyone get a license number?"

"I'm afraid not, Nurse Draper. They were all focused on bringing Dr. Barnes into the ER and giving him immediate attention."

"And you've called the police?"

"Yes, ma'am. I spoke to the desk sergeant and then spoke directly to Chief Dietrich. I gave him the driver's name—Jim Jeffers—and told him that Mr. Jeffers said that he would be making a delivery in Los Angeles and then driving to Las Vegas."

"And is he sending someone?"

"Yes, ma'am, he said that he would send one of his lieutenants, I suppose because Dr. Barnes serves as the Medical Examiner for Laguna Beach. They work with him all the time."

"Yes. Thank you, Dorothy. Let me know immediately of any further developments. I'll be waiting for the results of the ER team's evaluation."

Lieutenant Tom Deaton arrived seven minutes later. He was greeted just inside the door to the ER by Nurse Sarah Ritter. They still dated occasionally, but each had moved on psychologically. More than friends but not quite boyfriend/girlfriend, there was still some perceptible warmth.

"We don't know anything yet, Tom. They're doing some bloodwork."

"Is he awake?"

"No, he's comatose."

"Comatose?"

"Yes, I'm afraid so."

"They said he was found by the side of the road."

"Yes, beside the 5. That's what the truck driver said at least. Did they tell you he was naked?"

"No, they didn't."

"He was dirty and unshaven. He looked like an abandoned, homeless person."

"Who's in charge of the ER, Sarah?"

"Dr. Rawson. Emily Rawson."

"Is she with him now?"

"I think she's waiting for the results of the bloodwork."

"Thanks."

He found her, badged her and introduced himself. She was drinking coffee from a cardboard cup and offered him some. "Thanks," he said and sat across from her at a desk in the corner of the ER.

"He was nude, Lieutenant. I can't remember the last time I saw Len Barnes without pressed slacks, starched shirt and a tie. He was unkempt. He looked like a derelict."

"Any wounds or marks on the body?"

"No significant bruising or puncture wounds. His body was dirty but there were no signs of trauma except for ..."

"Except for?"

"Some marks around the ... anus. No tears or significant abrasions."

"Really?"

"Yes, but no sign of sexual assault. There was nothing unexpected on the swab. There are any number of possible explanations ..."

"I understand," Tom said. "And he's comatose?"

"Yes ..." Just then a nurse approached them. "What is it, Leslie?" Dr. Rawson asked.

The nurse looked at Tom before speaking. "This is Lieutenant Deaton, Leslie," Dr. Rawson said. "He's making enquiries concerning Dr. Barnes."

"Hello, Lieutenant," she said. He smiled and said hello in return. The nurse handed Dr. Rawson a slip of paper and said, "Dr. Barnes's blood alcohol level is off the charts, Doctor."

The doctor looked at the numbers and stood up. "I've got to go," she said. The nurse waited for a second before following her. "Alcohol poisoning," she said to Tom. "It can shut down the body's involuntary functions."

"Like breathing," he said.

"Yes, and the gag reflex. It stops you from choking. If he begins to vomit ..."

"I understand," he said.

"We'll do what we can. Dr. Rawson is excellent."

"Thanks, I appreciate that," he said and went outside to make a call.

THREE

Her cell phone went to voice mail; he left a message and tried her office phone. No answer. He checked her departmental number and hit the call button.

"Department of Anthropology," a female voice answered.

"This is Lieutenant Tom Deaton of the Laguna Beach PD. I need to speak with Dr. Cornell immediately."

"Just a second, Lieutenant. I'll try to track her down."

She returned in thirty seconds. "Dr. Cornell is in class, Lieutenant. I can give you her cell phone number if you wish to leave a message."

"I've already done that," Tom said. "It's an emergency. I have to speak with her at once."

"She's teaching in another building and I'm here alone with the work/study student. I'll ask him to run over and ask her to call you. Just give me a number where you can be reached."

In the meantime he called Chris Dietrich and briefed him on Len Barnes's condition. Seven minutes later Sally Cornell returned his call.

"Tom, it's Sally, what's up?"

"Hi, Sally," he said, not trying to alarm her. "When was the last time you talked to Len?"

"Last Saturday," she said, her tone becoming suspicious. "I'm coming up to see him tonight. What's happened?"

"As far as I know he's not in immediate danger, Sally. He's in the ER at Saddleback and receiving good care."

"Give me the whole story, Tom," she said.

"He was found early this morning on the side of the **5** by a truck driver, who brought him to the ER. There are no signs of significant injury, but his blood alcohol level is high and he's … he's in a coma, Sally."

"Tom," she said, pausing, "Len doesn't drink."

"That's what I thought," he responded.

"What was he doing when the driver found him, just lying there?"

"Facedown, actually. He wasn't wearing any clothes, Sally. He hadn't shaved in several days and his body was … dirty."

"That makes no sense at all," she said. "I'll be there as fast as I can."

"I'll call you if there are any changes," Tom said. "In the meantime, drive carefully. I'm here with the attending physician and my friend Sarah is working in the ER, so I'm up to date on all developments and doing all that can be done."

"I understand," she said. "I'll see you soon. Thanks so much for calling me."

He went back into the ER and asked one of the nurses if there had been any personal effects found with Dr. Barnes.

"No, Lieutenant; he was found … completely … alone. The truck driver wrapped him in a blanket that he had in the bed in his truck. You know those big semi's; they have a sleeping space behind the driver's seat … "

"Yes," Tom said. "Where is the blanket now?"

"It's in a box over by the nurses' station. We thought the driver might come back for it."

"Has it been cleaned in any way or shaken out?"

"We didn't really have any time to do that, Lieutenant."

"That's good," he said. "I'm glad you didn't."

"We've all seen CSI, Lieutenant."

"I understand," he said. "Thanks."

"It's smudged and there's some grit, but there may be something else still on it. They can find a lot these days."

"Yes," he said. He refilled his coffee cup and called Detective Hector Campo.

"What can I do for you, Lieutenant?" Hector answered, checking the caller i.d. before speaking.

"Dr. Barnes, our ME, was found by the side of the **5** this morning by a truck driver. He's in a coma, but that's not for public consumption. I'd like to talk to the driver. He was en route to L.A., almost surely from San Diego and his next stop was Vegas. No one got his license number; he left the hospital while they were taking Len into the ER."

"Do we have a name?"

"Jim Jeffers."

"I'll check with the major companies and see what I can find out. It may take a little while …"

"I understand," Tom said. "I know how many trucks there are heading toward L.A. on the **5**."

"Is Dr. Barnes stable, Lieutenant?" Hector asked.

"I'm not sure that's the right word," Tom answered. "He's not moving. His body is functioning, for now."

"I'll start calling those companies," Hector said.

"One other thing," Tom said. "Would you send a patrolman to pick up something. It's a blanket. Dr. Barnes was wrapped in it by the truck driver. When he was found he wasn't clothed. Forensics might be able to find something on it that would be helpful."

"I'll do that, Lieutenant. I'll have him call you on your cell when he's approaching the hospital."

FOUR

Tom persuaded Sally Cornell to leave the ER lounge for a few minutes to get something to eat. "We can go out," he said, "or go to the hospital cafeteria."

"The cafeteria's fine," she said. "I don't have much of an appetite. Maybe just some coffee …"

"They're using the word *stable* now," Tom said. "That's a step up."

"With alcohol poisoning it's not just a matter of time," she said. "You know the clichés … sleep it off … walk it off … things don't just get better. Sometimes they get worse. If there's alcohol remaining in the stomach it can take awhile to get into the bloodstream. Still and all, it should be through him by now …"

"I never saw him take a drink," Tom said.

"A month and a half ago … when I was given that award by UCSD … Len came down. There was a reception. The only nonalcoholic thing that was offered was some kind of nasty punch with foam floating on it. The department sprang for some decent wine and the chair brought in part of his single-malt stash. Len took one of the plastic cups and filled it with water at the drinking fountain. It wasn't that he couldn't tolerate wine or Scotch and it wasn't that he didn't like the taste … it was more of a professional thing. He thought of himself as always being on call and wanted to be ready to enter the operating room at any moment. Damn it. I'm talking about him in the past tense …"

"Like a pilot," Tom said, "only they stop drinking 24 hours before a flight. One of my college friends flies for Delta now. He's always looking at his watch. If it's 24 hours and 10 minutes until his flight he won't take a sip from a beer. 'I don't want to leave any of it, so I won't start on it,' he'll say."

"So let's be straight about this," Sally said. "If he had alcohol in his system someone forced him to drink it. Either that or he was suffering so deeply (or about to suffer so deeply) that he took it as an anesthetic."

"Sometimes a small amount can hit a non-drinker hard," Tom said, "but a non-drinker would be unlikely to drink enough to cause alcohol poisoning. He'd pass out first. And Len would know all about the quantity and its likely effect. It's not as if he was a teenager breaking into his father's liquor cabinet …"

"Something terrible has happened," Sally said. "I know it …"

"You talked to him last on Saturday. What did he say he was doing? I checked with the hospital; he wasn't scheduled for any surgeries …"

"He was going to take a couple days off," she said. "He wanted to look for a new condo. His is great for just him, but when I visit it's a little cramped. And he wants me to leave more of my things there … you know him, Tom; he's very conservative. It's his way of saying that he wants to take our relationship to the next level."

"And you're fine with that …"

"Absolutely, but I didn't want to push … he said he was thinking about getting a larger place, a place where we'd be more comfortable. I told him I thought that would be great."

"So he was househunting."

"Yes, but I'm not sure he had actually contacted a realtor. A lot of the properties have models that you can visit. He wanted to do some initial looking, gather some brochures and then talk to me about it."

"I doubt that he made it," Tom said. "I looked in on him briefly. I'd say he had at least four days of whisker growth. He wouldn't have talked to builders' reps or realtors without shaving."

"No, he's always 'on'," Sally said. "He's *Dr.* Barnes, surgeon. I don't mean that he's arrogant or self-important. He just wants to project that professional posture. 'You never know who may need me to operate on them,' he'd say."

"So he'd cleared his calendar to do the initial screening; then the two of you would huddle before moving on to looking seriously at possible properties."

"Exactly," she said, "but something happened first and he was unable to do that."

"But what?" Tom asked. "And if *you* don't know, who would?"

"No one that I can think of," she said. "This was something out of left field, something totally unexpected."

"Two possibilities." Tom said. "Either he walked into something unexpected or ..."

"Or someone dragged him into it."

"Yes."

"Tom, when the ER team is comfortable with it ... I want to examine him."

"I'll make that happen. You're our consultant as well as his friend."

"I brought my things. I'll get them from the car."

FIVE

Hector called to report on the Jeffers search. "He must have given a false name, Lieutenant. I've talked to every major company that does business in sunny southern California and none of them have a driver named Jeffers. One Jeffords, but his first name was Norman. One Jephorson. Also named Norman; what are the odds on that? Anyway, I've got a Plan B. I'll talk to the people at Saddleback who saw him and try to put something together using CompuSketch. While I'm doing that I'll ask one of the uniforms to get the email addresses of the company dispatchers; I'll shoot the picture to them and see if any bells start to ring."

"Excellent," Tom said. "How soon can you get here?"

"Let me chase down a laptop with the software … maybe twenty minutes."

"I'll have them ready for you when you arrive. Anything from forensics on the blanket?"

"Not yet. I told them to call you directly."

"Good. See you in twenty."

Tom and Hector had joked about the updated version of their facial identification software and the workshop they sat through with the artist from UCI who kept drawing pictures of his cousins and brothers-in-law to illustrate standard criminal faces. Now Hector would be putting his classroom knowledge to work.

Sally was sitting in the ER lounge, waiting for the green light from Carol Draper to do her personal examination. "She's a forensic anthropologist," Tom had told her. "She works with the LBPD and the LBPD ME on a regular basis. I need to have her opinion."

"I was under the impression that she was a *personal friend* of Dr. Barnes's," Nurse Draper responded.

"It won't cloud her judgment," Tom said. "And it's not as if she's going to operate on him."

"Very well," she answered, "if you think it best."

Ten minutes later forensics called. "Lieutenant, Officer Emerson here."

"Yes, Susan. What have you got?"

"Not a great deal, I'm afraid. The dirt smudges on the blanket are consistent with the dust and grit we see in this area. A little head and body hair from two different donors, probably some from the truck driver and some from Dr. Barnes. No blood, no semen, not even any saliva. No vomit (thankfully) …"

"How about alcohol?"

"Nope," she said. "And no food crumbs or tobacco. A tiny bit of deodorant residue, probably from the truck driver. There was a grease stain, smaller than a fingertip, probably from the truck driver. And no insects or evidence of insect presence. As these things go, it was very clean. A blanket from the back of a truck … you could find a whole world of nasty there. We'll keep looking, Lieutenant, but so far there's nothing here that would occasion any big surprises. If you could bring us some of Dr. Barnes's hair, we could confirm that some of what we found here is his."

"Will do," Tom said. "Thanks."

"Always a pleasure," she said and clicked off.

Tom freshened his coffee and called Chris Dietrich. His phone rolled to voice mail and Tom left a message, bringing him up to date on their progress, such as it was. When he returned to the ER lounge, Sally was gone. He went to the 'room' off the ER, a space enclosed with a sheet that afforded some privacy to Dr. Barnes. He pulled back a corner and saw Sally exploring Len's mouth with a tongue depressor and small flashlight. "I'm just getting started," she said. "I'll see you in the lounge in a little while. Give me at least thirty minutes."

"OK," Tom responded and walked over to Nurse Draper's station. He explained to her the use of the facial identification software and the fact that he needed Calvin Tompkins and the other orderlies and nurses who saw the truck driver to meet with Detective Campo and help him create an image of the man's face.

"Certainly," she said. "I appreciate the fact that that Mr. Jeffers or whatever he called himself took the trouble to bring in Dr. Barnes. Not everyone would have done that, but at the very least he could have given us proper contact information. There's a small meeting room in the corner of the ER, Lieutenant, just over there (pointing). I'll have them there when you need them."

Tom checked his watch. "Detective Campo should be here in about ten minutes."

"They'll be ready."

"Thanks very much," Tom said.

"Dr. Barnes is a fine man, Lieutenant," she said. "We're prepared to do everything that we can to help you find whoever did this to him. I've known him personally for eight years. The strongest thing I've ever seen him drink is a caffeinated cola drink. If you ask my opinion …"

"Yes … ?"

"Someone was trying to put Dr. Barnes in a compromising position. They were trying to humiliate him, to destroy his reputation, to ruin him personally and professionally."

"That is certainly consistent with the evidence so far," Tom said.

"Then we must do everything that we can to find that person and bring him to justice. Such behavior is … completely unacceptable. It's intolerable. It's … disgusting."

"I agree, Nurse Draper."

"I'll ask Sarah to keep you informed," she added, "unofficially, of course."

There are few secrets here, he thought to himself as he returned to the lounge.

Twenty-five minutes later Hector approached him, carrying a laptop. "It wasn't too difficult," he said. "They all agreed. He looks like Owen Wilson with a normal nose. Have a look …"

"Even the hair and eyes look like him," Tom said. "And no baseball cap or sun glasses. That helps."

"I would have liked a unique cap," Hector said, "but if he had one he left it in the truck cab."

"Good work," Tom said.

"I'll shoot the image to the dispatchers ASAP," Hector said. "When I know anything I'll let you know."

"I'll be here," Tom said.

SIX

Sally was still conducting her examination of Len's body. Tom checked his phone for any messages and then picked up one of the wrinkled magazines from an adjoining table. It felt as if it had been handled by a thousand people, none of whom had washed their hands within recent memory. He thought about the *Field & Stream*, but he wasn't in the mood to look at hunters holding up the heads of dead deer. He passed on the *AARP* magazine, even though it touted itself as enjoying the world's largest circulation. Instead, he picked up a year-old copy of *Sports Illustrated*, most of whose predictions for the 'coming' season had proven to be false. He liked the 'Faces in the Crowd' section, with the accounts of high school athletic prowess, kids in the boonies breaking records and conquering teenage awkwardness at the same time. So many seemed to be clean-cut, fresh-faced and from Iowa …

"Tom." The word interrupted his concentration and he looked up to see Sarah Ritter standing above him.

"Sarah … sit down."

"I can't. I've got a five-minute break, just enough time to throw down some coffee." The ER urn was empty, so they went to the machine in the hallway.

"I'll buy," he said, checking the prices on the dispenser as he reached in his pocket for coins.

"Just black for me," she said. "I don't know what that stuff really is that passes for cream."

"The 'whitener'?" he answered. "You probably don't want to know."

He handed her the first cup. She held it in both of her hands, warming them against the cool air of the ER and the draft of the hospital corridor. The thin wisps coming off the surface smelled vaguely like actual coffee.

"I wanted to tell you ... "

"Yes ... ?"

"I wanted to tell you that I told them to wait before they cleaned him up ... that there might be some evidence that the police would want to collect ... but they thought it best to clear away the dirt and clean up the matted hair, in case there was a wound site that might go unnoticed. And they *did* have the blanket ..."

"I think the blanket will be fine," he said, "not that there's much evidence there, but anything of value would probably have transferred to it. Better to save his life first and solve the case later, assuming that there is a *case*."

"I don't think he would have chosen to go for a drunken, naked walk by the side of the freeway, do you, Tom?"

"No, not Len Barnes. We get addle-headed nudists on an occasional basis, but never with his standards of behavior and sense of responsibility."

"Anyway, I wanted you to know that I tried to protect the evidence, whatever there was of it."

"I appreciate that. By the way, I just talked to Nurse Draper. She said that you'd keep me up to date on his condition ... off the record, of course."

"The Draper gossip network is better than anything the KGB, Stasi, CIA and MI6 have even hoped to develop. Her theory is that an Emergency Room is a little world unto itself and if she is to run that world (and she *does* believe that *she* runs it), she has to understand it in all of its details."

"In a police station like that the officers would leave false clues and leak false information, just to bait the watch commander or desk sergeant."

"I can't say that it hasn't happened here also," she said, releasing a slight smile. "Anyway, I have to get back to work. Thanks for the coffee."

"You've only taken two sips."

"Sometimes I only take one," she said. "Unless you anesthetize your mouth first …"

"I understand," he said, "it's pretty rank."

"And such small portions," she added, as she turned and walked down the hall.

"Joking in the darkness; it's what they do," he said to himself as he returned to the lounge.

The *Sports Illustrated* was gone, but there was no one else sitting in the lounge except for an elderly couple and a young Latina woman with an infant in her arms. His cell phone twitched and he went outside, setting his coffee cup on the arm of a wooden bench. "Deaton," he said.

"Susan Emerson, Lieutenant," the voice said. "We found something else on the blanket, but it's probably no big deal."

"What have you got, Susan?" Tom asked.

"Just the slightest trace of alcohol. That's no surprise, of course, not if he had been drinking or if someone had forced it on him. There *was* enough of it to transfer to the blanket. Just a tiny, tiny amount."

"Can you tell what it was—bourbon, scotch, gin?"

"We're in a pretty speculative area here, Lieutenant, but we think it may be mother-in-law's vodka."

"The kind to keep her quiet?"

"Yes. People put it in punch. It's 190 proof, but they have to call it something, so they call it vodka. It's basically pure alcohol. What did that writer say, 'Candy is dandy, but liquor is quicker'? This stuff would be instantaneous."

"Thanks, Susan, that's very helpful."

"I figured you'd want to know, Lieutenant. If we find anything else we'll give you a quick buzz … but probably not as quick as the one this vodka would have given Dr. Barnes."

He took out his book, made a note of Susan Emerson's call, finished his cup of coffee and returned to the lounge. Sally was there, pacing. She looked upset.

SEVEN

"I need to talk to you, Tom," she said, "right away, someplace private."

"Let's find a quiet corner in the cafeteria," he said. "How is Len?"

"His vital signs are good," she said, "but there's no indication of awareness. I talked to him on the off chance that he might hear me, even if he couldn't acknowledge it …"

They found a table that was open but hadn't been cleaned. Tom removed a tissue from his pocket and wiped it off. "Coffee?" he asked.

"Yes," she said. "Thanks."

He returned with it and sat opposite her.

"Why didn't you tell me what had happened to him, Tom?"

"You mean the slight abrasions …"

"Yes."

"I didn't think they were severe enough to indicate some sort of sexual assault. I thought there might be a more mundane explanation …"

"Like cheap paper or something …"

"Yes," Tom said. "There's another possibility though."

"If he wouldn't ingest the alcohol orally …"

"Yes," Tom said. "It happened among the Russians, the ones who were tired of waiting for the workers' paradise, the ones who lived on vodka rather than hope—the desperate ones in search of an instant escape."

"Not quite like White Burgundy by candlelight, is it?" she asked.

"No, it's not," he answered.

"But it would work. If he resisted they could force it on him that way. All they'd have to do is get an enema bottle and hold him down. They wouldn't have to worry about the spitting and gagging."

"Did you find anything else?"

"I think you were right about the whisker growth. Either he was kept from shaving for about four days or he's been unable to do it for that long. He hadn't brushed his teeth for awhile. I got some of the plaque with a dental pick. It's in a plastic envelope. I don't know if your forensics people can get anything from it or not, but it's there at least. Len is pathological about oral hygiene. He brushes his teeth when he gets up in the morning, then after every meal (at least) and once again when he's getting ready for bed. He flosses every day too. Once again, he's either been prevented from doing it or he's been unable to do it."

"But he's eaten."

"Yes. He's not gaunt."

"Anything else?"

"He hadn't cleaned his ears either. He's got this device. It's like a tiny sword with a handle and a solid, round hand guard. Instead of a tip it has a little hollow plastic ring on the end. You put it in your ear and the little guard thingie keeps you from inserting it in too far. Then you clean the cerumen—the wax—with the little ring thingie. It looks like something you might get out of a vending machine for a quarter, but Len paid five bucks for it. He swears by it and uses it constantly."

"Nose hair untrimmed?"

"Yes. Yes, it was untrimmed, that is. He basically looks like your average person who doesn't care very much about his appearance. But Len isn't that average person. He shampoos his hair every morning and every evening; whenever it's available he likes to wash his hands with Lava. Constantly. It's like he's always doing autopsies or surgeries and hunting down some elusive bit of dirt or bacteria. He hasn't had the opportunity to wash them in awhile. I cleaned out the grit from under his nails. It's in a separate plastic envelope. Some of it was dust, the kind they found him lying in, but some of it was darker. Maybe your people can find something there."

"So ... I make it that he's been held incommunicado, against his will, for several days. Then he was stripped, forced to ingest enough alcohol to poison him and left by the side of the road. There were at least two individuals involved because Len weighs at least 185 pounds. If he was pulled out of a sedan or rolled off the back of a pickup and then dragged across the pavement or rolled down a hill in the grit there would be noticeable abrasions. He was carried by at least two individuals and then positioned carefully in the brush. They were creating an image, call it a ... tableau. They wanted him to be seen in the worst possible light—drunken, disheveled, dissolute ... pick your 'd' word. They wanted to create an appearance that was the direct opposite of everything anyone might think about in connection with Dr. Leonard Barnes."

"It works for me," Sally said.

"And they knew him," Tom added.

"With that much anger and vengefulness ... they had to have known him."

"And if they knew anything about alcohol ..."

"They didn't want him to recover," she said.

EIGHT

"And you can anticipate my next question," Tom said.

"Yes. Who?"

Tom nodded in agreement.

"I'll give it a lot of thought," Sally said, "but I can't promise much. His batting average on surgeries was one of the highest. He's never been sued for malpractice, at least not since I've known him and he's never talked about anything like that happening in the past. He's very private. He operates; he examines; he reads and he spends time with me. That's about it. No country club memberships, no golf tournaments, no wine club. Religious, but not church-going. Not a joiner. In demand with professional associations as a speaker, but not active with their administration. A very private man, Tom. Highly competent. Well-liked and loved but not 'out there'. I can't think of anyone who would want to hurt him ... but, like I said, I'll give it some serious thought."

"I'll have someone check on his surgical schedules, see if there was anything controversial or unpleasant."

"You have his office number," Sally said. "His chief assistant is named Marsha. She's very nice and very helpful, but like I said, I'll be very surprised if you find anything that jumps out at you on that front."

"Family?"

"Len's an only child; his father died years ago, his mother shortly thereafter. She was living in Ohio, I think. No children from his marriage; his wife died when she was young."

"Cause?"

"Cancer, I think. Why do you ask?"

"Nothing else *to* ask, I guess," Tom said. "There's *one* thing for sure, though …"

"What's that, Tom?"

"Whatever this was, we know what it was *not*. It definitely was not a random act."

"Maybe that's a good thing," Sally said. "A thief might have just shot or stabbed him and left him to die in an alley. Whoever did this felt that he was doing something cute, something that would have drawn attention. Because of that we were able to find him. Maybe now that he's here he'll have a chance to survive."

"Yes," Tom said. He paused before speaking again. "Talk to me about comas," he said.

"I don't know all that much," Sally said. "The word comes from the Greek, meaning *deep sleep*. It can be caused in a lot of ways—head trauma … stroke … in Len's case, intoxication. There are various scales to measure the level of consciousness. Nurses watch for signs: response to pain, eye or other movement, vocal responses … it's very important to prevent asphyxiation, so nurses talk about 'airway management' … sometimes people come out of a comatose state in a few days, sometimes in a few weeks. Interestingly, a profound comatose state can sometimes lead to a better recovery than a lesser one. Sometimes the recoveries are complete; sometimes the patient ends up in a vegetative state or simply dies. When there *is* a recovery it's usually gradual—the patient is awake briefly; he may say a few words. The next day he's awake a little longer … often, comatose patients are confused when they awake. They may suffer from dysphasia. It's not like in the movies where the patient opens his eyes, bolts upright and asks 'where am I?' So far Len's not showing any signs of awareness, but his body seems to be functioning well. They'll do brain scans and see if there's anything else at work here, but the alcohol seems like the most likely cause of his condition."

"Thanks," Tom says. "That's very helpful."

"You had a brain procedure, Tom …"

"Yes, but I just had pain, no loss of consciousness. And, thank God, I've been fine since. That was several years ago now."

"But when you feel tired or get a headache, you start to wonder …"

"Yes, especially in the beginning," Tom said. "It's hard to believe that you've actually been cured."

"After a lot of bad news it's sometimes difficult to accept any good news."

"Yes," Tom said.

"Len is always open to good news," Sally said. "Even when he's driving the California freeways he carries a set of binoculars with him. He's always looking at birds and trees. He's like an old-time doc, one from the sixteenth or seventeenth century; he talks about miracles and wonders; he talks about being alive to the world around him. When he comes back … when he wakes up … we've got to have good news for him, Tom."

NINE

"I've gotten a hit," Hector said. "The truck driver formerly known as Jim Jeffers …"

"Yes," Tom said.

"He's actually named Dale Wade. He works out of Phoenix, driving for Swift. His dispatcher is a guy named Kendall. Carl Kendall. No-nonsense, straight-arrow type. He i.d.'d him instantly. And he understood the deal right away. The competition is fierce, the federal regulations are strict and the drivers are on a very short leash. He said that he understood why his driver would want to do the right thing but also get out of Laguna ASAP. He also said that the company would cooperate fully. The driver is en route to Las Vegas now. If it's OK with us, they'd like him to complete that run. He'll then leave the rig in Vegas and shuttle back to Orange County tonight. He'd be available this evening, but I told Kendall that you'd want to talk to him in daylight, so he could show you precisely where he found Dr. Barnes and he could answer any questions about the site when you could both see it clearly. If that sounds good to you I'll have one of the uniforms pick him up at John Wayne and we'll put him up somewhere in Laguna tonight so that he's ready to go first thing in the morning. How about the Best Western? He'll be impressed that it has 'Dana Point' in the title."

"Perfect," Tom said. "Let me know where he'll be; I'll pick him up at 6:00, we'll grab some coffee and head down the highway."

Dale Wade was sitting near the check-in desk when Tom arrived. He seemed overdressed in dark wool slacks and a long-sleeve cotton shirt that had been freshly starched and ironed. He was clean-shaven, his hair was neatly-combed and there was the scent of motel soap and shampoo around his head and shoulders. "I'm Lieutenant Tom Deaton," Tom said, extending his hand.

Wade took his hand, covered it with his left and said, "Lieutenant, I hope you understand …"

"I understand completely," Tom answered, as they walked to the car. "Detective Campo spoke with your dispatcher, Mr. Kendall. He explained everything. The company is giving us their full support and we very much appreciate your personal cooperation."

"No problem at all," he responded.

"I brought a black-and-white," Tom said, unlocking the door. "If I turn on the light bar when we're at the site the drivers will all slow down by at least ten miles an hour and give us a wide berth."

"It's not too far," Wade said. "It was just above San Juan Capistrano. There was a golf course on the east side of the road."

"I know where you mean," Tom said. "The Marbella Country Club. There's an interchange just below. We'll get off and get back on the northbound side. That's fresh coffee there in your cup holder; help yourself."

"Thanks," Wade said. "That's very thoughtful."

"How did you see Dr. Barnes's body?" Tom asked, as he drove along the freeway. "I mean, at that time in the morning you were able to drive briskly, at least 65 and the light must have been fairly faint."

Wade tightened up. "I'm not sure, Lieutenant. I thought about that later … it was as if I was meant to see him …"

"A bona fide good Samaritan."

"Something like that. I just caught a glance with my peripheral vision. I saw what turned out to be his right arm. It was extended from the side of his body, as if he was reaching out toward something. At first I wasn't sure that it was a human body. You don't expect to see something like that there, especially not without any clothes. I signaled and then hit the break, driving off the pavement and onto the shoulder. I was pretty far past him at that point. I put on my flashers, backed up very slowly, leaned up out of my seat and confirmed that it actually was a human body there. Then I came to a full stop and went down to see if he was still alive."

The trucker told him to slow down; Tom feathered the brake and began inching forward carefully. "Wait, Lieutenant. Slow down … now … stop. About eight or ten feet over … right … there … see that scrub? He was right in the middle of it. It's still bent there on the side.

"It was like he was hidden in broad daylight. That early in the morning … the truckers are sipping coffee, trying to wake up and focus. They see something white like that on the side of the road … it doesn't really register … it's like it's newspaper or something. For some reason or other it caught my attention and I stopped."

Tom put on the emergency brake, turned on the light bar and they got out of the black-and-white. "What you did … " Tom said, "it was a good thing."

"Thanks, Lieutenant. He was right there. His right arm was extended and his left arm was laying against his side. I thought he would be shivering, but he wasn't. It was like he wasn't feeling anything, good or bad. His legs were parted and his knees were bent so that his toes were pointed in the same direction. His body was dirty but there weren't any wounds or any blood that I could see. I did brush some of the dirt out of his right eyelash. Maybe I shouldn't have done that … anyway, I could see that he was breathing and I didn't want him to open his eyes and get dirt in them. It sounds stupid now, I guess, but I drive with my feet, hands and eyes. I carry eyedrops with me all the time, in case my eyes get irritated. It's a big deal to me …"

"And he just appeared to be sleeping?"

"Sleeping very peacefully."

"And you signaled another driver to stop and help you put Dr. Barnes into your truck."

"Yes. When I thought about it later, I wondered why I didn't just call the police or a local ambulance. I guess I was thinking that here was a guy who had had a very hard night. Too much partying. Maybe dumped off by an angry girlfriend ... I don't know what I was thinking. I guess I didn't want him to get into any more trouble. It's not a crime to sleep like that on the side of the road ... well, maybe it's indecent exposure or something, but it wasn't as if he was aware of it ... it wasn't like it was a conscious act. Anyway, I just figured if it was me I'd want somebody to take me in to get some medical help, so that's what I did."

"You did the right thing," Tom said. "He was in a coma. He needed medical attention right away."

Wade smiled. "Anyway, I have a Danger Zone sign in the truck. I set it behind the rig and then walked along the burn, waiting for another truck to come by. As it turned out, the first one stopped ... another Swift driver, a guy named Ray, from Cincinnati. He helped me put the doc's body in my truck and he helped me cover him with a blanket I keep there. I strapped him in so he wouldn't move around if I had to brake fast. I thanked Ray, he left, I retrieved my sign, I checked my Garmin, found your hospital—Saddleback is it?—and drove him there. Then I headed for City of Industry to drop off my load of auto parts, picked up some valves there from a place called Inline and headed toward Las Vegas. You know the rest, Lieutenant."

"At any point did you or Ray see any indication that Dr. Barnes was conscious or *aware?*"

"No, sir, we didn't. He just seemed to be sleeping soundly."

"And did you clean up anything on him besides removing the dirt from his eyelash?"

"I may have brushed some of the dirt off of his chest after we picked him up and before we put him in the truck, but nothing elaborate. No soap and water or anything like that."

"Did you see anything on the ground near his body, anything, anything at all?"

"No, I didn't. Actually, I looked. I thought maybe he might have had something with him when he decided to lay down and go to sleep. There was nothing. I remember thinking that the ground was unusually clean. Usually you see *something*, some paper, some fast food wrappers, cigarette butts, something."

"How about footprints?"

"Not that I remember. The wind rearranges the dust and grit. And the **5** gets some heavy duty use ..."

He waited while Tom called in a forensics team, joking with them about the early hour and then giving them directions to their precise location. "If it's OK with you I'd like to wait here until they arrive."

"I understand," Wade said. "If anything's left you don't want to take any chance of it's being disturbed."

Tom opened up the back door on the driver's side and took out a thermos. "Refill on your coffee," he said. "I always want more than a couple of cups."

"Don't mind if I do," Wade said, retrieving his cup from the cup holder in the black-and-white as Tom filled the cup from the top of the thermos. "It's really strange, don't you think ..." he said, "a professional man and all ... he wouldn't be walking around naked like that. But who in the world would want to do something like that to him? I mean, I can understand somebody hating another man, wanting to hurt him. Shoot him, stab him, hit him over the head. Get some kind of revenge for something or other ... but this is such a screwy way to do it, if that's what the person was trying to do. It doesn't make any sense at all. But I guess that's what you're thinking too, right, Lieutenant?"

"That's right, Dale. But like I said, we certainly do appreciate your help."

"I couldn't tell you much, I'm afraid."

"You pinpointed the spot. We couldn't do that by ourselves. Maybe the forensics team will be able to turn something."

"I sure hope so," Wade said. "I sort of feel as if I'm a part of the case now. Invested in it, so to speak. I just wish I could help more ..."

"We'll call you if we have any additional questions," Tom said.

"Please do. Here, let me give you my cell number. I'm not sure where I'll be after I get back to Vegas."

A few minutes later the forensics team pulled up in an unmarked van. Their leader was a man named Jim Plant. "Didn't want to attract any unnecessary attention, Lieutenant," he said. "We're likely to be here awhile and the one thing we don't need is the press hovering over us ..."

"I understand, Jim. Can you spare one member of your team for awhile? I want to check Dr. Barnes's condo."

"Take Carol," Jim said. "She's the best duster I've got."

Tom and Carol Carlow checked in with the superintendent of Len's complex. He opened the door with his master key and Carol began checking the door knob and door frame for fingerprints. "Sometimes they lean against the frame, Lieutenant, you know ... while they're waiting. They usually wipe the knob when they leave but sometimes they forget to wipe the frame."

Tom checked inside. There was no computer but there was a modem and box for DIRECTV. Len must have had a laptop at home and a desktop at the office. With the wireless router he could work in any room in the condo. Perhaps he took the laptop with him when he left, but there was no way of knowing with any certainty. His car was missing from the numbered parking space in the basement of the complex and there were no car keys or, indeed, any other keys on the hook at the end of the line of kitchen cabinets. And no cell phone. It appeared that Len had taken everything with him and come back with nothing.

"Nothing on the door frame, Lieutenant," Carol said, "and nothing but smudges on the handle. Sometimes you can get a heel print, from the base of the thumb, but not this time. I'll check inside …"

Tom looked for other personal and professional items. Len's cellphone and wallet were gone and so was his pager. There was no coin purse or pile of coins, no tablet or iPod, though he had one of those power stations that recharges all of your electronic devices. The bed was made and the plates and cooking utensils were either in the cupboards or the dishwasher. Len was a good housekeeper. Tom checked the desk in the small, guest bedroom that Len used as an office. No notepads, no post-it notes, no day-timer book.

"I've got a touch of blood residue in the bathroom, Lieutenant," Carol said, "but that's no big deal. Probably just a little razor nick. There's nothing in the tub or on the walls. This place is really clean …"

"How about prints, Carol?"

"Just two so far. He must have a girlfriend."

"He does," Tom said.

"At first I thought he might have a housekeeper, but I think the prints are from a girlfriend. Housekeepers dust; men don't, as a rule. If you look at the nicknacks and family pictures on the bookshelf in the living room you can see the dust around them. They haven't been moved in a long time. There's also some dust on the shutters on the bathroom window. Men vacuum; they cook; they organize things; they make beds. They'll scrub out a sink or a bathtub and they'll clean a mirror, but they don't like to dust. Maybe a few men do; I don't know, but the vast majority don't."

"Anything at all look out of order to you, Carol? Anything that would suggest that someone was in the apartment who shouldn't be?"

"No, not really, Lieutenant. There are a lot of things that aren't here that I would expect to be here, but he probably took those things with him. If he was abducted, I would think it happened outside the apartment."

"I agree," Tom said. "Thanks for your help. I'll take you back to your team."

TEN

Len Barnes's assistant, Marsha Jasper, was an attractive, middle-aged woman with grayish blonde hair and bright blue eyes. Tom wondered how she worked the files, keyboard and telephone buttons with her carefully-manicured nails.

"Good morning, Lieutenant," she said as he walked into Len's Irvine office. "I've been expecting you. Would you like tea or coffee? I also have some herbal teas and packaged cocoa."

"Coffee, Marsha, if it's not too much trouble."

"It's no trouble at all," she said, standing and walking to the butler's pantry to the right of her desk. She spoke as she worked. "I've cleared Dr. Barnes's calendar, of course, so it's just me here today … and the paperwork." (She prepared his reports in his capacity as Medical Examiner and also handled his billing, insurance work and professional correspondence. She was half Della Street, half CPA.)

"I wish I had something positive to report," Tom said. "At least there's no further bad news."

"He'll be fine," she said immediately. "I've worked for Dr. Barnes for seventeen years. I have never met a man with that much personal discipline and general cheerfulness. Of course, he has to maintain his health. And his posture. Sometimes when he's operating he must stand for six or seven hours …"

"Yes, he's like a professional athlete," Tom said.

"Precisely. And everyone looks to him for leadership. He has to maintain his composure amid … well, there's no reason to whitewash it … amid all of that blood and those sharp instruments. He operated on me, Lieutenant, did you know that?"

"No, I didn't," Tom said.

"They say that you shouldn't operate on relatives or friends. You might lose your objectivity. Nonsense, I said. I wanted the best and Dr. Barnes is the best. He removed my gall bladder. Using a laparoscope, of course. You're aware of the fact that he's known for that. I had virtually no pain. Minimally-invasive, they say and minimally-invasive it was. The most impressive thing, I think, is his ability to handle all of the relationships …"

"The relationships?" Tom asked.

"Yes, the relationships. He's my boss, he's my doctor and he's also my friend. Each of those relationships is different and he has the personality and the professionalism to handle all of them. He's really quite special, Lieutenant."

"I know," Tom said. "As you know, I wanted to talk to you about other cases …"

"Unpleasant ones, you mean. Disgruntled patients. Lawyers. Lawsuits …"

"Yes …"

"Well, that won't take long, Lieutenant," she said, lifting the urn to pour his coffee. "Do you prefer it black or should I add a little half and half? I have some fresh. It keeps longer than milk and I always have some on hand."

"Just black, thanks," Tom said. She filled the cup and wiped a drop that had splashed on the edge with a small paper towel.

"First, Lieutenant, there has only been *one* lawsuit. Dr. Barnes's patients are always pleased with his work. You see that painting on the far wall?"

"Yes," he said, "the seascape … "

"It was given to Dr. Barnes by the artist. I'm told that the painting would sell on the local art market for upwards of $35,000. Dr. Barnes removed his thyroid and he gave him the painting in gratitude. Dr. Barnes's home is filled with gifts from grateful patients. He tries to say no to them, but they insist. They idolize him, Lieutenant. They simply idolize him."

"But there was one case, you said."

"Yes, but that man was nothing more than an opportunist. Dr. Barnes warned him about the operation. He told him what he might reasonably expect and what would be beyond the capacity of any surgeon. He spelled out all of the risks. The man insisted that Dr. Barnes proceed, which he did. The operation was successful beyond anyone's expectation, but the results were not *perfect*. Perfection would have been impossible, because of the man's condition. He then turned around and sued Dr. Barnes for $25,000,000."

"Successfully?"

"Of course not. Our insurer was outraged by the action and they decided that it was time to make a statement. Instead of using their usual house attorneys they hired Donald Fell."

"The criminal attorney."

"Yes, in Pasadena. They not only wished to win the case; they wanted to paint the bringing of the suit as a criminal act—which it most certainly was."

"And the result was … ?"

"The plaintiff lost the case and was ordered to pay court costs. They don't usually countersue for those, you know. Usually they just settle quietly."

"The court costs must have been substantial."

"In those days (that was awhile ago, remember), Mr. Fell was billing at $975 an hour."

"So the plaintiff would have been very angry at the result …"

"He was positively livid."

"How long ago was that, Marsha?"

"Thirteen years ago, Lieutenant. Thirteen years last month."

"And have you heard from him since?"

"Oh no, Lieutenant, he died shortly thereafter."

"And did he have any relatives who might still be angry over the case?"

"No, no. He was divorced from his wife and they didn't have any children."

"And that was the only lawsuit?"

"Yes, the first and the last. And the interesting thing, Lieutenant, is that Dr. Barnes never seemed to resent the man. He always said that it was his right to sue and that he could understand the man's feelings. Dr. Barnes said that he was wrong, of course (the man, that is), but he was sick and he wanted perfection in an imperfect world. Of course, the man had been abusing his body for years and, in some ways, got precisely what he deserved, but Dr. Barnes was generous—*very* generous, I thought—under the circumstances."

"And the man's name?" Tom asked.

"Brando," she said. "Oh, not Marlon Brando. He *did* consult with Dr. Barnes once, however. This was Harold Brando. He wasn't an actor. He was ..."

"A politician," Tom said.

"Yes, he was a member of the California Assembly."

"He was brought up on charges of taking a bribe, as I remember."

"He was not a nice man, Lieutenant. As I said, I thought Dr. Barnes was far too generous with him. Mr. Fell, however, was not ..."

ELEVEN

The call from the forensics team on the **5** came just as Tom returned to Saddleback Memorial. "Good news and bad news, Lieutenant, but not a lot of either," Jim Plant said.

"Tell me what you have, Jim, and we'll see what we can do with it."

"Let me cover the marginal stuff first," he said. "Miscellaneous junk and trash, food wrappers, cigarette butts, whatchacall the detritus of our civilization, but none of it really near the site itself. Ten yards away, fifteen, twenty … and it could have come from anywhere, what with the wind blowing from all directions. It's your call, Lieutenant, but we're thinking it's a real long shot that somebody would unload a naked body by the side of a potentially busy freeway and then stop to eat a Cheeto or smoke a Marlboro. It would have been drop and run or *put down carefully* and run."

"What else, Jim?" Tom asked.

"We found a small plastic bag that had some crack residue--just enough to turn the test liquid blue--and it's possible that whoever would be stupid enough to put a naked body in a shrub would also be stupid enough to use crack. However, the bitter truth is that there are a lot of stupid people out there and when they're finished with their treat of choice they often throw the container out the window. Anyway, there were no fingerprints on the bag and we found it at something like thirty-seven yards from the site …"

"How about the good news, Jim?"

"Well, it's good and it's bad, Lieutenant. We found a shoeprint, but it was actually a flip flop print. We had to brush very carefully, but we found some ridge marks. I'd feel comfortable saying that it was average to large in size, maybe a 10, say, and I'd be comfortable telling you that it could have been related to the finding of Dr. Barnes's body. The print was just to the left of where Dr. Barnes's left leg would have been."

"Left foot or right foot print, Jim?"

"Right, why Lieutenant?"

"Because when most people lift something heavy they use their left leg to provide the principal support. If one of the two people carrying the body—assuming for the sake of argument that there were two—was standing on the left side, holding the left side of Dr. Barnes's body, it's most likely that the brunt of the weight would have been carried by the left leg and the deepest footprint left would be that of the left foot."

"Works for me," Plant said. "Unfortunately I don't have a Bruno Magli size 14 with a heel plate and noticeable wear for you."

"That doesn't mean you haven't found something, Jim. Anyone who would wear an easily-identified shoe to a crime scene would either be a rank amateur or someone arrogant enough to believe that he could never be caught. What you've identified is either someone more professional or at least intelligent enough to leave a generic print. A hyper-generic print. Buy an el-cheapo pair at Wal-Mart or Target, do the deed, toss the flip flops in an incinerator and put on your Bruno Maglis or Hush Puppies or whatever … better still, buy a set of upscale flip flops, walk around on the cement for awhile, wear them down a little and then put them in your clothes closet. When the men in blue come calling, you tell them, 'That print couldn't be mine, Officer. I wear Havaianas and Havaianas only. You think *I* would put something cheap on *these* feet?'"

"I agree, Lieutenant. Unfortunately, I wish I had more for you."

"I do too, Jim."

"We'll test everything we have for DNA residue, but the simple fact is that most of the stuff found by the side of the road is thrown from car windows, not dropped by criminals perpetrating a crime."

"I understand," Tom said. "What about on the shoulder of the freeway? Any tire marks?"

"Marks on top of marks on top of marks, Lieutenant, but nothing clearly identifiable. We picked up a wad of gum there. No particular smell. It's not fresh and it's not Juicy Fruit. We'll check it out but I'm not optimistic."

"And nothing in the shrub or adjoining weeds?"

"Nope. We went over it branch by branch and leaf by leaf. By the way, it was your standard creosote bush; Latin name—*Larrea tridentate*. Lots of nice resin and a characteristic scent … unfortunately no forensic evidence.

"One other thing, Lieutenant … the blanket. We'll check the dust smudges on the blanket against the samples we took from the site next to the **5**. I'm assuming we'll get a match. If we find something untoward we'll let you know right away."

"Thanks, Jim, and thank the members of your team," Tom said.

"I will. Have a good one."

Tom slipped his cell phone into its holster on his belt and got up to get some fresh coffee from the cafeteria. He walked past the room to which they had moved Dr. Barnes to ask Sally if he could get her something to eat or drink, but when he got there Dr. Barnes was alone, breathing comfortably but still completely immobile.

He went to the cafeteria, greeted Joanne, the attendant with whom he was now on a first-name basis, filled a large to-go cup with coffee that smelled more or less fresh and paid the $1.59 tab. The coffee was very hot, but he sipped it around the edges, the way the Deaton family pets had sampled hot soup, and sat down for a moment to gather his thoughts. It didn't take long. They were pursuing every course imaginable at that moment, waiting for something to break but knowing that there were times when that just didn't happen. He called Hector and asked him to do a full-court-press check on Harold Brando, his relatives, exes, friends, associates, partners-in-crime, heirs and assigns.

"I remember that scuzzball," Hector said. "Wasn't he elected to the California Assembly Hall of Shame recently?"

"He probably should have been," Tom said.

"This could take awhile," Hector responded. "If you're picking up a string and seeing where it could lead … with a scumbag like him … it could lead anywhere."

"I need someone who would take revenge on his behalf, years after the fact," Tom said.

"That'll narrow the possibilities," Hector said. "Unless he left some kind of endowment to pay off people after he was gone it's unlikely that we'll find anyone. The kind of people he used to hang with … well, they're the kind that want payment in advance, preferably in used, unmarked bills."

"I don't think there are any blood relatives," Tom said.

"Well, *his* constituents (and I use the term advisedly) are likely to have moved on long ago to the next legislative gonef who was willing to *meet their needs* in return for some political or financial consideration."

"Right. Anyway, let me know."

"Will do. And Lieutenant …"

"Yes, Hector …"

"I ran into Chief Diedrich in the hall a couple of minutes ago and briefed him on where we are. He said that he knew you were busy. I told him that you were running the three-ring circus, but that you would call him the minute anything happened that could conceivably be of interest."

"Thanks, Hector."

By now the coffee had cooled enough for Tom to take bigger sips. He walked back to the ER lounge, stopping at Len Barnes's room on the way. He was still alone and there was still no noticeable change. When he got to the lounge Sally was there, pacing.

"I was looking for you," she said. She seemed agitated but optimistic. "He moved. Just a few minutes ago. He moved."

TWELVE

"I must have just missed you," he said. "I went by Len's room on the way to the cafeteria … "

"It was about six or seven minutes ago. I was sitting at his bedside, talking to him. Just aimless chatter, small talk—on the off chance that he could actually hear me. I wanted him to know that someone was there with him, that he wasn't alone, you know, lying there in the dark. Then, suddenly, I saw the tips of his fingers begin to curl. The fingers of his left hand, the hand closest to me. It was as if he was trying to take my hand in his, as if he was trying to find me, to reassure himself that I was actually there. I held his hand, hoping that he would move again, that I could feel his fingers squeezing mine …"

"And you don't think it was some kind of spasm?"

"It didn't look like that; it looked as if he was trying to grasp something in his hand. I don't know … I know it's not much, but it's something."

"Yes," Tom said. They were walking down the hospital corridor and had reached Len's room. When they got there Sally sat down beside the bed, took his hand in hers and began speaking to him. It was as if Tom had suddenly disappeared and that she had entered a separate space.

"I saw you move your hand," she said. "I saw it. Were you trying to touch me, to see if I was here or not? I *am* here."

Holding his left hand in her left hand, she scooted her chair sideways and put her right hand on top, gripping his more firmly. It was as if she was trying to wring information from him, even if the information was the faintest recognition of her presence and his awareness of it. She squeezed his hand and then patted it. "Can you feel that?" she asked. "Can you let me know? Just squeeze a little, not hard. I'll know that you know …"

She went on like that for several minutes. Tom stood in the doorway, not wishing to intrude but not wanting to leave. If there *was* some indication of consciousness or awareness, he wanted to see it. And if there was a word or words that Len was able to utter he wanted to hear them. It was interesting to him that Sally never used terms of endearment. She didn't call him Honey or Darling. The age difference between them may have yielded a different kind of relationship or at least a different form of communication that served as the basis for that relationship. Maybe it was the fact that she was a professor, that she was too sophisticated or self-conscious to talk to him the way Tom's parents had spoken to one another.

Sally was in her late thirties or early forties, Len in his late fifties. So, at least, Tom had assumed. He hadn't checked any formal records on either of them. Sally had spent the bulk of her career at UCSD; they had met through professional connections and Len had invited Sally to observe one of his more interesting autopsies. Hardly the basis for a traditional romantic relationship, it had evolved into a consultancy and then, finally, into something personal. The first indication that there was a romantic relationship came during one of her visits to Irvine when Sally stayed in Len's condo rather than in a local hotel. He was out of town at the time but she had her own key. Ever the detective, Tom noted that the key was in her leather case, not on a separate chain with an identifying tag.

Love among the doctors, or at least among the M.D.'s and Ph.D.'s. It was fascinating to watch her sitting beside him. Now she was moving his hair slightly, grooming him in a sense. No kisses or caresses, more like professional attendance or a relationship of (what would she have called it?) *reciprocal altruism*? Whatever it was, it wasn't demonstrative or gushy, but there was obvious care underlying it. He watched her lean over him, searching his eyelids and mouth for any sign of movement. If she could coax or wheedle the words, any words, from him, she would.

Finally she turned to Tom. "He *did* move," she said. "I saw him move."

"Like you said," Tom responded, "this will take time. He's not going to sit up and start in on a lengthy conversation with us. It's more likely to be gradual. A little movement today, perhaps more movement tomorrow. Eventually a word or two and then a sentence … "

"Yes, I hope so," she said. "I'm going to stay with him awhile, Tom. If you want to freshen your coffee, feel free."

He took that to be a request for privacy. He turned as he walked into the hallway and saw her move closer to him. She was holding his hand with hers but leaning closer to him, whispering something in his left ear. The terms of endearment perhaps.

His cellphone twitched. He checked the screen and hurried toward the exit. Where once the area beyond the ER doors was chiefly occupied by smokers it was now the principal domain of cell phone users. "Just a second, Hector," Tom said. "Let me put a little distance between myself and the rest of the folks here. What have you got?"

THIRTEEN

"Just an update. Your guy, Brando, Lieutenant …"

"Yes?"

"He didn't travel in very nice company."

"I didn't think he would," Tom said. "Who in particular?"

"A guy named Russo."

"Mark Russo?"

"You already know about the two of them?"

"I know about Mark Russo," Tom said. "Criminal entrepreneur. Totally amoral. Not that we expect paragons of morality from the criminal class, but Russo sets a new standard . A judge once called him 'utterly vile' but acknowledged that that might be an understatement. For a time he was working with the coyotes who were bringing in illegals. He rented them GPS systems, to help them find water or avoid developed areas. Sometimes he betrayed them to border patrols. Sometimes he trapped them and stole their money before betraying them. Sometimes he threatened to betray them and then jacked up his own fees. You hear about a guy whose word is his bond? This guy's word is totally worthless. You work with him once and you never work with him again, unless, of course, the price is right for him. I heard he was in the crystal meth business these days. What was his connection with Brando?"

"Political cover. Brando made calls, muscled local law enforcement, threatened them with reprisals if they didn't give Russo a pass. Russo contributed to his campaigns, sometimes with laundered cash, sometimes with gifts in kind, like selective stabbings or stompings."

"Cute. Where is he now?"

"Pelican Bay, in supermax."

"Good place for him. How long has he been there?"

"A year and a half."

"Pretty unlikely that he'd engineer some kind of revenge on behalf of someone who's dead and can't do him any good."

"Right," Hector said, "but it's not as if the scumbags in supermax can't communicate with the outside. They're still allowed to write letters and the hard core have complex codes that they use to direct their external operations."

"Easier to talk to people on the outside than on the inside," Tom said.

"Yes, though they've developed ways to do that as well. With a guy like Russo, though, there's one and only one motivator ..."

"Money," Tom said.

"Money," Hector acknowledged. "*Loyalty* is not a word in this guy's personal dictionary."

"Any other sleazoid connections?" Tom asked.

"Lots, but many are small time and when Brando died his usefulness basically disappeared. The only living relative, if you want to call her that, is his ex-wife Elaine. She lives in New Jersey with her second husband. She hasn't been quoted in public concerning her ex for about four years. All that she said then was, 'You mean that lying son-of-a-bitch?'"

"What's the husband do?"

"Quality control for a large farm. Part of the Birds Eye empire."

"Wonder how she met him; that seems like a long way off from her former life."

"Baha'i convention," Hector said. "Humanity as a global family and the earth as its homeland."

"Are they *allowed* to use the term *son-of-a-bitch*?" Tom asked.

"I don't know," Hector answered. "Maybe in his case they made an exception."

"But she's not likely to have given Dr. Barnes alcohol poisoning in her beloved husband's memory."

"No, she's not," Hector said. "And neither are any of his small-fry, former connections. Sorry I couldn't find anything more promising."

"I'm thinking that Brando is a dead end," Tom said. "The whole alcohol poisoning bit, the nudity, the side-of-the-road abandonment ... it's either some form of elaborate theatre or it's something very personal. This isn't the result of some obscure, years-old contract; it's more immediate. Whoever was behind this is out there, among us. He probably expected Len Barnes to die. Maybe he found out that he survived. Perhaps he's thinking about a way to finish the job. There haven't been any public notices of the crime yet, but let's post someone in plainclothes in the hospital—around the clock, just in case. I don't want to give this character a second chance."

"Will do," Hector said. "Any change in Dr. Barnes's condition?"

"Sally said he moved his hand. I didn't see it, but she's convinced that he did."

"She's not a dreamer type," Hector said. "She sees things pretty clearly. If she says he moved he probably did."

"Yes," Tom said. "She's with him now, hoping to see some other indication of awareness."

"That's nice," Hector said. "Tell you what, I've got an aunt who prays all the time. She's got good connections with the Lord; I'll put in a word with her. I'd pray too, but I think she's got a better chance of getting through than I do."

Tom smiled. "Thanks, Hector. Stay in touch."

He looked up at the date palms in the distance and the succulents that marked the garden walkways, the red and purple bougainvillea that the local businesses had planted to add color to their stucco walls--increase the amount of beauty in the world, maybe catch a potential customer's eye. The sun was bright, exposing everything to view except the perpetrators of his crime. He watched the traffic headed for

Oakbrook Village--couples, businessmen, teens who should have been in school, ladies who do inexpensive lunch, deliverymen, tourists killing time, hospital visitors looking for a break from the death or disease watch ... lunch at one of the chains, grocery shopping at Trader Joe's ... an afternoon matinee or just a temporary outing in the sun ... and just above them, the hum of the traffic on the **5**. What would they find next, lying in the weeds beyond its shoulder?

FOURTEEN

When he drove back to his father's cottage that night, his father was there. "I didn't expect you," Tom said. "I would have picked up something." His father had exchanged his usual boat clothes for wool slacks, polished leather loafers and a long-sleeve shirt with red pinstripes.

"Not a problem," his father said. "If you haven't eaten yet, we could go out." For several years his father Wayne had been living on his boat at the Newport Beach Marina, where he had worked for three decades before retiring as its harbor master. When Tom's mother died his father said that he felt closer to her there, on the boat that he had named for her, the *Katharine Elisabeth.* Tom had been living on his own, more modest boat at Dana Point when his father suggested he move into the family house. "I'd feel better if you were there," his father had said.

"I just stopped by to pick up one of my jackets," his father said. "The wind off the water has been picking up and it may drop ten or more degrees tomorrow. What were you thinking of for dinner?"

"I was just going to throw something simple together," Tom said. "Let's go out."

"Steak or Italian?" his father asked, "or both?"

"How about that place at the Fashion Island, what's it called, the Daily Grill?"

"Perfect," his father said. Good steaks, good martinis and lots of other choices."

"So what are you working on?" his father asked as they sipped their second drink.

Tom told him about the Barnes case.

"I know him," Tom's father said. "We consulted him when your mom was sick. He looked at all of her records, did his own examination, sat down with us and told us that her condition was inoperable. He seemed personally moved by her situation. Very nice man. Very caring. Very professional. We had already gotten the bad news from her family physician, but he encouraged us to get an opinion from a top surgeon. Dr. Barnes was so kind to her that it was almost as if he was conveying good news. It was the comfort, I guess. He's a very *comforting* man. Who would want to do something like that to a person like him?"

"I wish we knew," Tom said. "At this point we don't even have any promising leads."

"Nothing at all?"

"No, not a thing."

"Then it happened because of something *you* don't know about," his father said.

"Right," Tom said, not wishing to dispute the obvious.

"No, I mean it's most likely something that you *couldn't* know about. It's something *remote*, something that happened a long time ago. Maybe thousands of miles away. Maybe both. You've known Dr. Barnes for, what, five years … six? And really, how well do you know him?"

"Not all that well," Tom said, "but he has a friend, a woman. They're not engaged yet but they're very close. She doesn't have any ideas either."

"And how long has she known him?" his father asked.

"A few years," Tom answered, "maybe four or five."

"Well, that's my point. He's got, what, fifty years of life that the two of you don't know about? Whoever did this to him … it had to be because of something personal. Nobody would go to that kind of trouble if it wasn't personal. If you want to kill someone and dispose of the body, you just do it. You put a bullet in their brain, a knife in their throat or you bludgeon them with whatever object's handy. If you have to move the body you wrap it in a throw rug or put it in garbage bags and toss it from the car or the truck; you leave it in an alley or in the desert. If you've got a boat you put some cinder blocks on it and drop it in the Pacific. You don't force the person to ingest alcohol and you don't strip him and put him alongside the **5**. You wouldn't waste that time and you wouldn't risk that kind of exposure. Whoever did this could have been caught standing in a trucker's headlights or a highway patrolman's—who would want to do that?"

The waiter brought their steaks with the shoestring fries and vegetables. He refilled their water glasses and asked if they wanted any steak sauces or fresh drinks. When they thanked him and said no he told them to enjoy their dinners. As Wayne Deaton cut his skirt steak he paused to gesture and punctuate his points with the end of his steak knife. "Think about it," he said, "you've got a man who spends his days dispensing good news and bad news. 'We got all of the tumor, there was no sign of any spread; you should have a complete recovery … or: I'm sorry, we did all that we could under the circumstances … all we can do now is wait and pray.' It's his *job* to give a lot of bad news but that doesn't make it any easier for him. If he doesn't have to give bad news, why do it? If he has a lady friend he's not going to spend his time with her telling her about the bad old days or about people who hate him. Why should he?"

"Probably not," Tom said, "unless it came up in a way that he couldn't avoid telling her about it."

"Well, this is that point in time," his father said. "This is the time to connect the dots. You've got to know everything that he knows if you're going to have a chance of finding the person who did this to him."

"You're right," Tom said, "except that we've got a problem."

"He's comatose."

"Yes."

"Well then, there are two things you have to do and a third that you *can* do: *wait*, *pray* and find out everything that you can without his help. How's your steak?"

"Excellent," Tom said. "And your's?"

"Perfect. Even with broccoli and cauliflower."

They passed on dessert, but Tom ordered coffee and his father tea. "Lately I've been drinking the darjeeling," he said. "Sometimes the English breakfast. Your mother always preferred that. Tea doesn't keep me up the way that coffee does. The green stuff is supposed to be very good for you."

"That's what they say," Tom said.

"She wouldn't have gone for the steak, though," his father said. "Maybe one of those salads or pastas, the Cobb or the angel hair with the basic tomato sauce, maybe a cup of chowder or gazpacho in summer ... she would have liked this place."

"It's nice," Tom said, "but nothing has ever been as good as her cooking."

"She was like a magician," his father said. "You gave her a cut of meat, any cut, any size and suddenly the gravy would appear. And potatoes ... again, magic. She'd chop them up, add some butter, some salt and pepper, pop them in the oven and in a few minutes they'd be perfect. Then the vegetables ... always a little bit overcooked. We both preferred them that way."

"And the homemade rolls," Tom added. "And the pie with the scratch crust ..."

"Heaven," his father said. "We'll never have it again, but we can't sit and feel sorry for ourselves, not after forty-seven wonderful years."

"No," Tom said.

"This lady friend of Dr. Barnes's ..."

"Yes ... ?"

"Is it the anthropologist from San Diego?"

"Yes, it is," Tom said.

"I bet she can't cook like your mother."

"Probably not," Tom said.

"But if she's a good person …"

"She is, Dad."

"Then you've got to find whoever did this to the person she loves."

"Right."

"And if she loves him she'll want to be of help in that process."

"She's already helping, Dad."

"It may not be pretty--what you find out."

"I know."

"But you still have to do it."

"She knows that."

"If I can help in any way, you'll call me … ?"

"Absolutely, Dad. I'll call."

"Go find whoever did this and either put him in the ground or some place where they don't serve food like this."

"I will," Tom said.

FIFTEEN

The next morning Tom was at Saddleback at 7:00. Sally was in Len Barnes's room, sitting beside him. The shuttered light from the blinds shadowed across the edge of his bed. There were two empty cardboard coffee cups beside the lamp on his nightstand.

"Good morning," he said.

"Good morning, Tom," she said. "No major changes, but it's possible that there was a slight reaction last night. I was holding his hand and for a moment it felt as if he was trying to squeeze back. Maybe that was just wishful thinking ..."

"He's tough," Tom said. "He'll be back when he's ready."

She nodded.

"How about his vital signs?"

"Everything looks good," she said. "It's like he's in perfect health but he's exhausted and prefers to sleep."

"He's purged all of the alcohol from his system by now."

"Yes," she answered. "His doctor was in a few minutes ago. 'No news is good news,' he said. 'Len's stabilized. Now we wait.'"

"Can I get you a fresh cup of coffee?" Tom asked.

"No, thanks," she said. "I'm floating in it already."

"Let me get a cup and we'll talk," Tom said. She smiled as he left.

He told her about his talk with his father.

"Smart man," she said. "I think he must be right about the past. I wish I could be of more help."

"You can," Tom said. "Run down the basics of his life and career for me. I've got Hector going through the public record, but you'll know things that we won't find there."

"I don't know that there's all that much," she said. "He was raised in Ohio. His father was a chemist who worked for Procter & Gamble. I think he was much more than a lab technician; Len said that he thought about being an academic but decided instead to go into industry. I could understand that: less control over your own research but much better money. Probably a first-generation college student; I don't know that for sure, but that would be my guess. Anyway, he was a scientist, apparently a successful one."

"And Len followed in his footsteps in a sense …"

"Not directly. His mother and father were both great readers. They wanted him to have a broad, liberal arts education. He went to a magnet high school in Cincinnati and his parents then sent him to Kenyon, which wouldn't have been cheap, then or now."

"Big literary place," Tom said. "*The Kenyon Review* …"

"That's their forte, but they do science as well."

"And he chose the science."

"Yes, but he did do some work in the humanities also. I don't know what he majored in, specifically. I think it may have been some sort of interdisciplinary sequence, because he studied biology and biochemistry as well as chemistry and microbiology. He must have had a good experience, because he mentioned once that he had contributed some money to their new science quad. I'm not sure what he funded. It may have been bricks-and-mortar or it may have had to do with instrumentation.

"His father died when he was in college and he was able to finish with a combination of scholarships and loans. I know that he appreciated that help."

"And then he went to medical school."

"Yes. He killed the MCAT's but he was going to stay in town and study at the University of Cincinnati so that he could be close to his mother. She told him that she would be fine and that he should go wherever he wanted to go. He went to the University of Rochester, which gave him a generous scholarship. He flourished there and they tried to persuade him to stay on for his internship and residency, but he came back to the Midwest."

"Ohio?"

"I think he was offered something at Case Western, but he went to St. Louis instead, to Barnes-Jewish. He said he'd had enough snow at Rochester and didn't want more of the same in Cleveland."

"Was his mother still alive then?"

"Yes, I think she had actually remarried, but she died young and unexpectedly, I think while he was in St. Louis. A car accident, I think."

"And from St. Louis he came to California?"

"Yes, but not right away. I think he was in private practice there for awhile. I know that he met his wife in St. Louis."

"And she died young as well."

"Yes. Cancer. She was very young. Under forty. It's not something he talks about very much."

"But no children."

"No. They had intended to start a family, I think, but then she got sick and all of those plans were put on hold."

"So he's been single for a long time."

"Around twenty years," she said.

"That's a long time," Tom said, "but it's not as if he hasn't been busy."

"I tease him," she said. "I tell him that it's time for *him* now, that he's earned it. The thing is, he loves what he does. He doesn't feel some overwhelming need to travel or spend money. He wants to do surgery and he loves being your Medical Examiner. I've felt very awkward with him ..."

"In what sense?" Tom asked. "If you're comfortable talking about it ... "

"In the sense that he seemed to recognize that we had a good relationship and that something had been missing in his life, but that he hadn't really considered that *we* were an option for him. I didn't want to twist his arm or be *insistent*, I just wanted him to be happy. The problem was that he was already happy and hadn't thought about the fact that he could be happier still."

"Possibly because his parents and wife had died young."

"Yes, I think he had reached the point of being comfortable on his own. It's not that he's risk-averse; it's more that he came to believe that that kind of happiness just wasn't in the cards for him. He considers me a *surprise*, I think." As she said that she reached out and held his hand. There was no response, but his breathing was easy and he seemed at peace.

"What are you going to do, Tom?"

"I have to talk to Chief Dietrich," Tom said, "but if he'll approve the travel I'm going to fly to Ohio and start working my way through Len's life, talk to as many people as I can, try to find something that happened, something that might have created an enemy who would do this to him."

"I've got your cell number," she said. "I'll call you immediately if there's any change."

"Good. And I'll stay in touch. I don't know how long I'll be gone, maybe a week, maybe longer. I'll keep the plainclothes officer nearby, in case whoever did this tries to ..."

"Finish the job?" she asked.

"Yes," he answered.

"Len has a lot of friends here," she said. "I've spoken with some of the orderlies. They're keeping an eye out too."

"I'll be back as soon as I can," Tom said.

SIXTEEN

The Deatons were from Kentucky, he thought, as his plane landed in Greater Cincinnati Airport, but their part of Kentucky was farther south and far more rural. The area near the airport had grown with the airport and was now a long swath of chain hotels, strip malls and fast food restaurants. When he picked up his rental car another customer asked him if he was going to take the ferry to Cincinnati. He said no, not being aware of a ferry's existence or location. Having lost three hours on the flight, he stopped at a local chain, Frisch's Big Boy, had a sandwich and a piece of cheesecake, and checked into his hotel, a part of the Hilton group of properties. He slept unevenly and rose earlier than he had planned.

The next morning he was in the Hamilton County Courthouse when it opened. Amid all the tile, marble pillars and high ceilings, he saw a corner at the base of the southwest stairs with a sign, designating the former site of a blind newsman's stand, with a black and white photograph of him dispensing a package of candy or cigarettes while his dog—a huge, black German shepherd—slept at his feet. On the second floor he found a clerk in the Recorder's Office, who took him through the records of deeds and mortgages and then directed him to the plat books. Robert and Ellen Barnes had resided on Julmar Drive on the western side of the city. Their house was near the Western Hills Country Club. As he flipped through the pages of the plat book, looking for major intersections, he saw Anderson Ferry Road. If only he had known that yesterday, he might have taken the ferry across the Ohio to his actual destination.

He set his phone app for the Barnes address and followed its directions across the 8th Street Viaduct and into the city's western hills. The area overlooking the city was decayed but eventually the frame houses with ramshackle roofs and gutters and rusted automobiles gave way to neighborhoods of brick cottages and four-family apartment buildings. Julmar Drive was a cut above the surrounding norm and just below it was the former residence of Marge Schott, a large Tudor manse now surrounded by new, upscale development.

The Barnes home was brick and stucco, very nicely landscaped with a large, narrow lawn running down to the street. He estimated its current value in the area of $500,000, probably $2,000,000-$3,000,000 in Orange County. He knocked on neighbors' doors for forty minutes before he found a resident who remembered the Barneses. Her name was Irene Taylor. She asked to see Tom's badge and inspected it carefully.

"Dr. Barnes was a fine person," she said, "and so was his wife, Ellie. Their boy Leonard was very well-behaved. He used to cut our lawn. They were all very studious, the whole family ... I suppose someone has told you that Dr. Barnes was a chemist. He was responsible for the improvement of some of P&G's key products. He used to bring us samples to try. The company was very interested in its consumers' opinions. Sometimes he brought soap powders, sometimes cake mixes. They would always be marked simply: either "A" and "B" or "1" and "2". They came in plain packages. We were then asked to try them and tell the company which product we preferred. The Barneses doted on their son; they bought him a used car so that he could get to Walnut Hills."

"Was that his high school, ma'am?" Tom asked.

"Yes, it's way over on the other side of town, on Victory Parkway."

"Something has happened to Dr. Barnes, ma'am," Tom said. "Dr. *Leonard* Barnes, that is."

"Is the son a chemist also?" she asked.

"He's a surgeon, in California."

"That's nice," she said. "I knew he'd end up doing something important, just like his father. What's happened to him, Lieutenant?"

"He was attacked. He's alive and we expect him to make a full recovery but he's unable to communicate with us at the present time and we're trying to determine who might have done this to him."

"You're looking for some sort of enemy, then."

"Yes, ma'am."

"I'm sorry, Lieutenant. I can't help you there. Leonard was a wonderful young man. He was the scholarly type, but I suppose you already knew that. He studied every night and every weekend. I don't even know if he dated or attended his proms. When his father died he spent a lot of time caring for his mother. She remarried later, but she and her second husband were killed by a drunk driver on the expressway. The young man dealt with a lot of tragedy, Lieutenant; it was all very sad ... but I'm sorry, I don't know of any enemies."

"Is there anyone else still living on Julmar who would have remembered them, ma'am?"

"Helen Anderson is still living, Lieutenant, but she's in a care facility in Mariemont. She has Alzheimer's. There's no one else, I'm afraid. I'm the Lone Ranger."

He thanked her for her help and drove to Len Barnes's high school. Approximately ten miles east, the facility would not have been directly accessible on the local bus lines. With all of the transfers Len would have spent hours getting to and from school each day. He wondered if his mother had driven him back and forth until he was old enough to secure a license. An assistant principal named Papp described the school's admission policies and test requirements. "We're one of the top high schools in America, Lieutenant," he said. "Families make sacrifices so that their sons and daughters can study here."

Assistant Principal Papp (his first name was Arnold) checked Len's records. "They were all on microfilm until recently, Lieutenant. Now they're online. They're alphabetical ... we have a lot of Barneses ... it was *Leonard*, wasn't it?" He didn't wait for Tom's response. "Ah yes, here it is; just a moment, I'll print it out."

Two sheets scrolled out of the laser printer. Papp checked them before handing them to Tom.

"An exceptional student," Tom said, as he studied the records.

"Yes, we have many exceptional students," Papp said.

"And all of the Latin ..."

"We still require Latin," he responded.

"I don't see anything concerning ... *deportment*," Tom said.

"If there had been any problems they would have been noted--here," he said, indicating a blank space on the second page of the forms.

"I'm trying to determine if Dr. Barnes had any enemies when he was enrolled here," Tom said, "or if he was involved in any controversies or altercations."

"Hmmm," Papp said, "since there's nothing in the formal record, let me do this ..." He made a few keystrokes and brought up a second database. "This is the file of newsletters and annual reports. We use it as a kind of informal history. It's searchable." He entered Len's name. "Let's see ... here are a few things ... Leonard Barnes received a citation for extemporaneous speaking as a member of our debate team ... he received a medal for his Molybdenum exhibit in a science fair, and, oh yes, he was salutatorian of his graduation class—1980."

"So he may have had people who envied him, but there are no records of any incidents ..."

"No."

"And are there any remaining faculty who would have been here at that time?" Tom asked.

"We expect our faculty to have master's degrees at least," Papp said, "so, given the age parameters, they would largely be retired by now. Let me think … the only individual who might have known him is Gerald Aronoff. Let me see Barnes's record for a second."

Tom handed it to him.

"As I feared," Papp said. "Barnes studied Latin and French. Gerald teaches Spanish. But let me just see …"

He asked one of the office secretaries to check Aronoff's schedule. He was between classes and she found him in the faculty lounge. He accompanied her to the office. He was well-dressed, with a tweed jacket, knit tie and meticulously-groomed mustache. He was cordial, but formal and told Tom that he had a faint recollection of Len Barnes but was unable to recall any unpleasant incidents in which he might have been involved. "I believe he attended Kenyon," Aronoff said. "I think he may have received a partial scholarship there."

SEVENTEEN

Kenyon is an hour above Columbus and Columbus is 100 miles north of Cincinnati. Tom was able to reserve a room at the Kenyon Inn and got on route 71 as the afternoon sun was beginning to set. As he drove through the northern suburbs of Cincinnati and into the darkening farmland beyond, he checked his cell phone. No messages. He put it in his shirt pocket so that he could feel it twitch if the traffic noise on the interstate crowded out its ring tone. It remained silent and still throughout his drive.

Gambier, Ohio seemed to be little more than a collection of isolated buildings with a college at its center. Tom checked into the Kenyon Inn, reserved a table for dinner and took a brief walk around the campus. The campus center was bisected by a walkway called the Middle Path, which ended in a series of residence halls. To the right was the science quad, more a corner or landscaped niche than a separate quadrangle. He entered Higley Hall, which included facilities for Biology, Molecular Biology and Environmental Science and searched for a plaque commemorating a gift from Len Barnes. He was unable to find one but then entered Tomsich Hall, which adjoined it.

There were groups of students working on research projects in two of the Biochemistry labs. The facilities were clean and well-maintained, the students expensively dressed. Outside the Chemistry department, near a corkboard with thumbtacked fliers from multiple graduate schools, was a copper plaque indicating the recipients of the *Robert Barnes*

Prize for Research. Several of the student names were asterisked; a label at the base of the board explained that the asterisks indicated that the students receiving the prize had also held the *Robert Barnes Scholarship in Chemistry*. Len's gifts had honored his father.

Returning to the Inn Tom looked to his left at the President's 'cottage'. The lights were all lit; a large catering truck was parked beside the residence. A group of staff, some in white jackets, some in business attire, were walking around busily in what appeared to be a dining room. Someone was about to be asked for a gift that would provide the endowment for another scholarship or academic prize.

Tom took off his windbreaker and put on a sports jacket for dinner. The menu was basic. He ordered some soup and glazed chicken with sweet potatoes. There were two couples at separate tables in the dining room. One was enjoying an expensive bottle of wine, perhaps as part of a birthday or anniversary dinner. The room was quiet, with just the hint of classical music in the background; the appointments were 1950's/academic and very comforting. He expected to sleep well after a morning and afternoon of interviews and three hours on the road, but he was restless and called Chris Dietrich's office number, knowing that at that time he'd get an answering machine. He reported briefly on his activities, put the phone on his nightstand and tried his best to sleep.

After a breakfast of juice, coffee and buttered toast he walked to the Registrar's Office, badged the receptionist and asked to see the person in charge of college records. The Registrar was a pleasant man named John Pierce. He was short and efficient and helpful. "This is a common occurrence for us, Lieutenant. Students need clearances for various forms of government employment. We see our fair share of law enforcement officers."

Although the adjoining room was filled with file cabinets the Registrar went to the desktop computer in a work station near his desk. "You did say 1984, didn't you, Lieutenant?" he asked.

Tom said yes.

"Some file in alpha order, but we're a little old-fashioned here; we still go by graduation year. Barnes … *James*… Barnes … *Anne* … Barnes … *Leonard*. Here we are. Why don't you pull that chair over, Lieutenant."

Tom sat next to him and looked at the computer screen. "This way we can see what we have and you can tell me what you'd like me to print out for you," Pierce said.

Again, Len Barnes's academic record was superb. The only B+ was in Sociology. "Probably didn't hold his interest," Pierce said. "This is an exceptional record. Much less grade inflation in those days, of course."

Sally had been correct. Len's major field was flagged and there was an indication that he had studied in an interdisciplinary sequence that was centered on biological science but then moved out in other directions. "Ideal pre-med sequence," Pierce said.

"Are there any other records?" Tom asked.

"Disciplinary, for example?" Pierce responded.

"Yes, or anything to do with student life," Tom said.

"If there had been any serious disciplinary infractions they would be part of the academic record. Some would be released with the official transcript; some would not. There are none on Dr. Barnes's record."

How about positive things, student activities, that kind of thing?" Tom asked.

"Much of that is informal, but let's see what we can find."

Pierce accessed the online yearbook records, which were passworded. "Here he is … nice-looking young man. The photographers really knew how to do lighting then, even when they were taking hundreds of class pictures. Let's see … he was active in the science society, the pre-med group and he ran cross country. We're known for swimming here, but it's nice that he participated in athletics of some sort. Let's just check this …" He opened a file containing the records of magazines and newspapers associated with the college and found reference to Len's doing a formal presentation for an accreditation site-visit team. "This is impressive," he said. "The college wouldn't trust its academic reputation to just any undergraduate student."

"This is nice as well," he said, indicating a picture of Len in graduation robes with a special gold sash. "He was a marshal at the commencement exercises. That would usually indicate that he had a grade point average among the top three of his class."

Pierce made more keystrokes and accessed more databases, but was unable to find anything else. "My guess (and, mind you, it would only be a guess), would be that Dr. Barnes was a very serious student. Not the Big Man on Campus type. Not what we call a 'collegian'—the hail fellow/well met social type. As these records go, there's not a great deal here. It's all superb, of course, but there's nothing involving, shall we say, 'high-spirited' behavior. Let me check one more thing …"

The Registrar went into the development records. "They call it 'advancement' now," he said. "Yes, look here. Dr. Barnes is a regular contributor to the annual fund and he endowed a prize for student research in Chemistry. He also endowed a scholarship for a student majoring in Chemistry."

"Are the dollar amounts there?" Tom asked, not seeing any as he looked over the Registrar's shoulder.

"On another page," Pierce said. "This is the announcement page, as it were. All smiles and champagne corks, with hearty thanks from the President and the department chair. The actual records are here," he said, completing some keystrokes. "The prize is supported by an endowment of $100,000 and makes possible an annual award of $5,000. The scholarship was endowed at $250,000 and pays out $12,500 each year."

Tom nodded and thanked him.

"You see," Pierce said, "he made the gifts to honor his father. If you look at the personal information in his academic record you see that his father died in Dr. Barnes's sophomore year. We keep careful track of the parents, of course. There's a parents' fund and other … *opportunities*. It's very common to see an individual receive a scholarship, as Dr. Barnes did, and then endow such a scholarship later when he has the means to do so. When he lost his father the college stepped in and provided him the aid that enabled him to continue at Kenyon. Now he's made that opportunity available for others. It's quite lovely when you think of it ..."

"Yes," Tom said, "it is."

"But like I said, a very serious person. He lost his father at an early age as well as at an early point in his academic career. He was *focused* as a student. There was little time or space in his life for distractions. So, at least, I would infer."

EIGHTEEN

"I'm driving through Erie, Sally," Tom said. "There's a nice bypass around Cleveland and then a more or less straight shot to Buffalo. From time to time the road rises and I can see the lake on my left. I'll be in New York state in twenty-five or thirty minutes. What's happening at your end?"

"Nothing new," she said, "and I suppose that's good in a way. I've talked to the officers guarding Len and they tell me that they haven't seen any evidence of suspicious activity. His condition is unchanged. No additional evidence of awareness but no setbacks either. He's completely rehydrated; his urine is clear. He's just … asleep. What have you learned, Tom?"

"Nothing that we didn't already know. He was an exceptional student and he's a very generous man. I've gotten a better fix on his family situation and I've seen the places where he lived and studied. Unfortunately, I haven't learned anything that would bear on the present situation."

"So you'll be at Rochester in what, three hours?"

"Yes. My phone app says a little less than that, but I'm going to stop on the Thruway and get some coffee."

"I really appreciate your doing this," she said.

"Thanks. I'm happy to. I only wish I could find something that would be of help."

"Yes. Good luck. I'm going to go back to his room now. Travel safely."

"They do rotations, you know," the dean said. "When he reached the surgical rotation he truly excelled. The record suggests that he was accomplished in all areas, but he was truly distinguished in surgery. David studied with him …"

The dean, whose name was Lawrence Bevin, nodded at the other individual sitting opposite Tom. He was also wearing a white lab coat. His name tag read *David Leventhal, M.D.* Leventhal was chief of surgery.

"Leonard *was* exceptional," Leventhal said. "Lawrence is not exaggerating the case. The other students in the rotation looked up to him as if he was an intern or resident. He was very self-assured and very knowledgeable. And he was blessed with fine hands. You've seen them, I assume."

"Yes, I've seen him do autopsies, for example. His fingers are very long and delicate but he's also very strong."

"A woman's hands," Leventhal said, "if the woman was also a pipefitter. Hands like that … they're a gift."

"So you were classmates?" Tom asked.

"Yes. They wanted Leonard to stay on, but he decided to go to Barnes. My good fortune … I was able to land the post that they had intended for him. I've never left."

"And there were no hard feelings," Tom said.

"No, none whatsoever. We're not always the prima donnas we're claimed to be, Lieutenant."

Tom smiled. Bevin turned aside, as if he might have disagreed. Leventhal noticed it at once. "Oh come now, Lawrence," he said. "I didn't say that we can't be demanding, when our patients' welfare is at stake." Both were smiling now.

"Actually," Leventhal said, "Leonard operated on my wife. This was when he was at Barnes. She needed some exotic stomach surgery; there's no one I would have trusted more. We're colleagues. I wouldn't say that we're close friends, though there's never been any animosity between us.

We have great mutual respect. We've developed different specialties. I do reconstruction, for example. Leonard attacks disease."

"Were there any other students or other individuals who might have had ... conflicts ... with Dr. Barnes?" Tom asked.

"There's nothing in the official record that would suggest problems of that sort," Bevin said. "David ... ?"

"No, nothing that I can recall," he answered. "It's a personality thing in a way. Leonard is not a person who sees things or *takes* things in a personal way. He's always about the work. When there were discussions, debates even, about treatments or techniques he always focused on the patient and the medical issues at hand. He *depersonalized* it, if you will. He conveyed a sense of respect and created an atmosphere of collegiality but then discussed the points at hand rigorously and specifically. It's one of his great strengths, Lieutenant. He's able to create an atmosphere in which everyone is encouraged to do his best work without involving issues of ego or personality.

"I wouldn't say that Leonard is *without* personality. I believe that he is very centered and grounded. If I was pressed I would say that it has to do with the fact that he lost his parents when they were young and then he lost his wife. Where some might have collapsed into themselves or simply fallen apart professionally, he *focused*. He didn't *harden* himself; he's a very warm person, as you probably know. He simply became stronger ... and concentrated intently on the work."

Tom let that sink in before speaking. "This has been very helpful," he said.

"I hope you'll let us know when he comes out of the coma," Leventhal said. "He would be a great loss ..."

"I will," Tom said.

The discussion ended with some small talk about the city's convoluted highway system, with congratulations to Tom on his ability to negotiate it and find them. They then told him that he would have some difficulty in traveling to St. Louis, with his choice of multiple connecting flights through Detroit or Chicago. Bevin suggested that he consider driving. He thanked them for their advice as he left, but the weather was clear and he was able to book seats through Chicago on United. Each flight was delayed but he reached St. Louis in the early evening. He turned on his cell phone as soon as he landed, hoping for messages, but except for a commercial text from his carrier there were none.

NINETEEN

"We still send special patients to him, of course, but it's very different than having him here with us."

Tom was having lunch with the Barnes head of general surgery, Dr. Timothy Mallen, at the Chase Park Plaza, a block north of the hospital. Tom had a spinach salad; Mallen was eating scallops. Tom had put on a tie that morning; Mallen was dressed in an Italian suit with an understated silk tie.

"The patients loved him and the University loved him. They funneled all of their major development prospects toward him and he never let them down. It's funny when you think about it ..."

"What's that?" Tom asked.

"I grew up in a small town in Illinois. The orthodontist there used to come up to former patients at the mall or in restaurants and ask them to show him their teeth. 'Good, good', he'd say. Half the kids in town had been his patients. Like an old OB-GYN who had delivered most of the residents and heard their first cries. With Len it was similar: you walk into a gathering of notables in St. Louis and the room is filled with people whose gall bladders he removed, whose appendectomies he'd performed and, yes, whose cancers he'd eradicated. He was the surgeon of choice, Lieutenant; still is, but for southern California now."

"And did you know him well when he was here, Dr. Mallen?"

"I can't say that we were close friends; we were junior and senior colleagues, albeit young colleagues. I was interning when he was the senior resident. When he went into private practice I continued to see him, but not as often as before."

"He principally operated at Barnes."

"Yes. He also had a clinical appointment on the med school faculty. That involved a lecture here and there and an occasional seminar."

"I told you that he had been assaulted."

"Yes."

"Can you think of any individual who might have had an altercation with him or some ongoing form of conflict?"

"With Len? No. He's a very nice man, as I'm sure you know, but he's also the most professional individual I've ever met. He doesn't have time or room in his life for bickering or ego."

"There's nothing in the school or hospital files," Tom said.

"I'm not surprised. I can't say that there weren't … exchanges. There are always consultations and lively discussions with regard to treatment, particularly with the instrumentation and the drugs available to us now, but Len's focus was always on the patient. If there were arguments they were never heated and they were always, what would you say— *depersonalized*. He always generated a culture of mutual respect, though expecting the highest possible standards, of course. The interns followed him like puppy dogs. He didn't abuse them and they always learned things from him."

"Is there anyone else I could talk to at the hospital, someone who was particularly close to him?"

"I can't think of anyone. The best person would have been John Toensing. He and Len were both at Barnes together and then set up a practice in west county. Unfortunately, John died last year."

"How did he die, Dr. Mallen?"

"Non-Hodgkin's lymphoma. Len was here for the funeral, actually."

"And what happened to the practice?"

"When Len left, John took an associate, a nice young woman named Carlin. Janice Carlin. She got an offer from Mayo in Phoenix, where her parents live. When she left, John continued on his own. The practice was then sold to a surgeon from Chicago named Bartell. Jim Bartell."

"So they could still have records from the time when Dr. Barnes was there."

"They should. I don't know whether or not Jim has moved their offices. Len and John were on Lindberg Boulevard, just south of the Plaza in Frontenac."

Tom thanked him for his time and help, picked up his rental Camry from the valet parking attendant, and drove into Forest Park. He parked beyond the traffic flow and checked the address for James Bartell, M.D. on his phone. As he searched, the ring tone sounded. The caller i.d. flashed on the screen: Dr. Sally Cornell.

"Sally, what news?"

"He was awake, Tom. Only for a moment, but he was awake. His eyes fluttered for a second and he was able to speak."

"What did he say?"

"It didn't make much sense," she said. "He said, 'F-f-first floor.'"

"First floor?"

"Yes."

"As in the first floor of Saddleback?"

"He wouldn't know that. The drapes were closed and he wasn't awake long enough to look around and get a sense of his surroundings."

"It must be important in some way," Tom said.

"Even if it isn't, it's all we have at the moment," Sally said. "Where are you?"

"I'm about to leave for the offices of Len's St. Louis surgical practice. I hope to be able to check their files."

"And nothing new at your end?"

"No, just more of the same: Len's a wonderful man and a wonderful surgeon. He didn't say anything else to you?"

"No, I can't be sure that he was actually talking *to me* or just voicing something."

"I understand."

"There seemed to be the slightest hint of recognition."

"In what way?"

"After he spoke …"

"Yes?"

"I kissed him and it felt … it felt as if he was trying to kiss me back. Then he was asleep again."

TWENTY

Dr. Bartell had renewed the lease on the Lindberg office suite, just south of an upscale mini-mall, on a major artery. The epicenter of west county shopping, the Plaza Frontenac was anchored by Saks and Nieman's and included an art house cinema and several popular restaurants. Patients would appreciate the proximity of their doctor's office, particularly those who were concerned at the possibility of major surgery.

"Dr. Bartell was in surgery this morning," his nurse/receptionist said. "His first afternoon appointment is in an hour and thirty minutes. He'll probably be here in an hour or so."

Tom badged her and explained the reasons for his call. Her name was Estelle Gregory. "Dr. Bartell and Dr. Barnes met at Dr. Toensing's funeral, Lieutenant, but they were not previously acquainted," she said.

"How about you?" Tom asked. "Were you here at the time of Dr. Barnes and Dr. Toensing's partnership?"

"I certainly was," she said, "and I miss both of them. Dr. Bartell is a fine surgeon and a fine man as well. I've been privileged to work with all of them. I also heard from Dr. Carlin recently. She's established her own practice in Scottsdale."

"And you have access to all of Dr. Barnes's files …"

"The files have been culled and reorganized, Lieutenant. Some are in storage. What are you interested in, specifically?"

"As I indicated, I'm investigating a case concerning Dr. Barnes."

"Yes …"

"Dr. Barnes has been assaulted …"

"Oh, my," she said, "is he alright?"

"He's comatose but his vital signs are good. He's exhibited some degree of awareness for a brief period."

"Do you know what happened to him?"

"We know that he was poisoned, but we don't know the identity of the perpetrator."

"That's absolutely horrid."

"Yes, ma'am, it is," Tom said. "That's why I'm here."

"How can I help, Lieutenant?"

"Dr. Barnes is highly regarded by everyone who has known him. I'm trying to find an individual with whom he might have come into conflict, someone who might have a motivation for revenge of some sort. So far I've learned nothing that's been of help in this regard."

"You should have come here first," she said.

"You know of such a person or persons?"

"I do," she said, "but Dr. Barnes asked me not to speak about it."

"Under the circumstances I think he'd understand, ma'am. You have to speak for him, since he's unable to speak for himself."

"Yes," she said. "I understand. Would you like some tea or coffee, Lieutenant?"

"If you're having some, I'll join you," Tom said. "Either would be fine."

She invited him to sit at a table in the waiting room and brought in two cups of tea. "It was quite some time ago," she said. "After Dr. Barnes's marriage and after the establishment of his practice with Dr. Toensing. The man's name was Nathan Fox. He was a doctor as well."

Tom made notes in his pad, took a sip of his tea and asked her to go on.

"I don't know the initial details. This man Fox did something that deeply offended Dr. Barnes, something … personal."

"Did he specify what Fox did?"

"Not to me. Fox was an associate of Dr. Clement's … Charles Clement, a surgeon."

"And is Dr. Clement still in practice?"

"No. Dr. Clement died four or five years ago. I'm not sure that he would have talked with you anyway. The entire affair was kept very secret."

"Circling the wagons?" Tom asked, tentatively.

"I wouldn't put it that way," she said. "Dr. Barnes spoke with Fox and he spoke with Dr. Clement, disclosing the nature of the act or actions which he found offensive. Fox resigned and left the city. I presume that he continued to practice medicine, but I don't know that and I don't know where he went when he left."

"Whatever he did must have been serious," Tom said.

"Yes. I know that Dr. Barnes was prepared to report him and have his hospital privileges revoked."

"Because of something personal."

"Yes, Lieutenant."

"And the hospital would have been Barnes-Jewish."

"Yes, Lieutenant."

"I spoke with officials there and none were aware of an altercation between Dr. Barnes and Dr. Fox. They weren't aware of any form of conflict."

"No, they would not have been," she said. "As I said, it was all done very quietly."

"It might have even been Dr. Barnes's word against Dr. Fox's …"

"Yes, Lieutenant, but Dr. Barnes's word was, well, beyond challenge."

"And he might have had a witness," Tom said.

"Yes, he might have," she responded.

"And this Nathan Fox was a surgeon."

"Yes, he was."

"Did you ever meet him, ma'am?"

"Only once."

"How would you describe him?"

"Arrogant, self-absorbed, *proud*—in the worst sense of the word."

"You didn't care for him, then?"

"No, Lieutenant, I didn't."

"But you have no idea where he went."

"No, Lieutenant, and under the circumstances I don't think he would have wanted that information publicized."

II

THE FIRST FLOOR

TWENTY-ONE

Tom's first call was to Hector. "Nathan Fox, M.D. He was practicing medicine with another surgeon in St. Louis. That man's name was Charles Clement. Something happened between Fox and Len Barnes. Something personal. It must have been significant, since Len basically ran him out of town. He gave him the choice of leaving or waiting to have his hospital privileges revoked after Len brought formal charges within the medical community."

"Any other leads or additional information?"

"No, sorry, Hector. You know everything that I know."

"I'll put on the full-court press: find him, find out what he's been doing, find out where he's been in the last couple weeks. I'll also brief the chief."

"Good. I'm on my way to the airport now. I'll be back as soon as I can."

His second call was to Sally. "Nathan Fox, M.D.," he said. "Does that name ring any bells?"

"No," she said. "Is this a person who had dealings with Len?"

"Yes," Tom said, "bad dealings, apparently. Whatever happened was described to me as being *personal*. The person didn't know any of the details. She said that Len threatened to file formal charges against him and that Fox chose to leave town instead."

"Leave St. Louis."

"Yes. Fox had a surgical practice there, with privileges at the same hospital as Len. This was at a time when Len was in private practice with another surgeon, a man named Toensing."

"Any idea of what happened between them? Anything at all?"

"No, sorry. I was hoping that you might know something."

"Len never mentioned him to me. It must have been very serious. Len's not gossipy but he's also not purposely secretive."

"Perhaps he thought you would be offended. Fox may have done something that Len thought was really perverse."

"I'm an anthropologist, Tom. We're pretty much immune to shock."

"I understand," Tom said, smiling silently. "He probably figured it was over and done with and there was no need to talk about something unpleasant."

"It may have had to do with his wife," Sally said. "He doesn't say a lot about her. I know that he was deeply in love with her. I think he feels that if he talks about that to me it might hurt my feelings in some way. I don't push it. My own feeling is that it makes him more attractive as a person. I wouldn't want to enter into a relationship with someone who didn't feel things deeply and take commitments seriously. I love the fact that he loved his wife. I told you that he sees me as some kind of *surprise*. He doesn't articulate that, but that's what he feels, I think. He had a great love. She died. Time passed. He became accustomed to his new life, not thinking it could involve someone else, someone new. I'm the unexpected second act and I'm completely comfortable with that."

"And, of course, you had a life before you met Len," Tom said.

"Only in a manner of speaking," she said. "I've been in graduate school and an Anthro department. There *were* those conventions in Kankakee and Kalamazoo …"

"Cucamonga was always my own special memory," Tom said. "Anyway, he's in full head-over-heels mode now, I think, so he's enjoying the second act with you."

"Thanks," she said. "When will you be back here?"

"Tonight, I hope," he said. "I'm en route to the airport now. I may have to bounce around a little with connecting flights. Any new developments?"

"Not since he spoke. He looks very comfortable though. That sugar water must be agreeing with him. If he awakes again I'll ask him about Nathan Fox. In the meantime, travel safely, Tom."

"Thanks," he said.

Tom was lucky. There was space available on the next United flight to Denver and on a later flight from Denver to John Wayne. Lambert Field had seen a lot of change in recent years. Once upon a time it was the old TWA hub, but TWA had been swallowed by American, which had closed a set of gates rather than inviting in additional competition. United was on a separate concourse, along with a collection of other carriers that operated a small number of gates. He cleared security, grabbed a bagel and a cup of coffee and called Chris Dietrich, filling in the gaps from Hector's briefing and informing him that he'd be in first thing in the morning, unless he was needed that night.

He then called Hector. "Nothing yet," Hector said. "He's gone to ground, which is a good thing, I think. Something major happened. I like that in a potential suspect."

"Yes," Tom said. "Stay on him. I'll be in late tonight if you need me. Otherwise, I'll be in at first light or a few minutes later."

On the flight to Denver he began writing down possibilities: Fox had lied about Len to a patient. Fox had broken a promise to Len. Fox had violated protocols and somehow blamed Len. Fox had plagiarized from Len's work in a journal article. Fox had stolen one of Len's patients. Fox had stolen the records of one of Len's patients. Fox had misrepresented his services and overbilled. Fox had abused an intern. Fox had abused a resident. Fox had blamed Len for abusing an intern or a resident. The thoughts ran from the serious to the silly. Fox had misappropriated drugs.

Fox had hit Len's car in a parking lot and failed to leave a note. Fox had taken credit for one of Len's medical accomplishments; Fox had stolen food from Len's cafeteria tray. The longer the list got the more apparent it was to Tom that the list could be endless. Moral turpitude covers a very long list of potential actions. Estelle Gregory had said that Fox's actions were *personal*. That did not materially shorten the potential list, since Len could have been aware of or tangentially involved in nearly any act that Fox might have committed. Or someone could have told him about it. Len was a highly-respected member of the medical community. He could have been brought in on a case and then Fox lied to him or lied about him or used him in some way or another.

In Denver Tom had a roast beef sandwich and a bag of chips. He was tempted by the Coors tap at the bar, but had coffee instead and continued to go over his notes. His flight to Orange County was delayed for fifteen minutes, but landed only five minutes past its scheduled arrival time. He checked his phone for messages. When there were none he collected his luggage and headed home, anxious for the next day to begin.

TWENTY-TWO

"Let me start with the *first floor* question," Hector said. Tom nodded and continued to sip his coffee. It was 7:05; he had gone directly to Hector's work station.

"Unfortunately, there's not much. I thought that it might be a film or book title, so I started with the IMDB and Amazon. Nothing. The only thing on Amazon was a jazz record. Instrumental, no lyrics, relatively obscure ... so I tried the Library of Congress catalogue: only one hit—the title of an eighteenth-century play by a writer named James Cobb. The catalogue lists it as a farce. I called a couple people at UC-Irvine; none of them had heard of James Cobb."

"Not very promising," Tom said.

"No, so I figured maybe I'm too far afield. I started checking phone directories. Again, a single hit. Turns out there's an English tearoom in Solvang ..."

"And it's on the second floor," Tom said.

"Bingo. We start counting at ground level; the Brits call our first floor the ground floor and our second floor the first floor. There's a picture on their website. It's a little tourist stop in a strip mall. Solvang is this plasticy place, bills itself as the Danish capital of America ..."

"Up above Santa Barbara," Tom said, "in the Santa Ynez Valley. Lots of timbering and windmills."

"Right. When you're tired of cheese, yodeling and pictures of cows and want a little Earl Grey, you go up to the second floor of this building opposite one of the principal hotels— the *King Frederik Inn*—and get some. *The First Floor* is run by two Latinos from Oceanside. They sell tea, tea towels, teapots, tea cups, tea bags, tea strainers ... all things tea. I called the City of Solvang PD and asked if they had ever had any issues with *The First Floor*. Talked to a desk sergeant named Herspring. He said that they sell some nice homemade shortbreads and that his wife goes in there to buy this Chinese tea that looks like little stars. You throw them into the hot water and they pop open. Nothing criminal, however, except for the price of some of their imported china."

"And no local scandals or reasons to get their name in the paper."

"No, just a puff piece when they opened, what--eight years ago or so."

"How about Nathan Fox?" Tom asked.

"Nothing definitive, but a little more promising," Hector said. "When he left St. Louis he went to Philadelphia."

"Philadelphia?"

"Yes. He had gone to a place called Hahnemann for medical school; it's now run by Drexel University. My guess is that he had old connections in Philly. He needed some help getting his career back on track and picked up the phone. Eventually he took jobs in a series of hospital emergency rooms and then changed his name."

"Changed his name?"

"Yes. He's now Nathaniel Cox. Correction: Nathaniel Cox, *M.D.*"

"He dropped out of sight, so you tracked him by checking his social security records."

"Yes. Chief Dietrich had to make the call."

"He patched his life together with some part-time jobs and then decided to make a fresh start."

"Right," Hector said.

"Where is he now?"

"I don't know," Hector said.

Tom just looked at him, waiting for him to continue.

"At first he was in Memphis, again working in ER's, maybe trying to get a gig at St. Jude's. That didn't materialize, so he moved to Dallas. He worked briefly at the hospital where they took JFK."

"Parkland."

"Right," Hector said, "but then he left and went to San Antonio, where he worked for an HMO."

"How long?"

Hector checked his notes. "Four years and two months. Then he disappeared."

"And you talked to the people at the HMO."

"Yes. They said that he was a reliable employee who gave a month's notice and left. He gave a forwarding address in Philadelphia, which turned out to be a mail drop. I checked there and they said that he was a reliable customer who stopped leasing the box a few months ago. I asked if they ever saw him pick up his mail there and they said that he had begun renting it years earlier and that none of the current staff worked there at the time of the initial rental so they don't know what he looks like. He paid his rentals a year in advance. He received relatively little mail, but someone always picked it up because it never accumulated to the point that they had to empty it and set it aside for him."

"Sounds dodgy," Tom said. "Good docs put down roots in communities, expand their patient base, get their pictures taken for local magazines."

"Yes," Hector said. "I tried to find out what he was doing ... like maybe the procedures that others didn't want to do. Maybe something for which he wasn't board-certified. Nothing there. He was a general *factotum*; that's the word one of the hospital administrators used. I pursued the issue with all of his employers. All of them painted him as Dr. Reliable. No Michael DeBakey, just a guy who stitched up cuts and prescribed penicillin."

"Maybe he was doing something else on the side," Tom said. "The official jobs were just covers."

"Very possible," Hector said.

"So you checked back with the Social Security administration …"

"Yes. As far as they know he's currently unemployed. The last job for which he made contributions was in San Antonio."

"And the IRS?"

"Minimal income. A few thousand last year."

"You have to file," Tom said. "They don't like it if you cheat, but the first thing they check on is whether or not you file. What address did he give?"

"The Philadelphia mail drop."

"And now he's cut himself loose from that."

"Yes."

"So he *has* disappeared."

"For now," Hector said.

"Maybe he's in the OC."

"I got his driver's license picture from Texas. All of the local jurisdictions have it. Your copy is in your in-box."

"Good work, Hector."

"I'd rather brace him than chase the paper trail," Hector said.

"So would I," Tom answered.

Tom refilled his cup and went to his office. He picked up Nathan Fox's picture from his in-box. A color head shot. Puffy cheeks, circles under the brown eyes, no hat, no glasses. His chin was tilted upward as if he was posing for a mug shot. His ears looked as if they had been pulled back and tacked to the side of his head. Dumbo surgery. A bad job.

TWENTY-THREE

Tom briefed Sally on Hector's research. She was eating solid food again—a salad with croutons. She removed the plastic wrapping and discarded it, going through the ritual of eating a real meal. She set the mini-tub of dressing aside. Tom was eating a ham and cheese sandwich, washing it down with hot coffee.

"He never mentioned anyone named Fox or Cox," Sally said. "And he never described an event that could have been associated with another surgeon. Nothing bad, that is. From time to time he talks about successes, but he seldom speaks of St. Louis. That's the distant past for him."

"And you've never been to that place in Solvang, *The First Floor*."

"No. We were in Solvang once on our way back from Santa Maria. We just drove through it to stop for gas. I noticed that restaurant that's featured in the wine movie; what is it—*Sideways*? It's right on the main road. But no stops for tea or tea paraphernalia. It may be something else …"

"What's that?"

"The 'first floor' reference. Maybe he was referring to his condo search. You don't want the first floor usually. Less security, less of a view. Unless there's no elevator. You don't want a third or fourth floor walkup either. Maybe he saw something he liked that he didn't expect to like. More convenience. More space for the money … I don't know, Tom. I'm grasping, I know, but it's what he was supposed to be doing. It would have been the first thing we talked about if this hadn't happened …"

"Maybe," Tom said, "but perhaps we're approaching this too *rationally*."

"You're probably right. A person coming out of a coma might say anything. Why would we expect him to be coherent? Maybe we should expect just the opposite: rambling non sequiturs, thought fragments, something from a dream or a nightmare ..."

"How are *you*, Sally?"

"I'm OK. I need to hear his voice again, feel movement in his hands, see his eyes open, see his face turn toward me."

Tom discarded the remains of his sandwich and got a second cup of coffee. Sally picked at her salad. "I've got to get back to campus," she said. "I've got a student who needs to see me. I'll be back tonight."

Tom checked with the patrolman who was in plain clothes. His name was Bradley.

"Any movement, Scott? Any change at all?" he asked.

"No, Lieutenant, sorry. The good news is that no one suspicious has been in the area. Whoever did that to him probably thinks he's dead."

"No press?"

"No. They're occupied with other things for the moment. And that's fine with me; I'm not complaining."

"That guy at the airport who broke through security ..."

"Yes, Lieutenant. He said he wanted to kiss his girlfriend good-bye and had forgotten to. How do you forget to do that? I don't know whether the authorities will press charges or not, but my guess is that he's going to be looking for a new girlfriend in the very near future. They interviewed the current one last night and she said she was embarrassed by his actions. She said she didn't want to be on the news. She just wanted to get to her meeting in Sacramento."

Tom smiled. "I'm going to sit with Dr. Barnes for a few minutes," he said. "Thanks for keeping an eye out."

"No problem, Lieutenant."

When he entered the room the blinds were closed. Tom opened them. Maybe Len would like to feel the sun on his face, he thought. If he gives any indication of awareness I'll be able to see him better, watch the lines around his eyes and mouth, the wrinkles in his forehead …

After a few minutes the sound of Len Barnes's breathing became fainter. His chest rose and fell and the blanket moved in a slow rhythm, but there seemed to be less sound. No rattling in his throat or lungs … there hadn't been anything noticeable earlier, but it was still reassuring. He seemed completely comfortable, completely at peace, even down to the hint of a smile at the edges of his lips. The room was cool, verging on cold. Sixty-eight degrees, possibly a degree or two less than that. Tom pulled up the blanket slightly. His own windbreaker felt good. He turned up the collar.

"Talk to me, Len," he whispered. "Talk to me. Sally will be back later. Probably by early evening. You're a lucky man, Len. She really loves you. No question about it. And she'll be here for you. We're here for you too, Len. We've made some progress. We know about Nathan Fox. But guess what? He's changed his name. He's Nathaniel Cox now. Were you aware of that, Len? Do you have any idea where he might be? What did he do, Len? You've got to help us. We're trying to find him. His picture is on the street, but we need to know more, much more. Unless something else breaks you're the only one who can help us."

Suddenly there was movement. Very slight movement, but movement nonetheless. Len Barnes sniffed, as if he were trying to catch his breath … as if someone had briefly covered his nose or tickled him. He sniffed and then he moved his head to the left, a slight jerk, as if he was trying to free his neck from a tight collar or a restraining hand.

"What is it, Len? What is it?" Tom asked. "I'm here. Tell me." He was speaking louder now and he put his right hand on Len Barnes's left, squeezing it gently. "What is it?" he asked. "What is it?"

Len spoke without moving or opening his eyes. "The first floor," he said. "Very odd. Never … before."

And that was all he said. Tom kept talking to him, kept squeezing his hand, but that was it. He sniffed again, more quietly this time, wrinkling his nose slightly and then he returned to sleep, his breathing even and comfortable.

"He spoke again, Sally."

"What did he say, Tom?"

He hesitated.

"Don't worry; I'm on the Bluetooth; I'm fine," she said. "I can talk."

"He talked about the first floor again," Tom said. "He said it was very odd and that it hadn't happened before … something like that … his exact words were 'the first floor … very odd … never … before'. I wrote down the words. We'll parse them, Sally. We'll turn them every way but loose."

"It's important," she said. "It's not random. He's trying to put together a single, coherent statement."

TWENTY-FOUR

"He's gone to the yellow tablets, Chief," Hector said. "He's drawing lines, writing and rewriting the words, jotting down synonyms, antonyms and the full range of possible meanings. He's moving between the dictionary and the thesaurus sites on the internet and drawing pictures in the margins. He's in full obsession mode."

"That's good," Chris Dietrich said. "When Tom's engaged like that we usually see impressive results. He told me that he was afraid that he was too close to it. You keep studying the same set of words over and over and you get farther and farther from their meaning, not closer."

"Then he paces," Hector said. "And gets coffee. Then more coffee. He's trying to come back fresh. Trying to clear his mind and see the words … *well* … as if he's seeing them for the first time rather than the fiftieth. I watch him and I learn. I know how to concentrate. I didn't know how to re-concentrate."

"Tom and I were talking," Chris said. "We both think Sally's right. It's as if Len has this one long sentence or paragraph that he's trying to articulate, but he can only give it to us a phrase or two at a time."

"It's hell to have to be patient, Chief," Hector said.

"It is indeed, Hector. It is indeed. What else are you working on?"

"I'm finishing up the paperwork on the drug bust, Chief. How can somebody be so stupid as to peddle product on the beach in broad daylight?"

"You've got to reach the customers," Chris said. "They're not there at night."

"Right. Anyway, I've got a court appearance this afternoon on those burglaries …"

"Off the Canyon Road, last April."

"Yes, sir. It's taken a long time to put it all together. We had to recover some of the property, then link it directly with the perps, then get the truck driver to roll over on the head guy …"

"What's up next for you?"

"Supporting Lieutenant Deaton primarily, but I'm also helping Lieutenant Brighton on his stat rape case."

"You ever miss the streets, Hector?"

"I'm there enough to remind me of them, sir. I like the plain clothes and the detection, but I can *revert* when I need to. Correction. When Lieutenant Deaton needs me to do that."

"How about unauthorized weapons, Hector? Should I be checking your pockets more often?"

"Probably, sir," Hector said.

Chris smiled. "When I was in the LAPD, just starting out in Robbery/Homicide … there was an old sergeant who was known for carrying unauthorized *implements*. During briefings he'd tell us all to make sure that we checked our tires before we rolled. I thought it was good advice, but it took me awhile to pick up on what he was actually saying. I asked another sergeant about it and he explained it to me. He said that when you drive through the Midwest and go to those truck stops on the interstate you find all kinds of interesting things for sale. One of them is the box of miniature baseball bats. They're used like nightsticks, but they're not advertised that way. They're very handy; they fit under the front seat of a truck, out of sight if the sheriff starts looking, but easy to pick up if you happen to have a sudden need for it. The side of the box says 'Tire Pressure Testers'."

"I didn't hear that, Chief."

"Hear what, Hector?" Chris Dietrich said and turned back to the file folder in his hand.

When Hector walked by Tom's office he saw that Tom had switched from pencils to magic markers, highlighting items on the lists he was compiling. He knocked on Tom's door and asked him if he was interested in some lunch. "The real stuff, Lieutenant, not *Taco Bell*."

"Thanks. Give me another twenty minutes," Tom said.

Forty-five minutes later they were eating rice, beans, and enchiladas. "It's just like Italian," Hector said. "Perfectly fresh, simple ingredients and no chintzing on the technique. Homemade sauces, high-quality protein."

"Works for me," Tom said. "It tastes completely different than the microwaved cardboard with the Velveeta or mystery meat."

Hector nodded and ate some more rice. "Any progress with the Barnes statement?" he asked.

"Nothing definitive," Tom said. "I have to proceed as if Len was aware of what he was saying and that what he was saying would make perfect sense, once he was able to complete the thought. I've got one big thing going for me ..."

Hector waited for him to continue. Tom was gesturing with his fork in between bites.

"He's a simple man. Wait, let me rephrase that. He's a man with a straightforward, simple life. He doesn't have fifty sideline investments. He doesn't have a large and complicated family, all of them making constant, conflicting demands. He doesn't live on a large property with a need for staff and constant maintenance. He's not a joiner. He doesn't have a garage full of cars or a motor yacht at Newport Beach. He doesn't have four or five kids whose lives are in various stages of disarray. He's a very simple guy. He cuts, he autopsies and he loves an anthropologist. When he says something, it should be equally straightforward. It shouldn't be echoing with a lot of possible meanings. What you see is what you get, so what he says should be just what he says and just what he means. The first rule has to be to keep it all simple."

"And you're closing in on something?"

"I'm trying to," Tom said.

TWENTY-FIVE

Tom put the sheaf of yellow papers on the back of his desk and shifted his chair toward his computer. Googling local realtors he found the name of Cynthia Nelson and called her office. "Cyndi Nelson's office; how may I direct your call?" an older female voice said.

Tom identified himself and asked to speak to her. The receptionist put him through.

"Cyndi Nelson," a younger voice said.

"Tom Deaton, Cyndi."

"You're interested in condos, in Laguna Hills ..."

"Not exactly. I'm interested in condos but in a different context. We were at UCI together, had coffee once or twice."

"You helped me with my physics course, assembled the weights and pullies, connected the circuits."

"I tried to," Tom said.

"I'm confusing you with somebody named Dieter," she said. "What's up, Tom? You want to have coffee again?"

"I'm at the Laguna Beach PD now," Tom said. "I'm working a case and I need some real estate expertise. With all of those signs on the bus stop benches and the *For Sale* signs in the neighborhood, how could I think of anyone but you?"

"It pays to advertise," she said. "How soon do you want to get together?"

"Today, if possible."

"Let me check here … I've got a showing in a few minutes. They're just window shopping at this point, so I probably won't be writing up any offers. Tell you what … give me a number where I can reach you and I'll call you as soon as I'm finished."

She called fifteen minutes later. "They cancelled. Too much sunshine today; I think they're going to the beach instead."

"Where should I meet you?" Tom asked.

"How about the Starbucks on the PCH at Dana Point?"

"Perfect," Tom said. "Twenty minutes?"

"Yes," she said.

He bought the coffee; they caught up on past times, calculating that they hadn't seen each other since a ribbon-cutting function eight years earlier. "I'm glad to see that you've been prospering," Tom said.

"Holding my nose above water in a tough market," she said. "How have you been?"

"Not so bad," Tom said. "We never know how well we're really doing until we see the crime statistics at the end of the year. That's the public's chief indicator. Lately we've been doing pretty well, I think."

"But you've got something on your plate now that involves real estate …"

"It might," Tom said. "I don't think it's directly related to real estate. Let me tell you the situation. I've got a person who's unconscious. We need to know where he's been recently but he's not in a position to tell us."

"And time is of the essence."

"Yes, exactly. We think he may have been looking at condos about a week ago, but we're not sure. What I need is a list of the likely condos he might have checked out. Then I can go to the listing agents and see whether or not he signed any of their Open House sheets or communicated with them directly."

"Location?"

"His office is in Irvine; he works around the area, particularly in Laguna Hills."

"Price?"

"I'd just be guessing. A million and up."

"How far up?"

"I don't know, maybe three to five million."

"Lifestyle?"

"Middle-aged man, busy professional in a committed relationship. No children."

"The ocean's the ringer, of course. Prices skyrocket the closer you are and the better the view."

"I think he was just beginning to look at things, trying to get a feel for the market. He wasn't ready to make an offer."

"If he's busy and he's wealthy he probably doesn't want a fixer. Not that there are many fixers in that price range in this market. With a significant other he probably wants some floor space, not just a view and proximity to the sand."

"I think he'd probably start with new construction. New projects with model units. He'd want a sense of what's available, what it's going to cost, what kind of features are being offered. I believe that he was looking alone and was then going to touch base with his partner."

"Big picture-type."

"Right. He wanted a sense of the range of properties, the range of amenities, the range of prices. Then he and his partner would get together and they'd home in on specifics."

"OK. Well, first off, there's a lot on the market and there's also a lot of new construction. Go figure, huh? What you hope to do is trace his steps, right? You're not so much interested in the properties as you are in his movements."

"Yes," Tom said.

"That makes it easier," Cyndi said. "It's pretty basic when you get down to it. Most realtors represent a set of properties already. If they can steer a client to one of theirs and not have to split the commission, life is good."

"Right," Tom said.

"There are also some —what would you call them?—extreme properties. They're not problematic properties; they just sit at opposite extremes on the feature scale: properties in the absolute best locations with top amenities but less square footage; properties a little more distant but a lot more generous with extra bedrooms and bathrooms; properties with a lot of units and wings and towers and choices; properties with fewer units and choices but more privacy … you get the picture."

"I do."

"When I have a client who wants to get a big-picture sense of the market I start by showing him the extremes; then I try to elicit a sense of his preferences and priorities and we start to get more specific. Make sense?"

"It does," Tom said.

"Why don't I make you a list of, say, fifteen to twenty projects with the names of the listing agents. I'll call somebody at our Laguna Beach office and ask them to put together a collection of folders for you. When these properties are developed the listing agents send folders and brochures to all of the area realtors. We can put together a collection very easily. Give me about an hour and a half. I'll email you the general list and you can have somebody pick up whatever folders are available on the properties on the list at our Laguna Beach office. I'll also email you the name of the person who will be your contact there."

"Terrific," Tom said. "That's exactly what I need."

"Now you owe me something," Cyndi said.

"Just name it," he responded.

"Drinks and dinner some time."

"I can do that," Tom said. "I'd like to do that."

"So would I," she said. "An hour and a half, then."

"An hour and a half," he responded. When she extended her hand he took it and also kissed her on the cheek.

"You always did live dangerously," she said, smiling.

"My hallmark," he said. "Think about where you'd like to eat."

The email came through in an hour and fifteen minutes. There were twenty-one properties on the list and the name of the Laguna Beach office contact: Dwight Healy. He explained what had happened to Hector. "She doesn't want any competition," he said. "That's why she asked a man to work with you on this."

"You think so?" Tom asked.

"I hope so," Hector responded, smiling. "You need to get out more, Lieutenant."

TWENTY-SIX

Dwight Healy was able to assemble a packet of folders for sixteen of the twenty-one properties. Some properties had nothing more than realtor contact information. The more ambitious and the more desperate offered folders, brochures and special bookmarks with website information. Under other circumstances it might have been interesting and enjoyable to study the floor plans and the staged models and see if there were any correlations between the seven-figure pricetags and the architectural and design realities. Maybe later, Tom thought. In the meantime he started placing calls to the agents representing the properties.

All of the agents who were available expressed a willingness to talk to him and share information without the requirement of a warrant. "I have to warn you," one said, "people don't always write down their actual names when they visit a property. They don't want realtors hounding them forever after. It's a kind of bait and switch, after all. When they visit a property the realtors learn that they may be in the market. Some people are just window shoppers, of course, but some are actually looking. If they don't buy the property they're inspecting they might buy something else. We get their names and then *home in* on them, you should pardon the expression ..."

"I understand," Tom said. "I've also got some pictures I'd like you to see."

"I'd be happy to take a look," the agent said. "Just keep in mind that the agent on the developer's brochure was probably not on site when the property was visited. Usually it's a part-timer, someone who's there to make sure that the doors are opened and then locked, the lights are all on, the brochures are on the kitchen counter and potential buyers have a sheet available for their name and contact information."

"But you would have a record of who was were, particularly for a recent, fairly narrow time period."

"We would," she said, "and we'd be happy to share that information. All that I'm saying is that this may require a little more legwork than you may have anticipated."

"I understand," Tom said, "and I appreciate your willingness to help. When can we get together?"

She agreed to meet with him in forty-five minutes. Her name was Lauren Reed; she was with Coldwell Banker Platinum Properties and she was actually on site during the period in which Len Barnes would have been looking. Unfortunately, he had not signed her sheet and she was unable to identify him from the photograph which Tom showed her. He thanked her and moved on. By the end of the day he had talked to eight realtors and four assistants, but failed to connect Len with any of the properties which they represented.

One of the realtors had commented on the fact that she had seen several significant prospects during that time period but one of the prospects was a woman, one was a man accompanied by his mother and two were married couples.

Later that day he was able to make appointments for the following day with six additional agents, scheduling those appointments as early in the day as possible. One person at Re/Max thought that Len looked familiar, though there was no signature or contact information on her sign-up sheet. "He was with his wife," the agent said. "She was complaining about the colors in the guest bathroom. I told her that that was only a model and that the room could be painted or papered in any fashion that she desired, but she just kept complaining and shaking her head."

"You're sure she was with him," Tom said.

"Oh yes, she kept approaching him and asking him how anyone could have such bad taste as to paint a bathroom that color. He just smiled politely and humored her; he actually seemed very nice."

Tom thanked her, checked her name off of the list which Dwight had been kind enough to prepare and grabbed a hurried lunch at a sandwich place near her office. He arranged three more appointments for that afternoon, but none panned out. Only one agent acknowledged seeing someone who looked remotely like Len and she said that he had been accompanied by a teenage son who sat in the living room area while his father toured the property, searching the apps on his phone and texting his friends.

The handful of agents remaining were available the following morning. Tom met with the first at 9:00 a.m. Her name was Gerry Hollis. Blonde and high-energy, she was meticulously dressed and coiffed. She worked for Prudential; the property she represented was a Newport Beach high rise with secure, two-car parking bays, 1800 square feet of finished space, ocean views and $1,595,000 pricetags. "To start," she said. "Upgrades are extra, of course. The model would be around $2,200,000, depending on the counter tops and the appliances chosen. Everyone wants a great kitchen but no one seems to cook anymore. I don't always understand things; I just sell."

Tom showed her the picture of Len Barnes.

"Oh yes," she said, "I remember him. Very nice man. Very quiet and sweet. I thought he looked familiar the moment I saw him. Then I realized; he took out my sister's thyroid. I mentioned the fact to him and he asked how she was doing. 'She's fine,' I said."

"Did he happen to sign your list?"

"Actually, he didn't, but he took my card. It was a week ago Monday."

"You're sure about the date."

"Yes. I'm not usually here on Mondays because I'm always here on the weekends. Sundays are our best day; I'm sure you knew that. Mondays I have one of our trainees house-sit the model. There's not usually a lot of traffic, but we're open if someone wants to see the property and pick up a brochure. That Monday the trainee was sick. She called me right before the property was to be opened and I had to jump in the shower, throw on some clothes, pin on my name tag, hurry to the office and be prepared to smile and shake hands."

"Do you remember what time of day he came in?"

"Early. Just after we opened at 9:00. He was here about thirty or forty minutes. He even made some notes on the brochure. I don't hound potential clients, particularly not in this price range. I told him I'd be happy to answer questions and then let him tour on his own. I saw him jotting notes as he walked between the rooms. He was particularly interested in cupboard space and square footage. I remember he asked me whether or not additional cupboard space could be built."

"And he came alone."

"Yes, he came alone but left with two other men."

"With two other men?"

"Yes."

"Did you see them?"

"Briefly. I went down with him to the first level. We have a unit there which is filled with boxes of brochures, construction material samples and signs. I needed to pick up some additional brochures. We said good-bye and when he left the property he was joined by two men out on the sidewalk."

"*Joined?*" Tom asked. "Did it look as if they were waiting for him there?"

"I can't really say," she said. "He walked out the door and I turned to unlock the door to the storage unit. Then I looked out at the last minute and he was walking away with the two men."

Tom took out the photo of Nathan Fox. "Was this one of the men?" he asked.

"I don't think so," she said. "Both of them had full heads of hair and mustaches."

"Caucasian?"

"Yes, as far as I could tell."

"Height, weight?"

"A little taller than the doctor, I think. Maybe a little bit heavier, but not obese."

"Complexion?"

"Hard to say in the bright sun, Lieutenant," she said, "and I was looking at them in profile."

"They were on either side of him when they walked away?"

"Yes, they were. I remember that. I remember also that they were wearing suits and ties; the doctor was dressed more casually."

"Anything else, anything else at all?"

"No, I don't think so. I'll call you if I remember anything more. I didn't make anything of it at the time because I wasn't paying that much attention."

"I understand," Tom said. He thanked her, left the building and paused on the sidewalk, checking for security cameras on the façade and under the porte-cochère. Unfortunately, they had been roughed-in but not yet installed and there were no cameras in the visitors' parking area.

He called Chris Dietrich and briefed him on what he had learned. "If Fox was there," Chris said, "he wouldn't have shown himself at the outset. Len would have recognized him and reacted."

"Right, Chief," Tom said.

"What are you thinking, Tom?" Chris asked.

"That this might be bigger than we thought, that if Fox *is* involved, he found and hired some muscle to intercept Len. That's a lot of trouble and expense."

"He would have needed help to restrain Len, poison him and leave him beside the **5**."

"Right."

"Good work, Tom. What's next?"

"I have a couple more real estate agents to talk to. I'll see if I learn anything else from them."

"Good. I'll see you when you get back to the office."

There were three remaining agents to contact, but Tom was restive. He had learned something new, something promising, and he doubted that the other agents would know anything, particularly since the time of Len's meeting with Gerry Hollis corresponded, on Sally's time line, with the start of Len's search. Perhaps it had ended there.

TWENTY-SEVEN

"I met with the remaining real estate agents, but none had had any contact with Len," Tom said. "Then I began to wonder whether or not I had elicited everything possible from Gerry Hollis. I called her back and pressed her on the details of the facial features of the two men. She agreed to do a CompuSketch with Hector, though she was concerned that she wouldn't be of very much help."

"And how did that work out?" Chris asked.

"Here are the sketches," Tom said, sliding the printouts across the table. "We did one with swarthy complexions, one with stark white. Very hard for her to determine in the bright sun. The swarthy could also be seen as a California tan."

"Noses, mustaches, dark hair. Mediterranean," Chris said. "Could be Italian, could be Middle Eastern. Could be ... just about anyone but Scandinavians."

"Or southern Californians?" Tom asked. "Indigenous, surfer types, that is."

"It's knowledge that we didn't have before," Chris said, "and we can congratulate ourselves all around on believing that Len didn't get drunk and end up naked, on the side of the road, all by himself."

"And they had been following him," Tom added. "This was the result of systematic planning, possibly even of sophisticated planning."

"What are you saying?" Chris asked.

"Well, Chief, it's one thing to hire two mooks to pick up a guy. They drive to his house or his place of business and just grab him by the neck and shoulders. If, however, you wanted to do something less obvious and heavy-handed or if the pickup spot was one in which there was a fair chance that you might be observed by witnesses, you'd want each of the muscle guys to be dressed nicely and have a plausible set of credentials. Good, forged credentials don't come cheap and they're not sold at Wal-Mart or Target. In this case, the person was picked up in broad daylight at a respectable, upscale place of business, at a time when he--the victim--was not expected to report for work. He was off, on leave or vacation, and no one expected to see him for awhile. If he ends up on the side of the road, loaded with alcohol, that could be plausibly interpreted as being the culmination of a long bender or lost weekend. And if you wanted some time to talk to him first, to taunt him or to humiliate him in some way, the fact that he was not expected back for several days would give you the leeway to do that without raising any suspicions or concerns."

"Right," Chris said, "but it wouldn't be easy."

"No, that's why I said *sophisticated* planning. Not CIA, super-snoop planning, but something more than 'let's do it on Tuesday' planning. You'd have to tap his landline or intercept his cell phone communications, hack into his email ... it would also help if you already knew about Sally and the basic elements of his private life. Hacking into his office email or even breaking in surreptitiously to check the schedule in his nurse/ receptionist's book would help ... if you really wanted to do it right, not just grab him off the street."

"Are the CompuSketch pictures on the street, Tom?"

"Yes, they are, Chief, but the details are sparse and there are no moles, tats, scars or defining characteristics. I don't have high hopes that we'll get any immediate hits."

"I understand, but some information is better than no information. What about his nurse/receptionist?"

"Marsha Jasper."

"Yes. Could someone have gotten to her? Could she have betrayed him?"

"I doubt it, Chief. She's been with him for nearly twenty years. They're very tight."

"What if she was threatened? What if she was told that it was all benign, that someone was planning a surprise party or a practical joke, something like that?"

"I'll check back with her, Chief, but my gut tells me that she would have said something. She's not a person who would be easily intimidated and she didn't seem edgy or jumpy when I talked to her, but I'll talk to her again."

"Absolutely not," Marsha Jasper said. "Absolutely not. No one approached me, Lieutenant, and Dr. Barnes's schedule is not something that someone could just waltz in here and read. He likes a hard copy, but the book is locked in my desk when he's out of the office. I keep an electronic copy, but it's passworded. *Carefully* passworded. This is very important information, Lieutenant, what with all the insurance company requests and the ambulance-chasing lawyers … no, you couldn't get at that information without a warrant or a very shrewd team of computer hackers."

"I'm not accusing you of anything, ma'am," Tom said. "My concern is that someone might have threatened you and that you felt that you or members of your family were at risk."

"I understand, Lieutenant. No offense taken. None whatsoever. And my family …"

"Yes, ma'am?"

"Well, if anyone had wanted to make a move on them …"

"Yes?"

"If they would have checked first they would have known that that might not be a very good idea. The members of *my* family are armed, Lieutenant. To the teeth."

"Yes, ma'am," Tom said. "Thanks again for all your help."

Tom updated Chief Dietrich. "That's good; it never hurts to check," Chris said. "Come to think of it, I believe I met her husband once at a birthday party for Len. Large, barrel-chested guy. He asked me about our service automatics. Said he liked a Sig P320, but preferred a .44 magnum Desert Eagle. 'Course, you walk funny with all that iron on your hip,' he said, 'but I find it comforting.'"

Tom smiled, clicked off and walked down the street, looking for a Starbucks. It didn't take long to find one. Through the traffic on the boulevard he could see another one on the opposite corner. He entered, felt the chill from the air conditioning and looked at the chart above the urns and pastry shelves. He felt awkward saying *small, medium,* or *large,* but he also felt awkward with that *venti* and *grande* stuff. "*Venti* is *twenty,*" a barista told him once. "Italian for *twenty*; twenty ounces." He still felt awkward.

"Yes, sir?" the man at the cash register said. "Sir?"

Tom was looking at his cell phone. He had turned it to *silent* while he was talking to Marsha Jasper and hadn't yet returned it to *normal/ outside.* There was a text message from Sally: "L spoke again. More this time. Call me ASAP."

TWENTY-EIGHT

"*The first floor? I didn't understand. It's fine, they said. It's fine.*"

"And that's all he said?" Tom asked.

"Yes," Sally said, shifting on the plastic chair in the ER lounge. "He found something odd about it. Something he hadn't seen before or hadn't experienced before. That's what he implied the last time he spoke. Now he says that he didn't understand, but that someone assured him that it was fine."

"He didn't understand because it was odd. Something about the first floor was odd."

"Yes."

"But he's with others now. He calls them *they*. We've just learned something else, Sally."

"Yes … ?"

"Len was looking at a property in Newport Beach. I spoke to the realtor. When he left the building she saw him accompanied by two men."

"Under duress?"

"She couldn't tell. She had turned to the side to do something else. When she turned back he was walking away with them."

"What did they look like?"

Tom handed her the copies of the pictures.

"These don't tell us very much, do they?" she asked.

"No, but look at the way the two men are dressed. If Len had intended to meet with them for some recreational purpose it's likely that they would have been dressed less formally. This would have been about 9:45 or 9:50 in the morning--too late for breakfast and too early for lunch, assuming that the two men were businessmen--and who else dresses that way on a weekday morning except businessmen?"

"People trying to look like businessmen," Sally said, "or at least trying not to look like goons who were abducting someone."

"Precisely," Tom said.

"So it's possible that these two men took him somewhere, to a first floor somewhere."

"Yes."

"I knew that he would never drink so much alcohol that it would poison him. I knew that he was coerced."

"Yes," Tom said, "but they didn't take him to a bar. Just about every bar I've ever seen has been on the first floor. Not every one, of course. The stylish ones are on the top floors sometimes, but it would never be considered *odd* to find a bar on the first floor. That's assuming that they wanted to get him drunk voluntarily, rather than ... *force-feeding* him."

"Yes, I agree," she said, "but Len said that they said that it was *fine*. When he said it, it was as if 'they' were reassuring him. They were persuading, not forcing. They didn't say, 'shut the hell up and like it' or 'deal with it' or something like that. He found something to be odd and they assured him that it would be fine."

"Yes," Tom said. "And that doesn't sound like coercion or at least not violent coercion."

"At least not yet," Sally said. "They might have started with requests and assurances and then moved on to demands and threats if he refused to cooperate."

"True."

"The one thing they weren't doing was showing him real estate," Sally said, trying to force the hint of a smile.

"No. And there was no initial violence. He walked away with them; he wasn't dragged."

"But they were on either side of him, according to the realtor."

"Yes," Tom said. "They may have shown him a weapon or threatened him in some quiet way, but they didn't assault him and he walked away in a manner that didn't raise any concerns in the mind of the realtor. She simply thought that they were meeting him there and that the three just walked away together."

"How would they know that he was going to be there? They must have been following him or they must have had access to his schedule …"

"He walked into the property unannounced," Tom said. "The model is always open during business hours; there's no requirement to make an appointment or some special arrangement. I've spoken with his nurse/receptionist …"

"Marsha Jasper."

"Yes."

"Tough cookie; very protective."

"Yes, she assures me that no one could have gained access to his schedule easily and that no one approached her concerning it."

"So it's most likely that they were following him."

"Yes, I think so."

"And no one has identified the men from the drawing yet …"

"No," Tom answered, "but as you said, there's not much there."

"I'd like to talk to the realtor."

"I'm sure she'd be happy to help, if she could. I stood on the spot where she did, however, and I saw the field of vision available to her. When she turned to look at Len she couldn't have seen him and the two men for more than a fraction of a second. She remembered the bare outline of their faces and what they were wearing. I'd love to know more about their body language and their posture, the physical manner in which they were relating to him as well as to one another. I'm not sure that she can really be of any help there. Hector drew exactly what she described, so the men weren't talking. They were simply walking south, abreast, for a split second …"

"And there are no security cameras in the area."

"Not installed yet, unfortunately," Tom answered.

"At least it's new information," Sally said. "Thanks, Tom. Thanks very much. Now I think I'll go back in; I want to be there if he speaks again. What are you going to do?"

"Cast the net a little wider if I can," he answered.

TWENTY-NINE

The next morning Tom emailed the pictures of Len and his likely abductors to law enforcement officials in St. Louis, Memphis, Dallas, San Antonio and Philadelphia, along with the Texas driver's license picture of Nathan Fox, now Nathaniel Cox. He didn't expect a hit on the abductors, but he asked the department officers in all of the cities with which Fox had been connected to check and see if he had a rap sheet. Meanwhile, Hector combed through the internet and the online newspaper archives of the cities in which Fox had lived, searching for anything that might help advance the case.

There were no immediate responses that day. Late in the afternoon Tom grabbed a sandwich from the station vending machine and swung by Saddleback. Sally was in the room with Len. She was balancing a scholarly journal in her right hand and holding his hand with her left. "Thought I might as well get some work done," she said. "This way I can monitor him and catch up on articles at the same time."

"We're checking with the police in the towns in which we know Fox lived," Tom said. "Maybe we'll get lucky. Any new responses from Len?"

"He hasn't said anything," she answered, "but he seems a little restive. There's movement from time to time. I'm taking that as a good sign."

"Maybe he's dreaming," Tom said.

"Possibly," Sally said. "There's no doubt that there's active brain function. Any new thoughts on the 'first floor' business?"

"I think we may be missing it because it's too obvious," Tom said. "I think he was taken someplace. Whatever or wherever it was he didn't expect it to be on the first floor of the building. Whoever took him there reassured him that it was fine and that he shouldn't worry about it."

"Maybe he was taken to see Fox. He expected an office or apartment above street level. Instead they took him to commercial space or some public, open space ... I don't know ... "

"Possibly," Tom said. "Maybe they lied to him and told him they needed his professional help. Perhaps they told him he was going to an ICU for a consult. When it became obvious that he was on the first floor and that they were going to stay there he became suspicious."

"So he went off with the men thinking that they needed him professionally ..."

"Possibly," Tom said, "but it would still be suspicious. People wouldn't just walk up to you on the street. They'd contact your office and your office would either call or page you. I don't know ... it sometimes seems as if I'm getting close to an explanation and then, somehow, I think about it for a moment or two and it all falls apart."

"I appreciate your trying," Sally said.

"Just a second," Tom said. "My phone just twitched. I'll be back."

The call was from St. Louis, a sergeant named Terry Baxter. "You're burning the midnight oil, Sergeant," Tom said.

"I'm on duty tonight, Lieutenant," Baxter said. "It's pretty quiet so I checked the files on your friend Nathan Fox."

"Yes ... ?" Tom said, gripping the phone tighter and holding it closer to his ear and mouth.

"He was popped for assault. The charges were dropped but he was brought in for questioning."

"Assault?"

"Actually, sexual assault."

"That's interesting," Tom said.

"Somehow I thought you might say that," Baxter responded. "Actually, he was busted for what the statute calls 'deviate sexual intercourse'; I'll read you the definition of the crime. It is 'any act involving the genitals of one person and the hand, mouth, tongue, or anus of another person or a sexual act involving the penetration, however slight, of the male or female sex organ or the anus by a finger, instrument or object done for the purpose of arousing or gratifying the sexual desire of any person or for the purpose of terrorizing the victim.'"

"Sex … or terror," Tom said. "Which was it?"

"Maybe both," Baxter said. "He claimed it was a harmless pat, that it was *congratulatory*. He said that he misjudged her position. He was trying to pat her on the back but that he inadvertently touched her … lower."

"A nurse?"

"Yes. After a couple of hours of surgery. A difficult case. He said that she had done a great job. It was like a locker room pat. She said it wasn't a pat. He goosed her. She didn't use that word. She said he assaulted her … with his finger."

"But he was never convicted."

"No, it was a classic he said/she said. Unfortunately, there were no witnesses and if it was true it would have been a first offense. My guess is that she wanted to embarrass him professionally by bringing the charge. Whether it did or not, he was here for another year and a half. She moved on to another job. The investigating officer thought at first that she had been eased out, but she was actually just completing a master's degree at SLU …"

"Slew?" Tom asked.

"St. Louis University. We all call it SLU."

"Sorry."

"No problem. Anyway, she was just finishing up her master's and the new job represented a promotion."

"Anything else on Fox?"

"No, sorry, Lieutenant."

"How about the name of the nurse?"

"Deborah Patton. I've also got her address and current phone number for you."

THIRTY

Tom checked his watch. It was late in St. Louis and Fox's actions occurred decades earlier. Rather than upset her unnecessarily he decided to call her in the morning.

"Ms. Patton ..." he said.

"Yes," she answered, somewhat tentatively.

"My name is Tom Deaton. I'm a lieutenant in the Laguna Beach Police Department. We're investigating a case that may be related to the actions of a Dr. Nathan Fox. I understand that you were assaulted by him, some time ago."

"Yes, I was," she said. "Has he done it again?"

"I don't know," Tom said. "We're trying to contact him in connection with another case."

"But you haven't found him ..."

"Unfortunately not."

"I'm not surprised. He's probably gone to ground; knowing him he would have a lot of things to hide."

"I spoke with an officer in St. Louis," Tom said. "He briefed me on your case. I'm very sorry that that happened to you."

"Thank you," she said. "So am I. It *really did* happen, Lieutenant. There was less sensitivity in those days, but we're not talking about the dark ages. There *were* sexual assaults and they *were* prosecuted. As I'm sure you're aware, hospitals can be *special* places. There's a great deal of stress and a great deal of suffering. Physicians and surgeons carry heavy responsibilities. They're not always successful. Sometimes they do adolescent things to release the tension. Some are full of themselves and build up their own fragile egos by playing dominance games in the workplace. It's one of the reasons for the chronic shortage of nurses. It's not that too few are trained; the problem is that once they're in the workplace and experience unpleasant things they change careers or attempt to redefine their positions so that they're less likely to be harassed or belittled."

"I understand. I have a good friend who's a nurse," Tom said.

"I was actually on my way out of the system when Fox assaulted me. I was just completing a master's degree in health management. I was able to use my education and prior clinical experience to get a position in a pharmaceutical company."

"And you're still there?"

"No. Actually I went back to graduate school a second time. I'm working at the University now."

"At SLU?"

"Wash U, in their Institute for Public Health."

"It sounds as if you've done very well."

"Thank you, Lieutenant. I'm doing useful work that I enjoy while Nathan Fox appears to be hiding in a cave somewhere. That sounds like justice to me."

"Let me ask you some more questions, if I may."

"Sure, but I have to leave in about fifteen minutes."

"Do you know of any other individuals who were assaulted by Nathan Fox?"

"Not specifically," she said. "He was always a toucher, but I haven't heard of any other instance of his crossing the line the way that he did with me."

"What was his reputation at the hospital?"

"Capable surgeon, but nothing out of the ordinary. Arrogant. He told a lot of bad jokes. Borderline offensive."

"Personal relationships?"

"In love with himself, primarily. I don't know that he was ever married and I don't know of anyone from the hospital ever dating him. He was not a particularly attractive man."

"I've only seen a recent driver's license picture," Tom said. "The license lists him as 5'11" and 240 pounds."

"He was closer to 280 or 290 when he was here," she said. "Male pattern baldness, some acne scars … he wasn't exactly God's gift."

"Anything else?"

"He wore a back brace. You could see it when he was walking or standing in a particular position. It looked like a vertical board, just above the base of his spine. In those days he smoked cigars. He held them in the center of his mouth and rolled them back and forth as he puffed. He had thick, spongy lips. Some of the nurses called him *Buddha*. Behind his back, of course. I think he may have been a golfer."

"That's very helpful," Tom said, writing quickly in his notepad. "I understand that he left St. Louis somewhat abruptly."

"Someone said that he took *French leave*; one day he was here and the next he was gone."

"Do you know why he might have left?"

"No, I don't. And there were never any rumors. He just disappeared."

"Did you know Dr. Leonard Barnes when he was in St. Louis?"

"Briefly," she said. "Very nice man. Top surgeon. He operated on my uncle."

"Do you know of any relationship that Dr. Barnes might have had with Dr. Fox?"

"No, I'm sorry, I don't. I wouldn't expect them to have any relationship. The two were night-and-day different. Dr. Barnes was a gentleman. Scrupulously professional. A private man, but always polite and kind. I knew his wife as well."

"You knew his wife?"

"Yes. She died very young. Tragically, some would say. She was a sweet person."

"She worked at the hospital?"

"Yes, she was a Med-Surg nurse."

"How did she die?"

"Cancer. We didn't have the tools that we have now. There's never a good time to have it, but it's much better to have it now than to have had it then."

"I understand," Tom said. "Thanks very much for all of your help."

"I'm happy to assist in any way that I can," she said. "Good luck finding Fox. If I were you …"

"Yes, ma'am?"

"I'd be sure to wear protective gloves when I lifted up the rocks."

THIRTY-ONE

"Did you know that Len's wife was a Med-Surg nurse?" Tom asked.

"No, I didn't," Sally said. "I didn't even know her name until after Len and I had been dating for a month or more."

"I still don't know it," Tom said.

"Karen. Her name was Karen. He told me her surname once. I believe it was Booth."

"With an e on the end?"

"No, I don't think so. Why do you ask?"

"I don't know. I thought I'd just run it through the data sets, see if anything lit up. He's so private about these things … when I was going through his condo with Carol Carlow we looked at the photographs on his bookshelf. They were so … *generic*. A picture of his mom and dad. A picture of him with a dog. A picture of his graduation from high school. A picture of you … there were no pictures of his wife."

"He showed me one," Sally said. "I think he felt that it might make me uncomfortable to see her picture there every time I came to his apartment. He keeps it in a box in his cupboard. She looked very sweet, an inch or two shorter than Len, dark hair, athletic. She had a nice smile."

"How was she dressed?"

Sally paused, wondering why he would ask that. "Not in a nurse's uniform," she eventually said. Shorts and a blouse. She was standing next to him in the sun. I think it was in Forest Park because there was a museum in the background which I think was from the St. Louis world's fair."

"And you asked to see it?"

"Yes, it wasn't a big deal. He mentioned her in passing and I asked him about her name. I told him I'd like to see a picture of her sometime. No rush, no pressure. He went into his room, brought it out and showed it to me. I didn't press him about it. I could see in his expression that he still missed her."

"I'm just trying to understand the context," Tom said. "I don't mean to pry. I told you about Fox assaulting the other nurse in St. Louis ..."

"Yes ... "

"I just wondered if Fox had made some sort of pass at Len's wife or then fiancée. Perhaps Karen had learned of his assault on Deborah Patton or of someone else. That may be why Len confronted him and threatened to expose him."

"Possible," Sally said. "As I told you, I had to ask to even learn her name. He never mentioned Fox to me and never said anything about an altercation with another doctor in St. Louis."

"It's probably painful for him to talk about those days," Tom said.

"It is," Sally said, "but it's interesting that he never mentioned his wife's being a nurse. Knowing Len, however, it may not be so surprising."

"How so?" Tom asked.

"When he speaks of her it's always in private terms. It's always as *his wife*. He never describes her in any other context. I suspect that he's sensitive to the fact that there are a lot of stereotypes concerning doctors and nurses. Some of the stereotypes are anchored in fact, particularly those concerning the ways in which nurses are treated by doctors. It's a very hierarchic world, almost a quasi-military one; when you add sex to the mix it can become complicated in ... unattractive ways. Fox is a good exhibit A, I suspect. Anyway, I think that Len would try to avoid all those things--the stereotypes, the preconceptions, the jokes. The behavioral dynamics between a husband and wife are different than those between a doctor and a nurse ... sorry, I don't want to get all social sciency ..."

"Just so long as you don't talk about *reciprocal altruism* and *affect display* or *psychometric measurement*," Tom said, smiling.

"I won't," Sally said, smiling also. "You know what I mean, Tom. Doctors order nurses around (female doctors as well as male); doctors don't take nurses' diagnoses as seriously as their own; nurses hold down the fort, while doctors come in at the last minute and issue directives. It doesn't work that way with husbands and wives, at least not with successful husbands and wives."

"I know what you mean," Tom said. "And from what Deborah told me, Len is not the sort of person who would act autocratically with regard to nurses, so it would be expected that he would go out of his way to avoid any hint of stereotypical behavior with regard to his own wife."

"Right," Sally said. "He's above all that stuff. The one thing he's never lost is his own self-confidence. He doesn't have to buoy it up by reducing others. He's always the adult in the room. If he was a Jew instead of an Episcopalian they'd call him a *mensch*."

"I'll check on his wife," Tom said. "Maybe we'll get lucky. This whole case has been proceeding incrementally. No big breakthroughs, no big epiphanies. Just a slow and steady slog."

"Maybe he'll wake up tomorrow and tell us everything," Sally said.

"I wish he would," Tom responded. "I'm betting it would be an interesting story."

"Let me know if you learn anything about his wife," Sally said.

"I will," Tom responded. "And you let me know if he tells you anything more about that 'first floor' business."

Hector's phone rolled over to voice mail when Tom called, so he left a message concerning the internet and court record search for Karen Booth. He thought about returning to the office, but instead checked in with Chris, reported on his discussions with Deborah and Sally, and decided to have an early dinner and call it a night. The early morning hours were often the best, with a shadow staff in the office, the email traffic low and the phone buttons not yet lit up.

Instead of stopping for carryout he decided to phone for a pizza, get a quick shower in the meantime and then violate all diet and exercise rules by eating just before he went to bed. That would also permit time for a beer or two while he waited for the deliveryman to arrive. Better to violate all of the dietary rules than just a few: he'd go for the pepperoni *and* sausage.

When he pulled into the cul-de-sac there was a dark sedan parked in front of his house. The Saltons (on his left) were on vacation in Colorado. The Mintons (on his right) had already relocated to Portland and their Spanish-revival cottage was on the market. The other houses on the street were dark. "To what do I owe this honor?" he thought, as he unsnapped the holster strap on his service automatic.

THIRTY-TWO

As Tom approached the sedan from the rear the driver's-side window came down and a hand holding an encased badge and photo i.d. came into view. "Please don't shoot me, Lieutenant," a female voice said. "I'm on your side."

Tom inspected the credentials, secured his weapon and said, "Would you like to come in and talk?"

Special Agent Gwen Harrison accepted Tom's offer of coffee and sat on his couch, putting her purse beneath the coffee table. He had expected her to opt for the dining room table and a hardwood chair, but she chose comfort over efficiency, perhaps to mislead him. She asked him if she could help with the coffee in any way. When he said no, she sat back, resting her right arm on the sofa arm and stretching her left across the sofa back. Body language 101: I'm making myself comfortable. I pose no threat. I'm just here to talk and be friendly.

She passed on sugar and cream, as did Tom. He sat in the wing chair opposite the couch and said, "To what do I owe the honor of a visit from a member of the Bureau?"

"No big deal," she said. "I came here rather than create some attention-grabbing event at the office. Think of it as a courtesy call and an offer of help."

"With regard to what, specifically?" Tom asked, as he sipped his coffee but kept his eyes on her.

"Nathan Fox," she answered. "Your checks on him came to the attention of several of the Bureau SAC's and the Director asked me to touch base with you."

"The Director … ?"

"Well, that's Bureauspeak for the central Bureau authority. The Director wasn't tossing and turning in bed last night, worried about a bit player like Nathan Fox. Fox has spent time in multiple states and when bulbs lit up there, the Washington bulb lit up as well. The ultimate responsibility rests with the Director, so he dispatched an agent assigned to his office rather than one of the regional offices."

"So you're assigned directly to the headquarters office, not the D.C. field office."

"Right."

"That would strike some reasonable individuals as important, Agent Harrison; they might even infer that Fox could be a *very* big deal, big enough to result in a visit from a senior representative of the Director."

"Some would call me a go-fer, Lieutenant. I appreciate the honorific description, however. I'm just here to elicit any information that you might have and offer our help to you in your investigation."

"Do you know where Fox is?"

"We know that he last surfaced in Texas and that he has employed a mail drop in Philadelphia. We also know that he changed his name (legally, we understand) to Nathaniel Cox."

"But you don't know his precise whereabouts at the moment."

"No, unfortunately, we don't."

"And why is he of interest to the Bureau, Agent Harrison?"

"There's really no pressing Bureau interest," she said.

"You described him as a *bit player*; that suggests a larger drama."

"Poor choice of terms," she said. "I should have used another word, *inconsequential*, perhaps."

"Just when things were getting interesting," Tom said.

"Can you tell me why you're looking for him?" she asked.

"He may or may not be involved in a case we're investigating."

"Would you be comfortable telling me about it?"

"Of course," Tom said. "Our Medical Examiner was recently found unconscious by the side of the Santa Ana Freeway. His blood alcohol readings were off the charts. He was found in the early morning hours, nude. Since he virtually never drank, we believe—given some marks on the body—that he may have been forced to ingest the alcohol, probably rectally. He remains in a comatose state as a result of the alcohol poisoning. Since he is a highly-regarded professional and a trusted friend, we have assumed that his condition was not the result of some extreme behavior, but that his body was posed in such a way as to suggest that his condition was self-inflicted. We're now attempting to find an individual with sufficient motive to do something like this to him."

"To actually kill him (or attempt to) as well as publicly embarrassing him," the SA responded.

"Yes, the nudity also provides cover for the assailants, since there were no keys, cell phone or other personal items found with him that might link him to them."

"You say *assailants*, plural."

"Yes. We think it impossible for a single individual to remove his body from a vehicle and position it by the side of the 5. There were no drag marks in the soil and no marks on the body that would indicate that it had been tossed or dropped."

"And Fox?"

"Fox is the one individual we have been able to identify who may have had a motive for committing the crime."

"They had a personal connection, then."

"Yes. They were both practicing surgeons in St. Louis, approximately twenty years ago. We have received testimony to the effect that our M.E., Dr. Barnes, had an altercation of some sort with Fox and that he threatened to expose him to the medical authorities there. Fox opted instead to leave the city and abandon his practice."

"I needn't tell you that that was a very long time ago, Lieutenant."

"No, you needn't," Tom said. "Unfortunately, it's all that we have. Let me ask you a question."

"Certainly."

"How did Fox get on your radar screen?"

"Nothing significant, really. We had a request from the IRS to check on his whereabouts. There had been considerable fluctuation in his income over a period of several years and they wanted to talk to him. I assume that they were going to audit him, but I can't verify that. His financial situation set off some bells and they wanted to take a closer look."

"You'll forgive me, Agent Harrison ... may I call you Gwen?"

"Yes, certainly.

"And you should call me Tom."

"Of course."

"You'll forgive me, Gwen, but I have to admit to a certain degree of skepticism here. Fluctuation of income is not a very rare occurrence, particularly in the case of a physician who has worked in ER's and other medical venues on a contract basis. You're asking me to believe that the IRS enlisted the help of the Federal Bureau of Investigation in locating him?"

"Yes, but you must keep in mind that this was a matter of computers talking to computers. The Commissioner of Internal Revenue did not call up the Director of the FBI and make a personal request to find this individual. They have millions of such cases and thousands of individuals in upper income brackets whose filings are questionable. When they can't find those individuals they request help from the Bureau."

"And the Director sends one of his Special Agents a couple thousand miles across the country to meet with an investigating officer in a local PD, by parking outside on his street and waiting for him to drive home."

"You would have expected our computers to talk with yours."

"Yes."

"I can understand your skepticism," she said, holding her expression.

"And you would like me to let you know if we have any luck in locating him."

"Yes, we would."

"And if you find him in the meantime you'll let me know?"

"Yes, we will."

"I was actually going to order a pizza," Tom said. "Could I interest you in sharing some of it?"

"Yes, thanks, I'm starving," she said.

"Veggie?"

"Meat lovers," she said.

"I'll make the call," he said.

THIRTY-THREE

"How's the pizza?" Tom asked.

"Excellent," she said. "Good choice."

"So tell me," Tom said.

"Yes … ?"

"Did you talk to Deborah Patton before or after I did?"

"Deborah Patton?"

"Come on, Gwen. You've got bigger computers than we do, better access to records and red telephones than we have and you've got staff everywhere. There's a field office in St. Louis and I doubt that they dodge calls from the Director. I'm sure that they also cooperate and collaborate with local authorities."

"They do," she said. "Actually, we talked to Deborah Patton some time ago."

"*We?*"

"I did."

"So this is your case."

"If it is a case; at this point it's more like a set of separate enquiries."

"And would you be comfortable telling me about it?"

She smiled and took a sip of her Diet Pepsi. "Can I have another piece of pizza?"

"You can have all of it," Tom said. As he picked up her plate, opened the box and slid a slice of pizza onto it, she picked up her purse, unzipped its center section, and removed a photograph.

He put her plate down on the coffee table and she handed him the photograph. It was a candid shot of Fox sitting at a restaurant table with a younger man. Shorter than Fox, he was also smaller in stature. His nose was shorter than those of the individuals who had abducted Len Barnes and he lacked the neck and shoulder strength that Gerry Hollis had described. If they were goons, this individual looked more like a graduate student or young professional.

"His name is al-Barada." (She pronounced it *al-bereday*.) "Mahmud al-Barada. His cousin is Hakim al-Barada. Mahmud was a student; his cousin Hakim has been linked with a terrorist group in Yemen."

"Where was the picture taken?" Tom asked.

"In San Antonio. Mahmud was studying engineering at UTSA."

"And Hakim?"

"Last sighted in Pakistan, but suspected of being in London."

"And Fox's connection?"

"He was listed as Mahmud's physician in his student records."

"And have you spoken with him?"

"He left school at the end of last semester."

"Forwarding address?"

"A mail drop in Karachi."

"Did he graduate?"

"No. He's technically on a leave of absence."

"But nowhere to be found."

"Not yet."

"I hope he doesn't have a lot of incompletes."

Gwen smiled. "A or A- student, very consistent."

"The dangerous ones aren't stupid," Tom said.

"No, they're not, but it's not clear that Mahmud has any terrorist ties. Bin Laden himself had nice relatives, as I'm sure you know."

"The family endowed a scholarship at Harvard, I understand."

"Yes," Gwen said. "I'm not sure you'd want to list it on your resumé, though."

"But you're convinced that cousin Hakim is the real deal."

"Yes," she said. "He just hasn't acted on it yet, or if he has we're not aware of his direct involvement."

"So why would Mahmud sit down and break bread with Fox?"

"That's what we'd like to know. Fox was working for an HMO at the time, so he should have had an office in which they could have met. Fox isn't gay, so this isn't a date. Or if he is gay he goes out of his way to grope women and mask the fact. Anyway, we do know that there is a medical connection with Fox because Mahmud received treatment from him."

"Surgery?"

"Yes, an emergency appendectomy."

"Perhaps that's how he met him initially."

"That's what we think. Mahmud was enrolled in the HMO and when he needed treatment Fox was assigned. They call him Cox. 'Dr. Cox'--all very formal. The appendectomy happened several months before the photograph was taken."

"So it could be a medical consult or it could be ... something else."

"Yes."

"And you have operatives in Karachi looking for Mahmud and people in London looking for Hakim."

"Yes, they're looking for Hakim in Pakistan also."

"And you're casting around in hopes that I might have turned something on Fox."

"Right," she said, nodding and smiling.

"And you're disappointed that I haven't, but you're happy with the pizza."

"Right again," she said.

"Interesting that he's dropped out of sight."

"We think so too."

"And your fear is that the al-Barada boys might have something in the works and Fox could lead you to them, if only you could find him. Or them. Or both."

"That's it in a nutshell," Gwen said.

THIRTY-FOUR

"I understand that the people at the Bureau call you the *tracker*," Tom said. "Direct descendant of Lakota warriors, the one whose image they'd love to splash across the center of a recruiting poster."

"You've been playing me, Lieutenant Deaton."

"I wouldn't say that," Tom responded. "I'd say that your reputation preceded you, particularly in law enforcement circles."

"I didn't expect to meet with a small-town beat walker, but I didn't expect to be recognized that easily."

"I read the WaPo online," Tom said. "A lot of things turn up there. The line between government and gossip is often very fine."

She smiled and nodded. "Well, I figured we'd be working together; that's why I brought the photograph."

"You just wanted to get the lay of the land first," he said.

"Maybe," she said.

"You didn't want to work with someone who was *inattentive*. It's too dangerous."

"Yes," she said.

"So you're much more than a go-fer and you have a great deal of discretion with regard to the conduct of this case."

"Yes. By the way, I'm really enjoying this talk … "

"I am too," Tom said. "You don't want to be on that recruiting poster, do you?"

"Not particularly," she said. "I like to close the cases, but I don't want any of the successes to be about me."

"Too dangerous," Tom said. "When they start erecting statues of you there are other people who will want to pull them down, put their own in your place. Or they use the statuary to argue that you're all image when the purpose of the game is to achieve results. You joined the Bureau to be in the crime-prevention business, not the advertising business."

"Very perceptive, Lieutenant."

"I thought you were going to call me Tom."

"Tom."

"Want to hear some more about the case?"

"Yes, I would," she said.

"Any more pizza?"

"No, thanks."

"Drink?"

"I'm fine."

"OK. Dr. Leonard Barnes is a widower; his wife died some twenty years ago. After her death he left his practice in St. Louis and relocated to California. He's now a prominent O.C. surgeon and the LBPD's Medical Examiner. A few years ago he met a forensic anthropologist from UCSD; her name is Sally Cornell. She consulted on several cases and eventually they developed a personal relationship. At the moment," he said, looking at his watch, "she's sitting by the side of his bed, praying that he'll emerge from the coma and say something that will help us find his assailants. He's moved around a little and actually spoken several times. He's referred to being on a 'first floor' and finding that somehow odd. He's been reassured, however, that it's fine and that he shouldn't be concerned. The exact words were (in order): *'F-first floor. The first floor. Very odd. Never … before. The first floor? I didn't understand. It's fine, they said. It's fine.'*

"Len has a condo now, but when Sally visits it's a little too small. They've talked about him buying a larger place. Just before we found him on the side of the **5** he was beginning his condo hunt. We think he was looking at some new developments, basically to get a feel for price and size. We know that he visited one site in Newport Beach, but just as he left the building he met two men. The witness (the real estate agent) had turned her head away for a second and didn't see the initial encounter. What she did see was Len Barnes walking away from the building, between the two men. We did a CompuSketch of them, but it's not very informative. Muscle guys probably--taller, broader than Len; they walked away on either side of him. A few days later he turned up in the dirt and brush beside the 5. We figure that they abducted him and took him to some place on a first floor, the kind of place he didn't expect to be on a first floor. When he questioned it, they reassured him that it was OK. And that's as much as we know."

"And you've thought of every possible reference point or connotation for 'first floor.'"

"Yes. We've gone over it with Sally also."

"Comas are tough," Gwen said, "as I'm sure you know. He's consistent, though. What he's saying is important enough for him to repeat it, to qualify it, to clarify it. He's trying to communicate something and this is where he starts."

"That's my assumption," Tom said.

"Well, at the very least we can run it through the Bureau computers, do some data mining, check with our Homeland Security brothers and sisters ..."

"That would be helpful," Tom said.

"We can also show you some of the material we have on Mahmud. There's not much, but maybe it will suggest something to you."

"Wiretaps? Cell phone intercepts?"

"There's not much," she said, "but you can have a look."

"I said that you have better toys than us."

"Yes, but you also pointed out that these people are not stupid. They're not unaware of the fact that they could be observed or overheard."

"First thing in the morning?"

"Yes," she said.

"Have you got a place to stay?"

"There's a meeting in Newport Beach. At the Marriott. I'm technically signed up for it. It provides an excuse for my being in Orange County."

"At the Fashion Island."

"Right."

"My father and I were there the other night, at a nearby restaurant."

"Maybe you and I could check it out," she said, smiling.

"Years later, we could say, 'we'll always have the mall.'"

She smiled. "What's easier tomorrow? Your place or mine?"

"You'll have to do some encryption and downloading."

"Yes," she said.

"I'll meet you at the Marriott. I'll bring breakfast. Pick a time: 7:30?"

"Perfect. I'll see you then. Room 512."

THIRTY-FIVE

"I went out for the coffee," Gwen said. "Picked up four extra large. I don't trust hotels to keep it hot and the stuff that you make in your room with the two-cup urn thingie doesn't taste like anything remotely resembling coffee."

"More like bitter pond water," Tom said. "I brought some bagels. I hope you like sesame and poppy."

Gwen was dressed in a conference suit with a white blouse and thin gold necklace. Tom saw a warmup suit hanging from the hook on the back of her bathroom door, drying out after her morning run, presumably. She had brought some napkins from the coffee shop and put the hotel room saucers on the coffee table, to be used as plates. Tom had plastic knives, cream cheese and butter.

"Those look great," Gwen said. "And they smell good as well. Do you want to work while I get all domestic?"

"I can," Tom said.

"What we have is on my laptop screen," Gwen said. "There are two icons; one is a set of transcripts and the other is the sound from which the transcripts were made. You can use my earbuds there. One sound bite was obtained with a parabolic microphone, the others were done … electronically. Like I said last night, there isn't much."

While Tom prepared to work, Gwen elicited his bagel choices, spread some cream cheese on each slice, stacked them on the saucer and put them on the desk next to her laptop. She also gave each of them a cup of black coffee and ate a bagel while he read the transcripts and listened to the sound bites.

"It's clear that they either knew that they were being recorded or feared that they could be," Tom said. "They're very guarded; they're speaking elliptically, as if they've got some sort of shared code. That's important in itself. They're colluding--no doubt about it. These aren't social calls or social encounters."

"They're guilty as hell," Gwen said. "We just don't know of what."

"There's a lot of talk about projects," Tom said. "One seems to be personal, some kind of deal that the two of them are striking. The other appears to be related to them but not specific to them."

"Yes," Gwen said. "They're working on something larger, but they have some sort of personal side-deal."

"Exactly," Tom said, "but there's no indication of a time or place. They must have connected before you were aware of the relation between them. They talked about whatever it is that they're *not* talking about directly, here. They may have been in a completely secure location or they might have communicated with written documents. I'd much prefer to see a complete plan with timelines, blueprints and blood-on-the-hands photographs, but what you do have suggests that they're involved in something illegal, immoral or homicidal, possibly all of the above. If anyone once thought that Mahmud was nothing but a graduate student, it's now time to think again."

"I agree," Gwen said. "That doesn't mean he's functioning as a go-between for Hakim, but it does mean that they're talking about something besides Mahmud's blood pressure or cholesterol numbers."

"When I was in college I had this English teacher," Tom said. "Whenever we read something that was really difficult to understand or interpret, he told us to write down all of the things that we *did know* about the text. 'In other words,' he'd say, 'if you pay attention to what you *do know* it will help you find out what you *don't know.*'"

"Here's a good test case for you," Gwen said.

"OK. We know that Mahmud is an engineering student who has a cousin who may well be a terrorist. The cousin has temporarily disappeared. Mahmud has temporarily disappeared. Mahmud met Fox when his appendix ruptured (or was about to). Perhaps he knew him earlier, but it's unlikely that he would have found a way to create a diseased appendix just so that they could make a personal connection ..."

"Go on," Gwen said.

"After the emergency appendectomy the two of them stayed in touch. They started talking about projects in which the two of them could each play a role. They became partners or at least prospective partners. They developed a personal relationship, above and beyond that of doctor/patient. The doctor/patient relationship was purely accidental or so any reasonable person would assume. Hence, the two of them—together--were not on the federal radar screen initially. At that time they might have had some unobserved meetings and untapped calls. There were pre-op meetings, post-op meetings and follow-up meetings. Mahmud lifted his shirt and opened his belt; Fox checked his scar, palpated the surgical site, maybe said 'Fine and dandy' or possibly prescribed some antibiotics. All very cozy and professional, all beneath the radar and all possibly occasions for other plans and proposals, something off the books."

"Good. I'm liking this," Gwen said.

"The link is probably financial, at least initially. Mahmud wouldn't begin the relationship by asking Doc Fox what he thinks about Sunni and Shi'a relations these days. He'd say something like 'you're a great doc; how come you're not on Park Avenue?' Then if Fox told a tale of woe about how he'd been a victim of the politics of personal destruction Mahmud could come back with a 'maybe there's some way I could be of help here.' A grateful patient doing his bit. Then if Fox started to respond to the foreplay they could move to the next level."

"Good," Gwen said.

"So what about Fox himself? What do we know? He's a journeyman surgeon who can't keep his hands to himself. He's underemployed or at least thinks he is; he's arrogant enough to think that he deserves better and slimy enough to step over the line if he sees something that he wants (and thinks he should have) on the other side. He understands surgery, surgical practice, ER's, HMO's and all of the ways to make money practicing medicine at the edges of the profession …"

"And he might be attracted to some kind of payment-in-kind involving women as well as payment in cash," Gwen said.

"Maybe it's what they have in common," Tom said. "Mahmud's people have a lot of cash and some of the members of the family are dreaming about the virgins they're going to meet in heaven."

"I like your English teacher's strategy," Gwen said. "Did he give you an A?"

"Actually he did," Tom said.

"So would I," she responded. "How about another cup of coffee?"

"Sounds good," Tom said, "but we're not done yet. We've got to talk about Dr. Leonard Barnes."

THIRTY-SIX

Gwen replaced their cups. Before she sat down she looked out the window, commented on the bright sun gleaming off of the sea mist, and asked Tom if he was ready for another bagel. He offered to split one with her and she picked one with sesame seeds, putting more cream cheese on his half than hers. "Let's talk about Dr. Barnes," she said.

"Let's do," Tom said. "Len Barnes is from Ohio. His father was a chemist for Procter & Gamble. He was always brainy; he went to a magnet high school, an upscale private college in Ohio and private medical school in upstate New York. His parents died young. He did his internship and residency in St. Louis, married, and watched his wife die young, of cancer. He was highly respected and well-liked by all, except, one assumes, by Nathan Fox. He relocated to California about twenty years ago, where he does general surgery and serves as the LBPD Medical Examiner. Now in his late 50's, he's in a committed relationship with a UCSD forensic anthropologist."

"What's his specialty?" Gwen asked.

"You mean beyond general surgery?"

"Yes. What's he particularly known for? If I was a doctor in L.A. or San Diego, which of my patients would I send to him? What does he do better than anybody else?"

"As I understand it, a lot of his patients have standard problems. He does a high volume of routine surgery with uncommon skill. I did hear once, though, that he had perfected some laparoscopic techniques. Chief Dietrich and I were with him once when he was doing an autopsy. He was talking about the days before anesthesia. He said that eighteenth-century surgeons could perform major surgery in as short a period of time as a minute. Without anesthesia, speed was obviously important. And most who died died of infections rather than shock (as Chris and I had wrongly assumed). They didn't yet have a germ theory of disease, Len told us. He then said that he wasn't particularly known for speed, but that he *was known* for leaving tiny scars."

"That's interesting," Gwen said.

"In what way?" Tom asked.

"Some people may not want others to know they've had surgery. Or a particular disease. Ever see the picture of Lyndon Johnson showing his gall bladder incision scar? I doubt that that would happen today. Too much information."

"I think he wanted to assure everyone that he was OK. There were rumors of other possibilities--pancreatic cancer, heart problems ..."

"They remove gall bladders laparoscopically these days," Gwen said. "Four little incisions. You're back on the street in a day. The AD in the D.C. field office had his removed that way."

"Did he show anyone the scars?"

"No," Gwen said, smiling, "but he used it as a brag point to illustrate how he was back at his desk in a matter of days."

"So what are you thinking, someone might have wanted Len to perform surgery for them?"

"Possibly," Gwen said. "Someone who didn't want to go through channels."

"Perhaps someone who didn't want his presence known."

"Yes," Gwen said.

"Someone who wanted it done quickly and expertly. Mahmud asked Fox and Fox said, 'I know just the man.' But the man would never accept a referral from Fox. He would have had to have been compelled."

"He could have been given some bogus story," Gwen said. "For example, he might have been told that he was operating on a celebrity who wanted to protect his or her privacy, or possibly a high government official or world leader. For security reasons they wanted the surgery done quickly--before the publicist or press secretary made any formal announcements about the person's illness. Consider the possibilities ... "

"They could have concealed the person's identity," Tom said. "The patient would have been covered with sheets anyway. Someone in authority might have taken him into the operating room, shown him an exposed section of flesh and said, 'Do your magic, Dr. Barnes.'"

"Just a little mystification would do," Gwen said. "A little sleight of hand, a little misdirection. Let's say I tell you that you're going to be operating on somebody very special. You fixate on that, think you're in possession of top secret, privileged information and you fail to consider the fact that you might be operating on somebody altogether different. You're feeling so important that you don't entertain the possibity that you're being duped. The patient is horizontal. The head is north, but you're working south. There's a surgical cap on him. Facial hair has been removed. There's an oxygen mask in place, tubes running all over the place, nurses and anesthetists blocking your view ..."

"You think you're operating on a Middle East head of state but you're actually operating on the guy who plans to bomb his palace."

"It's a possibility," she said.

"But not on the first floor," Tom said.

"What do you mean, the first floor?" Gwen asked.

"Operating rooms are special. They have specific requirements for hygiene: special ventilation systems, special flooring systems. You want a floor that's comfortable to stand on for hours at a time, but you don't want a floor with cracks or seams or joints that can trap biological material. You want a place that you can keep squeaky clean, because we *do* now have a germ theory of disease. You want someplace *remote*--a low traffic area: no tourists kicking up dust, no orderlies rolling in gurneys from ambulances every few minutes, no other sick patients, no gift shops with flowers or coffee bars with trash bins. I've seen operating rooms in basements; I've seen them on high floors; I've even seen them on the second floors of hospitals, but you don't see them on the first floor."

"And that's what Dr. Barnes questioned. That's what caused him concern. And the people accompanying him told him not to worry, that it would be all right, that it was fine. But he's a pro and he knew they were wrong."

"That's what's haunting him," Tom said. "He's the consummate pro. Everything has to be right and this was radically wrong. He can't get it out of his head. It's the first thing he wants to tell us."

"But who was the patient?" Gwen asked. "Hakim al-Barada? One of his pals? Somebody on a mission, a mission that couldn't be jeopardized by illness, but a mission that was part of a timeline that couldn't be altered?"

"It all seems like a stretch," Tom said, "but it fits the facts, at least as we know them."

"Then the rest is easy," Gwen said. "All we have to do is find a first floor operating room--*somewhere on this planet*. When we find it we'll take it from there."

"That's all," Tom said. "Assuming the mission is big enough, the cost of a private plane would be no great impediment. Pop Len on the plane, close all of the window shades, fly in circles for a minute or two, then fly on course for a few hours, drive him in a darkened limo for a few minutes, ask him to put on some scrubs, wash his hands and let him do his thing. Then force him to exchange places with the patient. Pump him full of 190 proof 'vodka' and bring him home. He doesn't know where he's been. He doesn't know what he's actually done. All he knows is that he's been asked to operate on somebody on a first floor somewhere."

"Seems a little daunting," Gwen said, "but you know what we say in Washington: 'When the going gets tough ...'"

"The careerists transfer to the General Accounting Office."

"I like you," she said. "You've got the proper mental attitude."

"I like you too," Tom said. "Why don't the two of us go hunting together?"

III

PIGEON RIVER

THIRTY-SEVEN

"I want to go with you," Sally said.

"I'm afraid that's not possible," Gwen said. "We would have to sell that to the Bureau, which would then have to accept responsibility for you in the field. They won't do that and we'd lose a day waiting for their formal answer. I appreciate your concern for Dr. Barnes and I am very grateful for all of your help, but you're really needed here. Hospitals do their best, but there's no substitute for a loved one at the patient's bedside. In this case we need someone in whom Dr. Barnes would confide, someone who can speak to him when he awakes and elicit the right information. We've briefed you on what we know and you know the right questions to ask. You're indispensable *here*, Dr. Cornell."

"Tom?" Sally said.

"The Bureau can open doors that I can't," Tom answered. "I'll be there for you and for Len. We need you to be here for us."

"I want regular updates," Sally said.

"I understand; we'll keep you posted," Tom said. "And you do the same."

"Of course," Sally said. "Where will you start?"

"In San Antonio, with Fox's HMO. We'll also check with UTSA and see if they have any additional information on Mahmud al-Barada."

"Can't the San Antonio field office do that for you and save you some time?"

"They could, but we don't want to put a lot of agents on the street yet," Gwen said, "particularly if the case has national security implications.

I like to do these things personally. I want to hear the timbre of peoples' voices and see their eyes when they speak."

"I didn't mean to press you," Sally said.

"I understand. No need to apologize. The fact that you care deeply is important. You're our best … *consultant* here. I know that when Dr. Barnes awakes you'll be the best person to represent us."

"I'll call you immediately if and when I learn anything," Sally said.

"I liked that you said *when* he awakes," Tom said. "I'm sure Sally appreciated that."

"I really think that he will," Gwen said. "He has already on several occasions. He seemed to be resting comfortably but I sensed that he was frustrated, that he wanted to speak."

"Probably because of the eyelid movement and the fact that he seemed to be wrinkling his nose. I don't think he had done that in the past," Tom responded.

"I wonder what she *would* be like in the field," Gwen said. "Anthropologists spend a lot of time there; at least some of them do. They're used to working long hours and getting their hands dirty. I suspect she would be an effective in-fighter, particularly defending somebody she loved."

"Or seeking revenge on somebody who had harmed him. You know what they say: it's why we don't let women direct wars."

"Because they'd be too violent," Gwen said.

Tom nodded.

"Unfortunately, today it's all about the technology. If the three of us were walking into the field with spiked clubs, I'd be fine with her, but she hasn't had the training on the full array of instruments and weapons at our disposal. None of us have, not on all of the Bureau toys. We're also at the mercy of the politicians and we have to rely on the liaison personnel who interface with the other federal security agencies. It's supposed to be easier and more integrated now, but I'm afraid that's not always the case. I wish it was, but I can't assure you that it is."

"How soon do we leave?" Tom asked.

Gwen checked her iPhone and tapped the email message from Bureau headquarters. "We leave at 2:20," she said, "connecting through Dallas/Ft. Worth. There are no direct flights until tomorrow morning. I've got the numbers for our e-tickets. Aren't you glad you packed last night?"

"As a matter of fact, I am. Are you getting a Bureau car?"

"Renting," Gwen said. "I'll try to get something inconspicuous. Better to go for invisibility than to wear a target."

"Good point," Tom said.

He drove to John Wayne while Gwen texted and made calls. When she clicked off Tom told her about Hector. "If we need him, he's first rate. He's also fluent in Spanish."

"I'll keep that in mind," Gwen said. "Many of the SA's in the field office will be Spanish-speaking, but they'll also be known in the local community. That's both an advantage and a potential problem, depending on who we have to deal with."

"I had another question," Tom said.

"What's that?"

"About our cover story."

"You mean at the hotel?"

"Yes."

"We're booked in adjoining rooms, if that's what you're asking."

"Colleagues, then."

"Sounds very academic, doesn't it?" she said.

"Yes. If the rooms are booked through the government will they know that you're FBI?"

"No. They'll probably think that we're bank examiners or IRS. Do you have a green eyeshade?"

"I'll carry two pens in an outside pocket."

"That'll work," she said. "Let's find our gate, get something to eat and talk about how we're going to find these people."

THIRTY-EIGHT

Fox had worked for an HMO with four offices in greater San Antonio. Now entitled St. Anthony Healthcare, it had once been known as Alamo Healthcare, until its board blamed a shrinking bottom line on the connotations associated with the previous name. The Leon Valley office also served as the organization's corporate headquarters, so that Tom and Gwen were able to speak with Fox's superiors as well as with his colleagues.

There were, however, only two colleagues whose tenure had overlapped with his. The first, Dr. Milton Abrams, specialized in internal medicine. He spoke of "Nathaniel" professionally. "He was a highly competent surgeon," Abrams said. "We did not see each other socially."

The second, Dr. Sheila Waterston, specialized in family medicine. She was Asian and had probably married an American and anglicized her given name. "I didn't know him well," she said. "We only overlapped by a few months. He removed the appendix of one of my patients and removed an undescended testicle from a second. There were no complications. Both of my patients were pleased with their results."

"We spoke with Dr. Abrams," Gwen said. "He told us that he and Dr. Cox did not socialize. Did you ever have occasion to see him outside of work?"

"No," she said, curtly, as if the question had implied something inappropriate.

"We're trying to confirm his place of residence," Tom said.

"You should speak with the personnel director," she said. By now she was fingering the earpiece of her stethoscope and trying to catch a look at the chart she had been examining when Tom and Gwen entered her office.

"We'll do that," Tom said. "I can see that you need to get back to work."

She gave him a thin-lipped smile but did not invite them to stay longer.

George Birken was the HMO's Executive Director for Human Resources. He wore a brown wool suit, starched white shirt with gold cufflinks and a yellow tie. Most of his hair was gone, except for wisps and tufts of it at his ears and nostrils. He wore rectangular bifocals and kept records with a black fountain pen.

"Dr. Cox is no longer employed by Saint Anthony's," he said.

"We understand that," Gwen said. "We'd like to see his personnel records and we'd like his last known address and home phone number."

"We're not in the habit of sharing that sort of information without a warrant," Birken said, "but I suppose it will be alright. There's really nothing there to speak of." He turned in his chair, stood, walked to a file cabinet at the end of those marked **current** and secured Cox's file.

"As you can see," he said, "the file contains his application for the position, the initial offer letter that he received and the annual letters renewing his contract at the next year's salary level. There are only three of those; he wasn't here that long."

"Is it common for physicians to stay here for an extended period of time?" Gwen asked.

"No, not really," Birken said. "This is a holding-pattern position for most of them. Getting back to the file … if there had been any significant disciplinary issues there would be a record of them there, but in his case there were not. Here, have a look for yourselves …"

"Is this a standard salary level?" Gwen asked.

"Yes, for a surgeon," Birken said, with the slightest hint of envy in his voice.

Gwen pointed at the address of record in his file. It corresponded to the address on his Texas driver's license. He also gave the Philadelphia mail drop as his permanent address. The phone number in the file was for a cell phone; there was no landline listed.

"Did you know him well?" Tom asked.

"I barely knew him at all," Birken answered. "Most of my work is with the non-exempt staff."

"Did you ever have occasion to help him with personnel issues?" Gwen asked.

"I helped expedite the hiring of a nurse who worked as part of his surgical team, if that's what you mean," Birken said. "The fiscal office handled the electronic deposit of his checks and the issuance of his W-2. We collaborate because my office is responsible for fringe benefits. We have a menu system for benefits. Here, just a second ..."

He turned to his computer, executed a series of keystrokes, paused and then printed the summary screen. "You can take that with you," he said. "His check was deposited to a bank in Philadelphia. Funds for his 401(k) were deposited there as well. St. Anthony's provided his health care and vision care; he opted out of the dental plan. The long-term disability plan and basic life insurance plan are required."

"Any other perks or benefits?" Tom asked.

"No," Birken said. "It's all on the sheet there."

"Not much of a footprint," Gwen said. "I doubt that they threw a big going-away party when he left."

"Can we check on his bank account?"

"Yes," she said. "I'll call the Philadelphia field office. They'll be able to get back to us in a matter of hours. I'll ask the San Antonio office to check on the cell number. I'd be surprised if he didn't use burners for the important calls. Let's grab a cup of coffee; I'll make the calls and then we'll see what they've got here on Mahmud."

The medical records officer was a woman named Mildred Gates. Middle-aged and harried, she wore her glasses on the edge of her nose and wrinkled her brow as she pulled folders from file shelves. She asked to see both of their credentials before she would share Mahmud al-Barada's file. "As you can see," she said, "there's not much there. He was enrolled with St. Anthony's but only came in for flu shots and allergy shots. Dr. Cox removed his appendix. He would have been advised to come in for annual physicals, but he apparently declined to do so. That's not uncommon among the young."

"So he didn't have a regular doctor," Gwen said.

"A family practitioner—no," she said.

"Could we have a copy of the file?" Tom asked.

"I'd prefer that you take notes rather than copy the official file," she said. "I can give you a sheet of paper, if you need one."

"That's all right," Gwen said warmly. "We're very grateful for all of your help. Did you happen to know Dr. Cox well?"

"No, I didn't," she said. "His nurses brought the files to and from this office. I understand that he was a good surgeon. I believe I only spoke with him at any length once."

"What was the occasion?" Tom asked.

"We had a large group of visitors one day, representatives from companies who were considering offering our organization as a health option for their employees. The cafeteria was crowded and he asked if he could join me at my table. I said 'of course' and we had lunch together. He talked about seeing the Spurs play. He said something about the skills of some of their players and compared them with some players on another team. I didn't really pay a great deal of attention. I'm not interested in basketball; I really don't know what a 'power forward' is."

"I mapquested his home address," Tom said. "It's right nearby. Shall we check it?"

"We might as well," Gwen said. "There's not much here. It's as if he was a ghost rather than a doctor."

THIRTY-NINE

Fox's apartment was in a multi-purpose structure on Fosse Court, just off of Bandera Road, the main drag through Leon Valley. In the front of the building was a dark wooden sign, *405 Fosse Court*, with hooks for hanging plaques. The current plaque read: *Unit Available*. The building superintendent and general manager was a thin, elderly man named Ray Walbert. He sat in an open office next to the rack of mail slots just to the left of the building's main entrance.

"It's a mixed-use facility," he said. "We're about 75% retirees and 25% transients. Those are people who are likely to be here for anywhere from six months to a year or two. Some are military; some are people looking for something long-term who just light here for awhile. We've got one section that's like a long-stay hotel. Some are singles who come for several weeks or months while they're waiting for their families to join them; some are military families waiting on a spouse to return; some are here for short-term employment. There's a mix. Dr. Cox was actually here for four years or so. That's very rare."

"How so?" Gwen asked.

"Because the units are furnished and pricier than your average citizen would want to pay."

"Approximately … ?"

"Two thousand, five hundred a month," Walbert answered. "That gets you two bedrooms, a bath, kitchenette, and living/dining room space. We furnish utilities but the tenant pays for cable and internet service.

"And parking's free," he added. "There's a dining room downstairs, but the menu is simple and it's mostly used by the retirees. There's also a barber shop. A beautician comes in two days a week. And there are washers and dryers; coin-operated. We used to have a little in-house store that sold toiletries, detergent, snacks, that kind of thing, but since the *H-E-B* came in down the street everybody's been shopping there. Cheaper, of course."

"*H-E-B* is a grocery chain," Tom said.

"Yes," Walbert said. "Their motto is 'Here Everything's Better'. Kind of clever, don't you think?"

"It is," Tom said. "Could we see Dr. Cox's apartment?"

"As a matter of fact, it's vacant now," Walbert said. "We can go right up, if you'd like."

"It was just painted," Walbert said. "Not that he left it in poor condition. They're just easier to rent if they've been freshened up a bit. Feel free to look around, if you'd like. If you want to, you can have a look and when you're done just push in the button on the back of the door handle and come on back downstairs. No need to dead-bolt it or anything like that."

"Thanks very much," Gwen said. "We appreciate your help." Walbert gave them a salute with two fingers and left. After they each looked for a few minutes they sat down in the living room to talk.

"Clean, but not exactly the Ritz-Carlton," Tom said. "Pine and Formica, wear-forever sofa fabric, institutional plumbing fixtures. If it had cinder block walls I'd say it was a college dorm suite. Except that it's quiet, what with the tenants shuffling around in bathrobes and house slippers. Odd choice for a more or less wealthy, single man. Not for a short-term stay, but certainly for more than a month or two. Maybe he always planned to leave sooner but was never able to. It's not like he was twenty five or thirty, but still, this is not exactly where the action is. If it ever *was* here it left a long time ago."

"It wouldn't draw attention though," Gwen said. "It's not like he was livin' la vida loca, cruising the strip in his Beemer, trolling for short-term relationships."

"No, it's more like early retirement," Tom said. "Playing against type, I'd say. Maybe it was a front. Maybe he had another place for naughty times. Odd behavior, but maybe not, not if you thought you were being watched."

"Or if you were simply in a holding pattern," Gwen said. "The rent here would be nothing for someone on a surgeon's salary. Maybe he was saving for something or just waiting for a big score somewhere. For the average person … I'd bet on the former. He didn't run into Mahmud until recently and he'd been here for years before meeting him."

"It would also free him to do whatever he wanted to do," Tom said. "No grass to cut, no maintenance to perform. He could come and go as he pleased."

Gwen's cell phone twitched and she held up her hand in a 'hold that thought' gesture.

"San Antonio field office," she said. "No record of any recent cell phone activity on that number and sparse use earlier. Nothing suspicious."

"I didn't expect there to be any," Tom said.

The phone twitched again. "When it rains, it pours," she said.

"Philadelphia field office. His checks were deposited at *PNC*. Bills were paid electronically. Sums were automatically transferred each month from the Philly bank to a money market account here, at *Wells Fargo*."

"How much was transferred?"

"Three thousand a month, automatically. Sometimes larger amounts. Probably walking-around money. He could use local ATM's without paying fees. It looks as if he had a long-term relationship with *PNC* and then bounced money from his mother-ship account to wherever he was at the time. Nothing suspicious. No big deposits or big withdrawals in the last couple years. And no big bank account beyond a 401(k) which contains approximately $230,000. Basically just a rootless guy who preferred to stay that way."

"A commitment-phobe?" Tom asked.

"Sure looks that way," Gwen answered.

When they went back downstairs Tom asked Walbert if Cox had paid for maid service.

"As a matter of fact, he did," Walbert said. "It's optional, of course. He also paid for laundry service. We ask our tenants to contract for those services through my office. That way we make sure that the women are paid and there's no undercutting on price through special deals. He paid all those bills on time, just like he did with his rent."

"He paid electronically," Tom said.

"I believe he did," Walbert said. "Here, just a sec … " He made some keystrokes on his computer keyboard. "Yes, every month on the first, just like clockwork."

"And he didn't leave a forwarding address?"

"No, he didn't. I don't think he ever got any first-class mail here, just circulars and stuff. We didn't see much of him. But more important, he never caused us any problems. First-class tenant as far as we were concerned."

"We knocked on the door of the unit opposite his," Gwen said, "but there was no answer."

"Actually, no one lives there. There's a number on the door but we use the unit for storage. Dr. Cox liked that about his wing. Much more privacy. Surgeons work hard; I figured he needed his rest."

"Do you remember any visitors that he might have had?" Tom asked.

"They're not required to check in with me," he answered. "Only if they need directions. I saw him walk out once with a Middle Eastern man. That would have been about three or four months ago, I guess. Something like that. I figured he was probably a doctor, like Dr. Cox.

The doctors we get here these days are often foreign. I guess you knew that."

"A younger man?" Gwen asked.

"Yes, much younger than Dr. Cox. Thirty, maybe? Hard to tell these days."

FORTY

St. Anthony's had a contractual relationship with University Hospital, where Fox had operated on Mahmud al-Barada. Tom and Gwen skipped lunch, grabbed some coffee at a Texaco station, and drove to the hospital to question physicians, nurses and members of the surgical teams.

Billing itself as the lead trauma hospital for a 22-county area, University Hospital's emergency center accommodated more than 70,000 patient visits each year. In addition to its trauma center, the facility was particularly well-known for its organ transplant center. It was the kind of place where Nathan Fox might have felt very comfortable.

The head nurse in the surgery center, a woman named Helen Shields, introduced them to the staff nurses and indicated to them the location of the doctors' lounge. "They're in and out there, after surgery," she said. "They get off their feet for awhile, grab some coffee, consult with one another and collect their thoughts."

Two of the available nurses were familiar with 'Dr. Cox'.

"He was a good surgeon," one said. "He could be impatient and short-tempered from time to time, but most of them can be that way. I suppose you know that he did general surgery. He didn't do anything exotic or out of the ordinary. Most of the procedures were routine. Neurosurgery, orthopedic surgery … all of those kinds of things are done by specialists."

"A lot of the university students contract with St. Anthony's," another said, "so that the medical problems are those of the young. We see a lot of eating disorders, for example, and a lot of athletic injuries, problems related to binge drinking, trauma from auto and bike accidents, that kind of thing. The students don't fall down and break their hips or have a lot of type-2 diabetes or arthritis-related problems. The HMO agreement doesn't include plastic or cosmetic surgery, unless it's reconstructive and we have specialists who do that sort of thing. Dr. Cox would remove appendixes and gall bladders, do some colorectal procedures; he might remove a thyroid or parathyroid from time to time. He treated burns and removed tumors, usually things just below the skin--fatty tumors or tumors in muscles or other soft tissues ..."

"How about laparoscopic surgery?" Tom asked.

"No, Dr. Wetters generally does that."

"How would you describe Dr. Cox's personal behavior?" Gwen asked.

Both of the nurses shook their heads. "I'm not sure what you mean," one said.

"How was he in personal interactions, outside of the operating room? Kind, decent? Abrasive, abusive? Standoffish? Touchy/feely?"

Both of the nurses paused before speaking.

"Would you be more comfortable if we spoke with each of you separately?" Gwen asked.

"No, that's all right," the second nurse said. Her name tag read *Patricia Selmo, R.N.* "He could be just a little ..."

"Creepy," the first nurse said. Her tag read *Carol Hansen, R.N.*"

"In what way?" Gwen asked. "Did he hit on the nurses?"

"I could feel his eyes on me," Patricia said.

"He would pat the nurses from time to time," Carol said, "as if he was congratulating them on a job well done, but then he'd leave his hand there for awhile. On their backs or shoulders, for example. It never became a significant issue, but most of the nurses tried to keep him at arm's length."

"To your knowledge did he date anyone from the hospital?" Gwen asked.

"No," both answered, simultaneously.

"Were either of you here when he removed Mahmud al-Barada's appendix?" Tom asked.

"I was," Patricia said. "It hadn't burst, but he got here just in time. The patient had been complaining of lower-abdominal pain and Dr. Cox got him into surgery immediately. The surgery itself was pretty routine."

"Did you observe any interactions between the two of them?" Tom asked.

"I'm not quite sure what you mean. Dr. Cox checked him in and talked to him outside the operating room. By then the patient was on a valium drip and feeling no pain. Dr. Cox would have explained the procedure to him. I wasn't close enough to overhear him. I was just in and out, getting ready for surgery. After the procedure was done I'm sure Dr. Cox talked to him, but I wasn't there to observe it."

"How about as he recuperated?"

"I'm sure he visited with him, but again, I didn't observe it."

"I didn't either," Carol added.

"What about other surgeons?" Tom asked. "Who would have known him best or had the most dealings with him?"

"Dr. Hellstrom," Patricia said. "He's also on the staff at St. Anthony's. They worked fairly closely, I think. They would be on call for one another, that sort of thing."

"Is he here today?" Gwen asked.

"He's in surgery now," Carol said.

"How soon do you think he'll be finished?" Tom asked.

"He's doing a hemorrhoidectomy; he should be done in fifteen minutes or so. You could wait in the surgeons' lounge for him."

"Thanks very much for talking to us," Gwen said. Tom nodded in agreement and then added, "You've been very helpful."

Hellstrom appeared in twenty minutes. He was still in his scrubs; his surgical mask was hanging over his chest. He had removed his gloves and washed his hands. The smell of the soap hung about him as he entered the room. He was of medium height, late fiftyish, his brown hair neatly combed, his eyes a dull blue. When he entered the lounge he made himself a cup of strong tea, to which he added some sweetener and a little milk from a glass bottle in the mini-refrigerator.

Gwen and Tom introduced themselves, badged him, and asked if they could speak with him for a few minutes.

"I need to speak with my patient in about fifteen minutes," he said, "but we can talk until then."

They asked him about his relationship with 'Dr. Cox'.

"I preceded Nathaniel at Saint Anthony's, so I knew him during the full period of his time there, what was it--three years or so? We both do general surgery. The HMO contracts with other surgeons for certain types of specialty work. Nathaniel and I would generally not operate together. We would consult one another regularly and we would trade slots with one another from time to time. In some ways we were like partners in private practice, but the financial arrangements were different."

"Were you personally close?" Gwen asked.

"We weren't fast friends, if that's what you mean," he answered. "We probably wouldn't have gone into practice together. Not that we didn't respect one another's skills ... there just wasn't a close personal bond. There was no animosity either."

"But you talked from time to time," Tom said, "beyond purely medical matters."

"Yes, of course."

"Did you socialize?"

"We had dinner together when he first arrived," Hellstrom said, "but not thereafter. Again, there was no animosity. I'm married; my wife teaches at Trinity University; we're both very busy."

"Did you like Dr. Cox?" Gwen asked.

Hellstrom seemed frustrated with the question, as if he was wondering why on earth she would ask him that. "He was a pleasant man. Relatively private. I always had the feeling that his position with St. Anthony's was a temporary one. It wasn't that they saw him as a fill-in; it was more that he saw himself doing other things. I was surprised that he stayed as long as he did."

"Did he say something to you about that?" Tom asked.

"He didn't express dissatisfaction with the position, if that's what you mean. He was not a complainer. He simply had other plans."

"Did he talk to you about them?" Tom asked.

"He did once," Hellstrom said. "He expressed an interest in management."

"Management?" Gwen said.

"Yes. I can't reconstruct the entire conversation. This would have been about a year ago or so. We were having coffee and he mentioned that he had spent a lot of time in various areas within the health industry. He had been in private practice. He had worked in emergency rooms and now in an HMO. He thought he should be putting that experience to use. I asked him what he meant by that and he said that he thought it was time for him to be managing such an organization rather than simply being employed by one. 'I could do a good job,' he said, 'because I understand the business end as well as the medical end.'"

"And what do you think he had in mind?" Tom asked. "What did he want to run?"

"Not an HMO," Hellstrom said. "From what he said, I thought he wanted to run something like an Emergency Care Center or, more likely, a Freestanding Emergency Department. The latter do procedures that the former can't do and they're often set up to do lab work and diagnostic work beyond that of the Emergency Care Center. They're open around the clock. Sometimes they're part of hospitals, extensions of them, if you will. Sometimes they're separately managed, but have a direct relationship with an acute care hospital. In other cases they're completely independent entities."

"Emergency Care Centers are more for those without insurance who want to talk to a doctor," Tom said, "right?"

"Yes, some of them actually charge by the problem. They'll repair a laceration, drain an abscess, administer vaccines, that sort of thing. A Freestanding Emergency Department is like an actual ER."

"And they would, what, serve a rural area?" Gwen asked.

"Yes, that's usually part of the concept. Hospitals might establish them to reduce the pressures on their own ER's as well as to provide local care for people in outlying communities."

"And did Dr. Cox actually say that he wanted to establish such a facility?"

"Not in so many words," Hellstrom responded, "but he talked about those entities and said that if they were managed properly they could be very lucrative as well as provide a necessary service. 'I know that I could make one highly profitable,' he said."

"That would be very expensive, wouldn't it?" Gwen asked.

"To establish one all by yourself? Oh yes. Space, equipment, advertising, the recruitment of staff … very expensive. Many millions."

"Freestanding Emergency Departments are heavily regulated in California," Tom said, "at least to my knowledge."

"They're very common in Texas," Hellstrom said.

FORTY-ONE

"Excuse the OCD," Tom said, "but I'd like to get on my laptop for awhile before we have dinner."

"I'm already on," Gwen said. "I'm eating the chocolate they left on my pillow; it's not bad. Knock when you're ready to leave."

Tom surfed for information on Freestanding Emergency Departments. Their numbers were growing: a 2008 story reported that there were just under 200 facilities in 2006 with a 23% increase from the previous year. There were problems with them, though. In some communities, for example, ambulances would only take patients to hospitals, not to FED's. Their convenient locations, however, meant that individuals preferred them to more distant hospitals, where the wait for actual care might be much longer. They were not in all states, at this point only around 16. They existed in Maryland, in Minnesota and Florida, for example, and, as Tom and Gwen had learned, in Texas.

They suffered from some limitations. For one thing, there were usually no backup specialty physicians available for consultation on complex cases and they lacked the kind of operating room facilities available in hospitals for such things as complex neurosurgery. Two facts caught Tom's eye, however, two facts that would have been of immediate and compelling interest to Nathan Fox: for the same type of outpatient visit, Medicare reimbursed medical providers $316 if the patient has been treated in an Emergency Department, $138 if the patient had been treated in an Urgent Care Center. The second fact would have been equally important: Emergency Departments were frequently located in emerging suburbs and exurbs, where they attracted an affluent clientele.

Some advertised themselves as boutique medical delivery systems, with better amenities and more user-friendly facilities. Sick children might be greeted with 'Frozen' dolls instead of Spartan waiting rooms and their parents with quick and polite service in upscale surroundings.

The medical personnel who operated and sometimes owned these facilities were usually ER docs, individuals skilled in treating certain problems under trying and urgent circumstances. For Fox: the big rock candy mountain.

Tom knocked on the connecting door to Gwen's room. She opened it, said, "Give me two minutes," and went into the bathroom to comb her hair and wash her hands.

They ate at a restaurant called *Marcella's*, a few blocks from the Riverwalk. It advertised *authentic* Mexican food and featured a large patio with cushioned chairs, votive candles in glass cylinders and twenty different brands of tequila. Gwen nodded approvingly at Tom's recommendation of a pitcher of margaritas and then ordered Chili Colorado. He opted for enchiladas with a Mole sauce, rice and refritos. The margaritas were smooth and cold and the space heaters on the patio cut the night air and glowed warmly against the dusky sky.

"Did you check on the Emergency Departments also?" Gwen asked.

"Yes," Tom answered, "but I didn't check on possible locations. At first I thought he'd go to a place with a large population with a lot of disposable income, a place like Plano, for example, but I googled hospitals there and the screen lit up with possibilities."

"I'm figuring something closer to home," Gwen said.

"The hill country?"

"Yes. Lots of benefits: money, expanding population and a nice place to live."

"Plus a vacation population," Tom said. "People would go to the Texas Medical Center for tertiary care but they'd go to the hill country to kick back. Then, if they needed care they'd go someplace close by, someplace inviting. They're away from their homes, away from their usual medical network; they've got the bucks; why not go to Dr. Nate's House of Health?"

"Retirees there also," Gwen said. "Something happens; they panic; they want something close by."

"Big space, though. On the edges of Austin and San Antonio and then a whole lot of territory to the west. How many counties--twenty?"

"Twenty five, according to the site I read," Gwen said.

"We'll need help."

"We've got it," Gwen said. "We can check with commercial realtors and see if any property has turned over lately that could be converted to medical space, also with contractors who could handle new construction at that order of magnitude."

"You're thinking that Mahmud fronted the bucks in return for something from Fox."

"Yes, or Hakim, with Mahmud as the middleman. Maybe Hakim's fraternity."

"Pretty big chunk of change," Tom said.

"They've *got* big chunks of change; the fraternity does at least," Gwen responded.

"Then what he was willing to do for them must have been important."

"Think of his risk," Gwen said. "Think about his expected earnings over the next fifteen or twenty years versus a long prison sentence."

"True. Millions. It still must have been important to them."

"Yes," Gwen said. "If this speculation is all true, it means that they were planning something big, not treatment for a sprained wrist so that somebody could lob a grenade into a high school football stadium."

"And if it's *big* big, they'd be willing to write off the opportunity costs."

"Maybe it was a step deal," Gwen said. "Some money up front and then more after the mission was completed."

"And Fox's major contribution was to deliver Len Barnes and force him to operate."

"Mahmud and Hakim's people could help with the *force* part. They'd be buying Fox's expertise and his willingness to front the operation."

"With his reputation on the line."

"Yes," Gwen said.

"If that's true, we'd better hurry," Tom said. "Len Barnes's work is done; they've already moved on to phase 2."

FORTY-TWO

"I can get some help from Washington," Gwen said. "I'd just as soon not work with the locals. They'd want to know why and as soon as the terrorist flag is raised (even if it's raised just a little) there would be ripples through the organization. Ripples have a way of reaching the media."

"I agree," Tom said.

"Assuming that Fox put the bite on Mahmud to help fund the project, where would they start?"

"Fox wouldn't buy a failed facility," Tom said, "unless there was some reason to believe that the operation failed for 'curable' reasons. He wouldn't want a business that failed because of poor medical practices or a flawed location."

"You mean too close to strong competition or too far from a possible clientele."

"Right. And if the facility was successful, why sell it to an outsider? If it were me, I'd put it in the hands of a trusted colleague and simply cash out or if the colleague couldn't foot the whole bill I'd let him run it and take back a piece of the action while I left to sit on the beach. I wouldn't put it on the market and wait for an over-the-transom bidder. That could damage the operation's reputation and the goose might stop pushing out the golden eggs."

"I agree," Gwen said. "I think we're looking at new construction. A conversion is unlikely. The comparative advantage of facilities like this is that they're spiffy and welcoming, medical facilities that resemble spas or luxury hotels rather than warehouses or minimum-security prisons. The architecture would be important. You wouldn't want to be in a converted Jiffy Lube or former appliance store."

"There's an old math problem that involves a traveling salesman," Tom said. "You set a given number of points on a map and then determine the route that would enable the salesman to move from point to point most efficiently and conveniently. It's amazingly complex, but businesses use a variation of it to locate facilities. If you're going to build a new Hilton Garden Inn or a new LongHorn Steakhouse you look at several things. The first is market; the second is probably the actual positioning of the facility to maximize the possibility of achieving significant market share. What competitors already exist in the area? Who lives around there or who comes through there? What are their income levels and what are their migration routes? Doesn't that sound like common sense?"

"Yes. The owner/operators of these facilities must also have some kind of professional association; that group could be of help. We could also talk to somebody at McKinsey or one of the other major consulting firms. They *live* for this kind of stuff. People pay them big bucks to solve problems or avoid them. I can imagine them working that traveling salesman problem you talked about. They have templates and protocols, scenarios … you come up with a problem and some serious cash and they come up with a solution. There may be an infinite number of potential problems, but there's a finite number of common problems and *where to locate your business* is as basic as it gets.

"Rather than us cast around, driving over 25 counties, we need to have our people comb through the building permits and property sales in those counties. I know someone in the Director's office who can commandeer some help from the business world … find some points, draw some lines, suggest some possibilities. I'll call in now. Order us some coffee. I'll be right back."

She returned in fifteen minutes. "They love it when you call them at home, after they've slipped into their jammies. It gives them a sense of drama, the feeling that things are happening, progress is being made, a spasm of hope that we're closing in on the bad guys."

"Maybe we are," Tom said.

"Sure," Gwen said, "but we've been doing the leg work. Now they get to ride in and wave sabers in the air."

"By waking up other people and telling them to hightail it to 9th Street and Pennsylvania Avenue."

"Not exactly like 'how the West was won' when you say it like that," Gwen said, "but it still gets their blood pumping."

"Now we can have dessert," Tom said.

"Fried ice cream?"

"Works for me."

"And some more coffee," Gwen said.

Suddenly Tom's phone twitched. "Funny," he said, "I would have thought you'd be getting the call."

"Tom?" the voice said. "It's Sally. Len spoke again."

"What did he say, Sally?"

"He didn't say very much, just a few words. He said, 'Couldn't see face. Wouldn't let me. Left my mark.'" She pronounced the words slowly, leaving time for them to sink in.

"Did he say anything else?"

"No, it was as if that was as much as he could manage. He said it and then went back to sleep. What do you think he meant?"

"I think Len was forced to operate on someone, someone whose identity was concealed."

"A criminal. Or … a terrorist."

"Possibly," Tom said. "All we can say is that it was someone who needed to keep his identity secret."

"Then it must have been someone prominent; Len doesn't know any criminals or terrorists."

"It doesn't make a great deal of sense," Tom said, "not if they fully intended to kill him afterwards. They probably just didn't want to take any chances. How is everything else?"

"Good," she said. "His vital signs are still strong. When he awakes he seems tired though, as if it requires a great deal of exertion to say a few words."

"Maybe it does," Tom says. "It sounds as if it's worth it to him. Remember: some people think that when you're comatose you can still hear things. Maybe Len's listening; maybe he wants to help and that he's doing all that he can."

"When he spoke he held onto my hand," Sally said. "He seemed to clutch tighter with each word, as if each word was very, very important."

"Each word is," Tom said. "I really appreciate your call; I wish we had more to report at this end. We're still trying to locate Fox. I'll let you know as soon as we learn anything."

He then said good night, clicked off and turned to Gwen. "Len was awake again. He said that he couldn't see the face, that they wouldn't let him, but that he left his mark."

FORTY-THREE

"Let me call in again," Gwen said. "We're working hypothetically here, but Dr. Barnes's statement *confirms* our working hypothesis. The Bureau will want to know."

When she returned a few minutes later Tom was surfing the web on his iPhone. She sat down and took a sip of her coffee. Tom started in without drinking his.

"He's talking about the sutures; he has to be. When he said he left his mark … he couldn't have carved his initials on the patient's chest or written something in ballpoint on his hand. They would have been watching him, making sure that he didn't purposely botch the operation. On the other hand, he would have been brought in because of his special expertise. He did something others couldn't do or he did it better than others did. If he was doing something special he could have added a fresh wrinkle, something they wouldn't automatically notice.

"Look at my phone screen. Look at the list of sutures … and that's just on one website. The *simple interrupted* stitch, the vertical and horizontal *mattress* stitch, the running or *continuous* stitch, the *chest drain* stitch and the *corner* stitch, the *subcuticular* stitch and the *Figure 8* … this is like a sailor tying knots. I'm betting that Len did something odd, something that would work, of course, but something that could be identified later, at least until the incision site had completely healed."

"We couldn't find the person that way, but once we thought we had found him we could confirm it."

"Yes," Tom said. "We'd need to know what Len did, unless, of course, the suturing was so unusual that any surgeon would notice it. I doubt that he would do something bizarre, because Fox would have recognized it as such, but he could certainly do something slightly out-of-the-ordinary. Besides, some surgeons allow their assistants to close; they're already in the lounge, getting a cup of coffee."

"It wouldn't be the *focus* of the procedure," Gwen said, "more like an afterthought, unless there were complications."

"Right. He might have varied the interval between the sutures, maybe did something fancy at the ends, something symmetrical. If he was challenged he could have defended himself by saying, 'Look, I'm the expert on this. My way *works*.'"

Gwen handed Tom his phone and he immediately resumed tapping. "Look," he said. "They would have wanted him to use absorbable sutures, unless he was using something that Fox could have easily removed. Their plan was to have Len do the work, then eliminate him. They wouldn't have wanted him to return later to check the incision site. Here's one company that markets absorbable sutures. They support the wound from what … 10 days or so to 6 weeks or more. And the absorption time is like two months to six months. The odds are that we have a little time in which to find the 'patient'."

"Maybe Dr. Barnes will tell us more in the meantime," Gwen said. "I should hear back from the Bureau on possible construction sites sometime tomorrow. Why don't we swing by UTSA in the morning and try to get an address for Mahmud. I've already checked; he's not in the phonebook."

The University was northeast of Leon Valley. The registrar's office was part of the library complex. When Tom and Gwen badged the receptionist she took them to the office of the registrar, a woman named Teresa Santos.

"The records are all online," she said. "Just a second … here it is." The screen was gray with lettering in white. It looked surprisingly old-fashioned.

"I believe I spoke with someone from your office earlier," the registrar said.

"Yes, that was me," Gwen said. "You gave us a permanent address in Karachi and informed us that he was currently on a leave of absence."

"Yes, that's correct."

"We'd like to know his local address."

"We would generally correspond with students by email," the registrar said. "Anything important would go to the permanent address. Still, I think I can get the local address, or at least the most recent local address."

"From the alumni association?" Tom said.

"Yes," the registrar answered, smiling. "They can always find you. Here, just a second … their site is passworded but I can get in."

A few seconds later the screen came up. The page colors were blue and gold with roadrunner logos amply sprinkled among the data. "Here he is … or at least here's where the association last sent materials. La Cantera. Just north of the University, by the mall."

Tom wrote down the address. "Is there an undergraduate institution listed for him as well?" he asked.

"Yes," the registrar said. "He has his undergraduate degree from Trinity."

"Hartford or San Antonio?" Tom asked.

"San Antonio," she said. "You could check with their alumni association also."

"That's what I was thinking," Tom responded.

Gwen called the Bureau as soon as they left the office. By the time she and Tom had gotten a coffee they were back in touch with her. "They can do this quicker than we could," she said to Tom, as she got out her notebook and pen. "Same address: on La Cantera," she said.

Tom had mapquested the address while Gwen was speaking to the Bureau. "Looks nice," he said. "From the looks of the things in the neighborhood, this would have been pricey."

"Let's check it out," Gwen said, "see if he left anything interesting behind."

FORTY-FOUR

The Manager for the *La Cantera Villas* was named John Williams. Dressed in a smart wool suit, he commanded a staff of two assistants and a full-time 'maintenance engineer'. "Of course I remember Mr. al-Barada," he said. "He was an excellent tenant. His unit is almost ready for rental again. Would you like to see it?"

"Yes, thank you," Tom and Gwen said in unison.

The apartment was located at the rear of the complex, away from the boulevard and overlooking a quarter-acre garden with a central fountain. Mahmud's space occupied 1500 square feet and included a living room, dining area, kitchen, den, two bedrooms and two bathrooms. The master bath had a stone walk-in shower and the guest bath had a jetted tub. There was a washer/dryer combination off of the kitchen, which had a six-burner gas range, double-door, stainless steel refrigerator, dishwasher, trash compactor, wine cooler, island and granite countertops.

"This is nicer than Fox's place," Gwen whispered to Tom.

"Money was no object," he responded, before turning to Williams and asking the rent for a unit such as this.

"$3750," he said. "That includes water, but not electricity, cable or wireless service."

"Nice apartment," Tom said.

"We have some one-bedroom units as well. They rent for $2250," he said. "We also have some townhomes."

"Not exactly like *my* college dorm room," Gwen said.

"No, nor like my daughter's," Williams said. "There *are* students capable of paying it, obviously. Or their parents are. Middle East oil money, probably. We get some Texas and Oklahoma oil money here as well."

They inspected the apartment but found no boxes of personal effects or documents crammed in crawl spaces. Everything had been stripped and sanitized. The smells of paint and disinfectant pervaded the apartment and there was a set of rollers, extension handles, trays and gallon cans of off-white latex paint in the master bedroom cupboard.

"Did Mr. al-Barada leave anything behind when he moved out?" Gwen asked.

"Not that I know of," Williams said. "Anything of value is returned to my office, so that I can contact the tenant. Trash is simply discarded. If there's any damage beyond normal wear and tear, I'm notified by the maintenance engineer, since we would then withhold part of the tenant's damage deposit. In this case, there was none."

"And did he leave a forwarding address?" Gwen asked.

"I believe he left an address in Pakistan."

"In Karachi?"

"Yes," he said, "that's right."

"Did you happen to notice if he moved himself or was moved professionally?" Tom asked.

"I didn't. All I know is that he vacated the apartment by the set date. As you can see, this unit sits at the back of the complex, so I wouldn't have seen the truck from my office window."

"I thought you might have noticed it when you were walking the grounds," Tom said.

"Sorry, no. I can ask other members of the staff, if you'd like me to."

"We'd appreciate it if you would," Gwen said.

The maintenance engineer thought that he had seen a small van, but he wasn't certain if it was for al-Barada's unit or for one nearby. He was also unable to remember the specific moving company. Tom and Gwen thanked both of them and returned to their car.

Both reached for their iPhones as soon as they sat down. There was a huge array of moving and storage companies in San Antonio. Interspersed with the A-list national companies were the mom and pop local operations and the dubious fly-by-nighters. There was also a list of storage locker facilities commingled with the list of moving companies. Tom got out the notepad from his hotel room and started writing names and numbers. He gave the first sheet to Gwen and kept the second for himself. "I'll step outside," he said, "so we don't have to talk over one another."

Fifteen minutes later Gwen lowered the window. "I've got him," she said. "He moved with Allied, the one on Green Mountain Road." Tom set his phone app and they drove east on the 1604 loop.

"It wasn't a large move," the agent said. Her name was Mary Ellen Buckworth; she was tall and businesslike and wearing both a cell phone and a pager and carrying a clipboard with the al-Barada file attached. "A couple rooms of furniture, no appliances. No piano, grandfather's clock, or any large items. There were two boxes of clothes—in the large boxes, the ones with the steel bars across the top that you can hang clothes on. A box of books, a couple boxes of kitchen ware, not much else."

"Most people with that small of a load would just move themselves," Gwen said.

"That's right," the agent answered, "especially in this economy. Of course, he wasn't really moving. He was putting his things in storage, so we represented one-stop shopping for him, which made everything much easier. Besides, it's not all that expensive. We have to compete with the guys in the neighborhood who own a single truck."

"Are you saying that his things are all here?" Tom asked.

"They sure are. Would you like to see them?"

"We'll get a warrant," Gwen said.

"You're from the FBI?" the agent asked.

"Yes, ma'am."

"And he's a foreigner from the Middle East?"

"Yes, ma'am," Gwen repeated.

"This is Texas, honey. If that badge is real you don't need a warrant to check out a couch, chair, mattress and a couple of boxes."

FORTY-FIVE

Allied made some large floor space available and the forensics unit from the San Antonio field office spread a fresh white sheet across the floor and taped it at the edges. They then unrolled al-Barada's oriental rug and combed it for hair samples and any other evidence that they could find. It was an Afghan rug, commemorating the victory of the mujahideen over the Soviets. Featuring images of the weaponry used, from tanks to hand grenades, it included a map of the country and the Soviet escape route to Uzbekistan, on which wheeled and tracked vehicles were exiting rapidly.

His furniture was positioned along the periphery of the sheet. Most was solid wood and had been purchased locally; the drawers were examined and the surfaces dusted for prints. The sofa and reading chair--both Natuzzi Italian leather--were set apart and the cushions, creases and cushion supports were combed and vacuumed.

"It isn't likely that there will be any DNA on file," Gwen told Tom, "but if we collect samples from different individuals we can demonstrate relationships later, particularly if we're claiming collusion and conspiracy. Unfortunately, the moving men probably put a lot of fingerprints on the hardwoods; they'll have to be identified so that they can be excluded. I want the print people to go over the books and papers in that one large box. As soon as they finish we can take a look. In the meantime I'm going to call Washington and see if they've made any progress on the real estate front."

"I'll get us some coffee," Tom said. "I saw a kitchenette in the hallway beyond the agent's office."

"Here, I'll make some fresh," Mrs. Buckworth said. "You could float a horseshoe in that goop." The cabinet contained pre-measured packets of coffee, color-coded for decaf or regular and sweetener and whitener packets, all provided by a local service. Tom noticed that the urns had been cleaned regularly.

"So you think you got yourself a bad guy?" she asked.

"Too early to tell," Tom said. "Everything is at a very preliminary stage. We do appreciate all of the help you've given us."

"Well, we're happy to. If he's gonna blow something up, it could be us or one of our neighbors. We want people like you to have every chance possible to stop him."

An hour and a half later Tom and Gwen were back at their hotel studying some of the documents that al-Barada had put in storage. Among them were a day-timer book and a folder of class notes.

"Just looks like engineering stuff," Gwen said. "Bridges, arches, highways, information on materials … it could be helpful if you were trying to learn what to blow up and what to leave in place, what would give way under what kind of stress and what wouldn't, that kind of thing. What I'm saying is that the notes are all *general*. There are no specifics like blueprints of prominent existing structures or bomb designs. His notes look pretty much like what the notes of his classmates would probably look like. And there are no comments in the margins, no jottings in the back of the folder, no phone numbers, web addresses, mailbox numbers."

"Not a lot here either," Tom said. "Notes on when certain class projects were due, a Dr's appointment labeled 'Dr. C,' a reminder here and there to pick up milk or bottled water."

"No romantic life, I assume," Gwen said.

"No. No female names with phone numbers, no reminders to pick up corsages or Whitman's Samplers ..."

Gwen smiled. "Maybe they'll have something in Washington. My contact was meeting with the director; his assistant said he'd call back later in the morning. I just checked for emails or texts. Nothing yet."

"Here's something," Tom said. "A notation that's several months old. Just two initials: P.R. I doubt that it means Public Relations. Not that he and his cousin wouldn't care about that; I just doubt that they'd call it that."

"You mean like, 'Remember to call Omar and Ali at Al Jazeera'," Gwen said.

"Right," Tom responded. "He may have been thinking it, but he wouldn't have written it in the way that we would. 'Remember to CYA; always check first with al-Zawahiri.'"

"I agree. Anything there in Arabic?"

"No. That's interesting, isn't it? Maybe it's part of his act. Mr. Non-Threatening. Just another kid from the other side of the world who idolizes all things American."

She nodded without speaking.

"I'm surprised my guy hasn't called yet," Gwen said. "They said 'late morning'; it's early afternoon there now."

Ten minutes later her phone twitched. "Here we go," she said. When she answered she told her contact that she was with Tom. "Can I put you on speaker?" she asked. She waited for his reply, clicked up the volume and put her iPhone on the coffee table.

"We have something that just might be promising," he said. "Probably a long shot, but it's the best of a bad bunch."

"Go ahead," she said. "We're all ears."

"It's a project in the hill country," he said. "Zoned commercial, but a short distance from a series of upscale residential properties. A development was planned but then either the funding fell through or the developer decided to cut his losses. The original plans called for a series of McMansions around a man-made lake. The homes were going to be on small lots and at the edge of the development there would be upscale commercial space: restaurants, shops, that kind of thing. In between the mansions and the strip mall there was a freestanding building. Very grand. They were going to use it eventually as a club house for the residents; in the meantime they were going to use it as the welcoming facility for potential buyers … you know, the kind of place where they set up displays of building materials--countertop choices, upgrades, that kind of thing. A place where they'd ply you with cheap wine and try to persuade you to sign on the line that is dotted."

"And the building was built but nothing else," Gwen said.

"Bingo. The developer halted the project and put the club house on the market. Since that portion of the space is zoned for commercial use there were a lot of possibilities."

"How many floors?" Gwen asked.

"Just one, I think. There's a high gable, but the building is long and wide. I'm guessing that there's a large open space with a high ceiling where you enter. There's also a fancy porte-cochère out front. You can see it on Google Earth; I'll send you the image."

"And the property was recently purchased?" Gwen asked.

"Yes, a couple of months ago. Small down payment, we think. The deeds always say something like 'for one dollar and other considerations' and even if they require tax stamps some people put on more than are required just to keep the suspicious guessing. In this case the MLS had the property listed for a million five. The mortgage was for a million two fifty. They probably talked them down a little and then put 5-10% down on the purchase price. We can get more information from the realtors involved; I'm just giving you the public record stuff at this point."

"Who's the mortgagor?" Gwen asked.

"Corporate entity. They call themselves *Executive Health.*"

"As in 'bring your MasterCharge or Visa'."

"One of the things that caught our eye."

"Good work," she said. "And you'll continue to follow up on the realtors involved, while we drive there?"

"I'll call the moment I know anything."

"Then all I need is the address."

"It's on Lakeview Drive. It would be, wouldn't it? No lake as it turned out, but how many elms and maples and cherries are left on the city streets with those names? It's in a town called Pigeon River."

"P.R.," Tom whispered, as Gwen nodded.

She was already putting on her jacket and checking her automatic as he hurried into his room.

FORTY-SIX

As Gwen drove, Tom worked his iPhone. "North northeast, convenient to San Antonio and not all that far from Austin. The nearest serious hospital is in New Braunfels. Pricey homes, lovely views, significant acreage. It's where *I* would locate, if I were Fox."

"Close enough for business, far enough away to help him stay under the radar," Gwen said. "Mahmud or one of his friends may have helped with the down payment, but Fox probably could have swung it himself easily enough."

"I'm thinking it's a step deal, at least as Fox understands it. Mahmud says, 'You do this for us and we'll do something for you, maybe help with the instrumentation and the casework, cover the mortgage for a couple of months.' Fox figures that if he scratches their backs now they'll scratch his as well. Of course, they could simply use him and abuse him. Once he's outlived his usefulness to them they could cut their losses and move on."

"Depends on whether they'd need him in the future," Gwen said. "Maybe he becomes the surgeon of choice or runs the surgery of choice for all the little wayward bomb throwers in North America. Dangerous, though. Once they thought that the Bureau or Homeland Security had figured it all out Pigeon River would be toxic."

"Right," Tom said, "they're probably playing him and he thinks he's playing them."

The facility was easy enough to find, as was the local commercial realtor. Gwen's contact in the Director's office had called with the contact information and the realtor, a man named Sandy Kingman, had agreed to meet them at the site. He was dressed for the restaurants that require 'casual chic' clothing and weighted down with cell phones, pagers, and clipboards. He drove a metallic silver Lexus RX350. When they asked about his client he responded promptly.

"A nice young man," he said, "a representative of the corporation."

"*Executive Health*," Tom said.

"That's right," Kingman answered. "They were looking for a site for their operation somewhere in the hill country. I told them that I had the perfect place for them."

"Did you ever meet with any other representatives of the company?" Gwen asked.

"No, I didn't. He checked out the facility, took a lot of pictures and told me he'd be back in touch. He called about a week later and we started the negotiations with the seller."

"Could you describe the man?" Tom asked.

"Yes, his name was Hardison. Bob Hardison. Tall, thin, clean-shaven, about 30 or 35. Athletic-looking. Said he was a golfer."

"Texas accent?" Tom asked.

"No, not that I remember," Kingman said. "I figured they were an out of state concern."

"Did they ever show you any information on the company?" Gwen asked.

"No, not really. That's all between them and their mortgage company. I just show the properties and try to sell them. I can refer buyers to some local lenders, but a big outfit usually has its own sources of funding. Not my business. So long as the seller gets his agreed-on price and I get my commission, we're happy here."

"Any guess as to Mr. Hardison's national origin?"

"I don't know. English, I guess, with a name like that. He had blond hair and blue eyes. We went out to lunch once and we each had barbecued pork. I don't know if that helps you or not ..."

"It does," Tom said. "What was the final purchase price?"

"Million three fifty."

"So all they put down was, what--100K or so?" Gwen asked.

"That's right."

"That's what, 6, 7% of purchase price?"

"Somewhere in there," Kingman answered.

"That seems low," she said.

"All a matter of risk, I suppose. Medical facilities generally make big money. The company was basically buying a shell. They'd have to have the resources to improve it and if they defaulted they would have been defaulting on an improved property. In the meantime the building stays the same. It's not like a tiny house that they're going to move into with a menagerie of dogs and cats and kids throwing toys against the walls. Besides, as I recall, the mortgage rate was on the high side. Not through-the-roof high, but a couple steps above sweet. That would have been a further motivator for the funding agency."

"And do you have keys to the building, Mr. Kingman?" Gwen asked.

"There are keys," he said, "but they're not mine. Mr. Hardison asked me to recommend someone to keep an eye on the place. We've got just such a person. There's a lot of business for caretakers around here, what with all of the vacation properties. Purchasers want one-stop shopping. Our man actually works out of an office on our site. His name is Dave Richardson. I picked up the keys from him before I came over here to meet you."

"We appreciate that," Tom said.

"Nice exterior, don't you think?" Kingman asked.

"Very," Gwen said.

"They're looking at thousands for the signage that they'll need," Kingman said. "Something eye-catching but also reassuring. Something that says 'you'll be safe here and may even enjoy your stay'. I recommended a guy in New Braunfels; he did the sign for our company."

He unlocked the right side of the front double door. The foyer was half-ballroom, half-hunting lodge. There was a lot of dark wood paneling and a lot of multicolored stonework. "This would all have to be muted a little," Kingman said, "but some gray paint would do wonders. I'd probably partition the space but try not to lose the effect of the high ceiling. Put in some leather furniture, maybe a little coffee shop. They're everywhere now—in grocery stores, libraries, you name it. Dark and warm equals comfort. Also a good way to kill time. You're waiting for your loved one to have his gall bladder removed … why not rest a spell and get yourself a Caramel Macchiato or a Toffee Nut Latte?"

"Is this the only finished space?" Tom asked.

"The rest rooms are both in; they're just down the hallway there to the left," Kingman said. "There's also a room just beyond, down the same hallway. We can see it if you'd like."

The room was large, at least 25' x 25'. "I believe this was going to be a room for the billiard table. They were thinking about walnut paneling and a small bar area. The light's in but nothing else."

"Would you mind if Lieutenant Deaton and I looked at this room on our own?" Gwen asked.

"Of course not," Kingman said. "It's all yours. Enjoy yourself. I'll be out in the entry area. Take as much time as you need."

"Look here," Gwen said. "There was a mat of some kind. You can see the outline in the dust on the cement."

"Probably where Len would have been standing. Keeping him comfortable or keeping his feet from sliding in the blood."

"No floor drain, of course," Gwen said. She reached in her purse and retrieved a small bottle of luminol. She sprayed it across the center of the floor. "Hit the light," she said.

When he did, Tom immediately saw the blue glow.

"The iron in the hemoglobin," Gwen said. "If I'm not mistaken there'll be some hairs on the floor as well. I'm going to get the forensics team here ASAP. See what else we can find."

"Sad," Tom said, "being operated on under a billiard table light."

"Probably deserved it," Gwen said.

"I was thinking of Len," Tom said.

"Oh. I can tell you one thing … " Gwen said.

"Already there," Tom answered. "Sloppy clean up. They were in a hurry."

Gwen just nodded as she reached for her phone.

FORTY-SEVEN

They were in Gwen's hotel room, thinking about dinner, when the call came in from the forensics team. Gwen put them on speaker.

"There must have been a fan in the room," the head of the team said. His name was Dan Stephens and the sound of his voice was slightly high-pitched. He seemed to be trying to control the urgency which he felt. "Makes sense. The A/C wasn't hooked up, so a fan would have helped make the room more comfortable. It blew the detritus against the opposite wall and into the break between the wall and the flooring. The quarter-round or other molding hadn't been installed yet, so there was a nice little trench in which to collect things. We found some hair. That of two of the people in the room corresponds with the hair of two individuals who had been in the presence of Mahmud al-Barada's oriental carpet. There's other hair as well, but that could have come from anybody—realtors, contractors, potential buyers, painters, drywallers … like I said, it was a nice little collecting trough."

"How about fingerprints?" Gwen asked.

"Some on the doorknob, a couple on the door frame. We think some were from the workmen, because there was white dust present, probably from the kid who sanded the drywall mud."

"How about the blood?"

"Group O, nothing rare. I can tell you this: there wasn't much of it. The cleanup job was sloppy. My guess is that somebody used something coarse like a paper towel and just spread the few drops that were there around. This wasn't a bloody operation. Whoever did it was clean and precise."

"So there was no bleach or other solvent that might have been used."

"Water is a solvent, of course, but there wasn't anything other than water there. The paper towel was probably damp when it was used. This wasn't some Tony Soprano/Christopher Moltisanti job. They didn't expect the area to be inspected and tested. More of a hit-and-run operation. They were in a hurry. They didn't even broom out the room; that's why the outline of the floor mat and the ridge lines underneath it were still visible in the dust."

"Talk to me about Group O blood," Gwen said. "It's very common, isn't it?"

"Yes, unfortunately. Over 60% of the world's population shares it. Really high in Central and South America—approaching 100%. Less common in Eastern Europe and Central Asia, but not unknown there. High in Western Europe, especially in populations with Celtic ancestry. It's also very high among Australian Aborigines."

"We're probably not dealing with an Aborigine," Gwen said. "How about in the Middle East? Is it common there as well?"

"Very. Sixty to ninety percent, depending on the country."

"No other blood found on the scene?" Tom asked.

"No, sorry."

"How about saliva or snot—something that might be tested for DNA?"

"No, they were probably all wearing masks, and whatever they brought in they also took with them. We checked the Dempster Dumpsters, the trashcans in the toilets and the smokers' stand outside the front door as well as the gravel and weeds in the immediate area."

"You'll check back with us if you think of anything else or come up with anything else," Gwen said.

"We will indeed," Stephens said.

"Many thanks," Gwen said, as she broke the connection.

"Would have required a lot of planning," Tom said. "It's not just a matter of sterilizing instruments and scrubbing the doctors' hands. My guess is that they'd want to keep this in the family, to the degree possible. The fewer the people involved, the smaller the risk. Fox may have played anesthetist, for example. Mahmud might have even played nurse or, at least, instrument handler. There must have been some practices and some run-throughs. If Len was brought in because of his specific skills, the procedure might have been laparoscopic. That means a whole set of instruments. Fox would be familiar with them, of course, and he would know how to obtain them. He also probably would have been hesitant to simply discard them, not if he was seriously thinking about setting up his own medical facility."

"We may be looking at a second storage site," Gwen said.

"Yes, possibly a mobile one. They could have put everything in a van and then locked it in a storage garage for future use. What did we say—twenty-five counties in the hill country and lots of urban sprawl?"

"Yes and that equipment could have been purchased over the internet using mail drops in multiple locations."

"I don't like the fact that they seem to have been in a hurry," Tom said. "Assuming that the person operated on is involved in a plot of some kind, the recuperation period would be reduced significantly by the laparoscopic procedure. You make a wide cut across a number of muscle groups and the person doesn't want to get up and move around for weeks."

"Doesn't even want to cough or visit the toilet," Gwen said. "You feel like the incision could pop open at any minute and spill your guts all over the place."

"Right, but with a few miniscule incisions, he could be back on the street in a matter of days. It was probably serious, though."

"Go on …" Gwen said.

"It wouldn't have been an emergency thing," Tom said. "When your appendix is ready to rupture you've got the sirens on and you're heading for the nearest emergency room. Back when I was a patrolman I took a guy to the ER who had problems with his gall bladder. He asked me to stop about every block and a half so that he could crack the passenger door open and heave his guts onto the curb or into the gutter. It wasn't a very precise activity. He was in pain and his body was telling him to get that gall bladder out as soon as was humanly possible."

"You're saying that the guy here had been diagnosed already and that they wanted a top-notch surgeon to do the job. We're not talking adenoids or tonsils."

"No," Tom said. "And a top-notch surgeon *here*. Not in Paris or London or Zurich. The *work* is here. And the person who was to do the work was diagnosed with something that could complicate or prevent the completion of the work."

"And it had to be done quickly," Gwen said, "and the recuperation period had to be brief because the *work* has been timed."

"Yes," Tom said. "A major terrorist event, assuming that that's what we're talking about, would take months and possibly years to plan, so the timeline makes sense. They start planning a year or two ago, plotting each step and arranging for the acquisition or construction of the precise material to be used in the event. You've got to get the material into the country and you've got to have the individual with the technical savvy to utilize it and accomplish the mission. You've also got to get that individual into the country. So think about it. The plans are in place; suddenly the key person starts feeling under the weather. A local diagnosis is made; it's not pretty and the clock is already ticking and there are no other good options. You've got to get the guy into the country and you've got to get him operated on. The best surgeon for the job is in the country. You could just kidnap him yourself and force him to do the job, but you wouldn't know whether or not he was doing all the right things. He could be a martyr, just like you, and do everything possible to kill your plan."

"You'd want somebody with the medical expertise to keep an eye on him, somebody sleazy enough to betray his country for personal gain or at least shady enough to do something for money that he knows is, at the very least, illegal."

"Yes," Tom said, "and it all worked. They *got* a top surgeon and the operation was successful. The plan is on again and their little patient is tanned, rested and ready."

"And we're geniuses for figuring all of this out and for getting this far with limited evidence," Gwen said. "The only problem is that we don't have a clue in hell as to who he is, what he's planning to do, where he intends to do it or where we go from here."

IV

KNOB NOSTER

FORTY-EIGHT

"We may finally have something," Gwen said. "The data miners have correlated the fragments of an email message with an event in Arizona. They pieced together various words and phrases and found a reference to a delivery on the 17th, the day before yesterday. On the 18th a team of border guards found an abandoned truck just outside of Nogales."

"Mexican … but in the commercial zone," Tom said.

"Right. Normally they'd trade off with a long-haul vehicle and then return to Mexico. Instead, they abandoned it, even though it appears to be in good condition, at least for a Mexican truck. It's drivable at least and the battery wasn't dead or the tires flat. When they opened it up it was full of boxes, but the boxes weren't full of merchandise; they were full of sand."

"Not a rare commodity in that part of the country," Tom said.

"No, we don't need to import any," Gwen said.

"So the Bureau figures that the sand provided enough weight to allay any suspicions when the truck was inspected electronically."

"Right. And it could also have provided the ballast that would keep the actual cargo from shifting."

"The actual cargo being a bioweapon, a load of Semtex, a container of fissile material …"

"Or all of the above," Gwen said.

"So the truck pulls off the road; it's met by another vehicle; the weapon is off-loaded and the truck is abandoned. Meanwhile the weapon is en route to its destination in a sedan, a van, another truck, a private plane, a donkey cart or ... whatever."

"All possible," Gwen said, "but I don't think we should assume that the target is necessarily near the entry point. The entry point was probably chosen because of its vulnerability, not because of its accessibility to the target."

"So you're saying that we're not that far behind whatever's being planned. They may have several days of driving ahead of them and some final preparations tacked on after that."

"Yes," Gwen said, "but there's no room for complacency in that timeline, particularly not if the cargo was as lethal as we're imagining it to be."

"Were the data miners able to come up with anything else?"

"Nothing directly relevant. The internet is filled with jihadist websites and the volume of email is, needless to say, staggering. Somebody did a guesstimate in 2017 and came up with the number of 269 billion per day. We're a long way from 2017. How many text messages are now sent every second? You don't have to dig very deep to find threats of horrific violence or raving tirades directed against the United States. The trick is to find the correlations, like the link between a delivery date and a very suspicious abandoned truck."

"But the problem is that when you're dealing with competent jihadists they're not going to telegraph their activities by describing them in direct and inflammatory language," Tom said.

"No, they're not. And they're not going to communicate in Arabic, if that's their native language."

"What's happening in London?" Tom asked. "Anything?"

"You mean in relation to Hakim?"

"Yes," Tom said.

"He was believed to be there, but I don't know that there were any confirmed sightings."

"And why would he be believed to be there?" Tom asked. "The Brits have more cameras in a block or two of central London than all of the Hollywood studios combined. Presumably they didn't see his smiling face as he cleared immigration or customs at Heathrow. Maybe there's a family home there? Somebody saw a light on? If they did they would have been in there in force in a matter of minutes."

"Good question," Gwen said, picking up her phone.

"Thanks," she said, in the process of ending the call. "No, we're still here in San Antonio. We don't want to leave until we have some indication of a possible target. We don't need *likely*, but we'd like to have *possible*. Right. Thanks again."

"Hakim's wife was seen there. People like Hakim ... they generally don't like the idea of their wives leading separate lives. If she was there it was assumed that he was as well."

"But they didn't follow her."

"No, they lost her. They picked her up on a security camera, which, in itself, is remarkable, given the fact that she was shopping at *Harrod's*."

"She could have left in any direction using any number of doors," Tom said. "There are taxis waiting outside or just dropping people off at each of the potential exits. She also could have slipped into one of the restrooms and changed her clothes, either covering herself up or uncovering herself in some unexpected way."

"Yes. Department stores are tough," Gwen said, "especially stores with a lot of merchandise in close quarters and displays that rise above the height of the average person."

"Good place to meet somebody, though," Tom said. He was futzing with his iPhone. "Over 111,500 square meters of floor space, 74,000 square meters of selling space, around 5,000 staff and 300,000 shoppers on a good day. If I'm going to meet somebody, that would work a lot better than a park bench in clear daylight. Plus it's a tourist magnet, which offers a lot of diversion and with shoppers from all over the world you see people there in multiple forms of dress, all of which could be altered in a toilet stall."

"Maybe she's his go-between," Gwen said. "He holes up somewhere with his computer and sends her off to pick up and transmit messages. It's certainly possible."

"And better work than going out on his behalf with fifteen or twenty pounds of C-4 strapped and bolted around her waist," Tom added.

"That would certainly be my preference," Gwen said.

"Too bad they couldn't follow her," Tom said.

"Yes it is," Gwen agreed. "Unfortunately, I don't have anything else, just some threats to bring death to the great Satan (and please forgive the sing-song) the occupier, the blasphemer, the crusader, the infidel, the oppressor, the filth, the scum, the vermin, the dog and the white devil."

"The white devil? That sounds like the title of a B movie from the thirties or forties."

"Actually, there was one or two emails that used that term. Not that big of a surprise, I suppose. They've tried every other way to insult us. Why not use some racial slurs and epithets? There *was*, after all, that jihadist rapper (what was his name—something or other like Abu Mansour al-Amriki. Maybe it was Amriki al-Mansour. I think I can find him on YouTube, in case you missed him." She keyed the URL for the site in order to show him.

"I think I saw him already," Tom said. "The white devil reference is more interesting."

"How so, other than that it's uncharacteristic?"

"Because it's the sort of thing somebody might say who was sufficiently aware of English expressions to know that it might work as an epithet but not sufficiently aware of our culture to have any sense of nuance or tone or context."

"Somebody who *thinks* they're using an acceptable term to convey scorn or hatred."

"Right," Tom said. "A *standard* term. Except that it's not a standard term. I can easily imagine it in one of Reverend Wright's sermons, but I could also see it as a type of firecracker or the name of a rock band. Black militants might rage against 'Whitey', but that's the kind of name we use for baseball managers, bass fishermen and NASCAR drivers. If a senator used 'white' in an epithet the media would reverberate for weeks, but standup comics and talk show hosts joke about how 'white' somebody is without anyone batting an eye. Race talk is a minefield because race is so complicated culturally; we use the terms in dozens of ways. Context, nuance, tone--they're crucial."

"You're saying that this could be a phrase used by a jihadist who didn't want to draw attention to himself, but just did," Gwen said.

"Yes, something like that. Where did you say the data miners found it?"

"They can't always say, specifically. They toss the net and see what gets caught in the webbing," Gwen said. "Sometimes the messages are encrypted and sometimes they just get small fragments. The white devil reference …"

"Yes," Tom said, "*whereabouts* did they find it?"

"Let me check," Gwen answered. She clicked on a desktop icon and then did a quick function/find search. "That's interesting," she said. "They found it within the set of messages concerning the delivery on the 17th."

Tom nodded, hit the power button on his laptop and waited as the screen came to life.

FORTY-NINE

"Actually," Gwen said, "the reference was to the *devil white man*."

"Thanks," Tom said. "Let me run some possibilities."

"I'll get us some fresh coffee," she said.

There was a forgettable film called *The Devil Wears White*, along with the more notable *Beat the Devil*, *Ride with the Devil*, *Shake Hands with the Devil*, and *Race with the Devil*. There were three or four foreign language films with 'white devil' in the title, one of which was X-rated and unlikely to be in a jihadist's collection.

Book titles were more plentiful, with *The Devil in the White City*, Webster's play *The White Devil* and titles referring to colonialism and other grand misdeeds. He checked on the Webster play: Elizabethan revenge tragedy with lots of feuding Italians, poisons and gunplay. Probably not the sort of thing that would have been in the core curriculum at Mahmud and Hakim's madrasa.

He tried *white man* and Whitman. He noted Kipling's poem "The White Man's Burden" and Whitman College, Walt Whitman, Paul Whiteman, the jazzman with the pencil-thin mustache, several *Whiteman* schools, Baum & Whiteman, 'the world's pre-eminent food and restaurant consulting company', a columnist named Lily Whiteman, a reggae singer named Raggamuffin Whiteman, Whiteman Trowels, Whiteman Equipment, Whiteman Park, the photographer Lisa Whiteman, the biologist Howard Whiteman, Whiteman.org, Dorit Whiteman, author of books on the holocaust, John Whiteman & Company, estate agents, the John Whiteman Harp Anthology, John Whiteman's Harmonica Collection, John Whiteman on Facebook, John Whiteman on zoominfo, John Whiteman the ecologist, John Whiteman the international speaker, John Whiteman the Managing Director, John Whiteman the mathematician, John Whiteman the blogger, John Whiteman the lawyer, John Whiteman the orthodontist and the Whiteman Foundation.

He checked out Malcolm X's ruminations on the white man as the devil and found links to a host of questioners who had wondered whether or not the white man *is* the devil. One (on an Islamic site) answered that the devil is real and he would love to have you believe that he is the white man, while, in fact, he is not human. Interesting, Tom thought; that hasn't kept anyone from calling us the great Satan.

He continued to surf and search, resisting the temptation to linger over particular sites and particular discussions. When Gwen returned she had a bag of bagels and cream cheese. "Do you have any idea how difficult it is to find authentic bagels in San Antonio?" she asked.

"No Krispy Kremes?" Tom asked.

"You need a little sugar jolt?" she responded.

"I need something," he said. "You did the right thing, though. Better boiled in water than fried in grease. And I appreciate your hunting for the real article."

"I don't know how real they are," Gwen answered, "but they'll be better than the stale bagels in the cellophane packages that they sell in the vending machines."

"With the little wooden spoons for the cheese," Tom said. "They remind me of the wooden scoops or spoons or whatever they were called that you got with the little tub of ice cream. Sometimes the ice cream (it was nearly always vanilla) would be frozen so hard that you'd have to hold the cup in your hand to warm it up and then scrape the scoop across the surface to try to loosen it up and give you enough for a decent taste."

"Thinking about the good old days, huh? Back before the hellish times when we could get authentic gelato on nearly every street corner."

"We've got very good ice cream at Laguna Beach," he responded, as she handed him a large cup of coffee and a bagel.

"Where I went they didn't have *grande* or *venti*," she said, "just large and extra large, with nothing on the menu using the words *skinny* or *dolce*."

"It smells great," Tom said.

"Here's the cream cheese," she said. "All they had were plastic knives, none of those little wooden scoop spoons that you like."

Tom took a long sip of his coffee and a bite of his bagel. "Hot," he said, "very hot. And the bagel ... very tasty. Very close to *real*."

He took a second bite and suddenly the room became quiet. Gwen asked him a question but all that he heard was a humming sound, as if she were endlessly repeating a single, dull vowel. It was as if something in his head had frozen time and concentrated his attention. A muffled chime was sounding and it was hitting the center of his brain like his cell phone alarm, rising in volume with each set of strikes.

"Stupid, stupid, stupid, stupid," he said.

"What? Who?" Gwen responded.

"Stupid."

"Tom?"

"Me," he said.

"Why?" she asked.

"Because I've been sitting here, staring at my laptop screen, taking the words *devil* and *white man* and running sets of possible combinations when the answer has been so obvious all along. Damn!"

"Damn?"

"Yes, damn."

FIFTY

"I hope you're going to include me in your little reverie," Gwen said. "Of course. It's so, *so* obvious."

She paused before responding, turned her head and thought for a moment and it hit her as well. "Whiteman Air Force Base," she said.

"Yes," he answered.

"The B-2 base. The stealth bomber—used to great effect in Sunni-dominated Kosovo as well as in Iraq and Afghanistan, facts that would *not* have gone unnoticed."

Tom was downloading information while she let the force of that possibility sink in. As he performed the key strokes, he summarized as he read. "Twenty remaining aircraft; one of them crashed on takeoff in 2008. The original plan was to build 130 plus, but they settled on 21. Twenty years old now, but they're still monsters. They can take off from Missouri, fly around the world, drop their payload and return home. They can be refueled in flight. They can be flown from forward operating locations. They can carry conventional and nuclear weapons ..."

"And they're expensive as all hell," Gwen said.

"A 'high value' target, that's for sure," Tom said. "Estimated cost for the full deal—development, procurement, maintenance, spare parts, facilities: 2 billion plus per aircraft. And that's in *1997 dollars*. I remember 1997 dollars. Nineteen ninety-seven dollars were good. Nineteen ninety-seven dollars bought a lot of stuff."

"If all 20 were at Whiteman, you'd be looking at a $50,000,000,000 target," Gwen said, "a target with symbolic value, a target of significant strategic importance."

"Plus the impact on the families at the base and in the local community," Tom said. "Assuming that we're talking about something with 'reach'—a biological weapon or some sort of dirty bomb, for example—you're looking at the destruction or neutralization of an air force base as well as a town. In the heartland of the country."

"The terror payoff would be huge; the message would be sent that no place is safe. And you wouldn't need a set of aircraft loaded with jet fuel; all that you'd need for a delivery instrument would be a car or a truck. How many people in the nearby town?"

"In Knob Noster ... around 3,000, but wait a sec ... there's also a state park nearby."

"They'd love to hit a state park," Gwen said.

"It gets worse," Tom added. "There are Minuteman silos there. Not operational, but available for tours, so there could be day visitors in their sights as well as local civilians and military personnel. There were ten ICBM's there at one time."

"VIP's love to tour facilities like that," Gwen said. "The good old days of the Cold War—yards and yards of reinforced concrete, *007*-movie bunkers with lots of lights, buttons and finger-locked toggle switches, sophisticated ventilation systems, nuclear weaponry, a couple of lieutenants with keys around their necks, capable of initiating Armageddon ... and then there are the B-2's themselves. Get on a simulator for a few minutes. Watch the computer screen as you fly over some bit of recognizable landscape, land the aircraft without incident, tell all your envious friends and relatives ... "

"Wait a second," Tom said, working his keyboard. "The base is available for tour groups but only between March and August and only on one day a month—always a Friday."

"When's the next tour day?" Gwen asked.

"This Friday," Tom said, as he scrolled. "Four days from now."

"How many in a group?"

"Forty, maximum," Tom said.

What's the protocol?"

"The reservations are made on a first-come, first-served basis, but they're made in advance, so if you want to be sure that your group gets in you'd have to apply months in advance, not days or weeks. Each group has to have a main coordinator and that individual has to provide an address, phone number and email address in addition to the full names of all guests attending, with their social security numbers. Any non-U.S. citizens have to be so identified when the reservations are made."

"Forty is a lot to coordinate," Gwen said. "If anyone tried to bring in forty fellow jihadists some item or other would surface in the background checks and immediately set off bells and whistles. I could imagine a set of dummied credentials for a handful, but not for forty."

"The main coordinator could be the ringer," Tom said. "He could then invite a group of other individuals to join him. There wouldn't be a shortage of interest. He could put an ad in a local paper inviting people to join him. Also, there's a maximum of forty. Maybe he's coming with a smaller group."

"I'll call the Bureau," Gwen said, "get the data miners to check on any calls or invitations for tours of Whiteman."

"There's another possibility," Tom said. "He could enter the base in a civilian delivery or service vehicle. He could do that *any* day. For that matter, if he had the right delivery system he wouldn't even have to enter the base."

"You mean fly something in," Gwen said.

"Maybe initially, but not for the final stages of the operation," Tom said. "They would be keeping a close eye on their air space and they wouldn't treat interlopers very gently."

"What are you thinking?"

"A mortar, maybe?" He was making rapid keystrokes as he spoke. "Here's an M30. It's heavy, over 600 pounds, but it's effective at over 7,000 yards. Say 4 miles or so. For a weapon that size though you'd need a crew. You'd have to transport it, assemble and position it, weigh it down, aim it, etcetera, but you wouldn't need a weapon of that size and you wouldn't need to fire from that distance. The rounds could be small; you could poop in a dozen or two and be back on the road in a matter of seconds. The possibilities are endless. You could find a local beer hall where the airmen hang out. Put some weapons under their cars and wait for them to drive back to the base. You could find out *who* provides *what* to Whiteman ... all military installations get supplies from civilian vendors and all have civilian employees. Their vehicles could be the unsuspecting carriers."

"It also depends on how high they've set their sights," Gwen said. "A truck filled with nitrogen fertilizer can bring down a building. A trunk full of plastic explosive could do that and more."

"Yes, but for maximum effect you'd probably want something nuclear or biological," Tom said. "If you want to take out the B-2's, the base, the visitors, the town and the national park you'd want something that could be detonated and spread across a wide area."

"A nice wind coming across the plains would help with that," Gwen said.

"And that would narrow things a bit," Tom said. "They wouldn't *plan* to set up east of the base, though they could potentially have winds from any direction."

"I've got to call the Bureau," Gwen said.

As she did, Tom continued to surf the web for possibilities. While the texts and images appeared on the screen he looked at the clock in the corner of his desktop as it counted off the seconds, minutes, hours and days.

FIFTY-ONE

"It looks daunting at first," Tom said, "but we're not helpless. The biggest problem will be masking our strengths, because the moment that Mahmud or Hakim or whoever it is that's fronting the operation feels trapped or threatened he might be tempted to detonate the device, release the agent or do whatever it is he's planning to do."

"Right," Gwen said. "We can't suddenly surround him with hundreds of Homeland Security personnel … unless we're prepared to sacrifice all of them."

"Let's think about other options. First, let's see if we can identify the vehicle that they're using. The more I think about this the more I believe that it would be highly unlikely that they would steal something."

"Why do you say that?"

"Because their operation disintegrates if they get caught up in small mistakes. They can't run stoplights; they can't suddenly be faced with a battery or alternator problem; they can't be picked up for an outdated inspection sticker or a burned-out license plate light. Any tiny problem could entail a check of the vehicle registration number. It's right there at the base of the windshield; one phone call and they're ruined. They'll want all of their documentation to be up to date and kosher and they'll want to be certain that their vehicle is operational and reliable."

"You think they'd purchase something new."

"Yes, or something used that's in very good condition. My guess is that they could have forged papers on themselves, but that they would have legitimate papers on the vehicle. They couldn't use their personal vehicles because the operation could be tracked right back to them, assuming, of course, that they intend to survive the operation."

"There wasn't a vehicle registered to Mahmud. There was to Fox, of course, but he wouldn't use his own vehicle and risk implicating himself in such an obvious way."

"And Fox would have absolutely no interest in a kamikaze run," Tom said. "He's about the money, not about martyrdom or the platoon of virgins waiting in heaven."

"No, he'd go for the virgins here and now," Gwen said. "So we ask local law enforcement to make discreet enquiries about recent car, truck and van purchases within a circle around Nogales."

"Yes. I'd bet that they'd make the buy in Phoenix. Easy access to the Phoenix airport from San Antonio. Easy drop-off point for a rental car there. Lots of vehicle dealers. Lots of choices and options. Tucson's also possible, but it's a much smaller town; we should still check both. My guess is that they'd go to a large-volume dealer, not to a fly-by-nighter with limited business. The latter would have far fewer transactions and a more vivid memory of his recent customers."

"I agree," Gwen said, "but Tom, I'm a little concerned about this …"

"I know what you're thinking. It's too rational, too logical," Tom said. "It doesn't account for their doing something stupid or unpredictable—like leaving their supply vehicle outside Nogales."

"No, it doesn't," Gwen said, "but I don't know … maybe leaving the truck there wasn't all that stupid. Some wouldn't pay any attention to it at all; they'd simply assume that it had been used to transport drugs or payment for small arms and it *is* true that there was nothing there (at least to the naked eye) that would link the truck to *them*. That's a battle zone anyway. Things appear and then disappear. With all of the opposition to allowing Mexican trucks on U.S. highways, it's a kind of don't ask/don't tell zone. People want cheap goods and cheap labor; they don't want unsafe trucks on the road and illegals consuming social services. We want to drive to our beachfront condos in Mexico or pop across the border to buy inexpensive pharmaceuticals but we don't want terrorists strolling into the U.S. on the other side of the turnstile. The problems are so much bigger than a single vehicle that single vehicles are easily forgotten. Still, I'm concerned. I like what you're saying. I just hope that the al-Baradas and the other members of their organization are as rational as you think they are."

"But looking for the specific vehicle isn't all that we can do," Tom said. "I think we should do everything that we *can* and then hope that one or more things work."

"Agreed," Gwen said.

"We can circulate pictures of Mahmud and Fox. Do you have a picture of Hakim?"

"Yes. A side shot, but it's a good image."

"OK. We get the Bureau to bring in local law enforcement and check with vehicle dealers in the local area. Maybe we'll get lucky. If we can identify the vehicle we can track it as it approaches its target. We can't surround the plotters with uniformed agents or Highway Patrol types, but if we could locate the vehicle on the interstate, for example, we could surround it with civilian vehicles driven by federal agents. Everybody drives five or six miles over the limit on the interstates; *they* can't, because they could be picked up. While they're driving the limit we surround them with cars, closing off the space around them. Then we bring in an aircraft that could blow them off of the road and let them decide how quickly they want to visit with those virgins."

"But if we can't identify the vehicle ..."

"We could still check them out," Tom said. "For example, we could set up road repair units on each side of the interstate. Narrow the traffic to a single lane, then check out each vehicle as it comes through. If Mahmud or Hakim is driving, we're set. If Fox is driving (which I would consider very doubtful), we'd also be set. We profile everybody. Take pictures of anyone who looks suspicious and run the images through your computers."

"And if they come in on a back road?"

"Close the roads at strategic points and canalize them—detour them back to the interstate."

"Anything else in your bag of tricks?" Gwen asked.

"We should definitely prepare the people at Whiteman. They're not going to have the B-2's on display at the side of the road. They could slowly relocate them to a distant site on the base."

"Slowly? You mean in case the al-Baradas are observing by satellite or drone?"

"Yes, we can't be too safe, even if it's more likely that they'd have an observer on the ground in the area."

"OK, so you've moved the aircraft to some distant point. What about the military and civilian population?"

"Notify the essential personnel who would be handling an emergency operation and have them prepared to respond quickly in the case of a strike. I don't like putting the population there at risk, but if we telegraph the fact that we're aware of their operation they'll simply postpone it and return another day. Or drive to the Plaza area of Kansas City or the Gateway Arch in St. Louis. Or the Royals' stadium or the Cardinals'."

"You'd need enough military personnel on hand to make it appear that everything was proceeding normally."

"Yes," Tom said, "but you could enhance security without making it too obvious. I would, for example, change the credentials required for entrance to the base."

"What do you mean?" Gwen asked.

"Nothing too overt," Tom said. "It could be as simple as a new bar code on an i.d. Your regular visitors and your trusted military personnel could be outfitted with one a day or two before, so that anyone on the margins would lack the new code and have to be issued one. That would give you the chance to check them out."

"You're worried that the al-Baradas could use someone else's vehicle or a dummied-up delivery vehicle."

"Yes. It would be one additional speed bump they'd have to negotiate and it would give us an additional opportunity to identify them."

"But if they were coming in as putative tourists …"

"They'd see everyone ahead of them in the queue being delayed for a moment or two, but then passing through. No big deal, they'd figure. It's visitors' day. Everybody's being a little more careful."

"And the number of visitors is strictly limited, so whoever had not been cleared in advance (local delivery vehicles, pre-screened military personnel) would be obvious."

"Yes," Tom said, "and it could all be low-key. New security precautions … no big deal. You could make some kind of announcement to the effect that there's an upcoming inspection of some sort and that protocols are being tightened."

"All in case the al-Baradas have somebody on the ground there, trying to scope out whether or not their operation has been identified."

"Yes, exactly," Tom said.

"So far so good," Gwen said. "I'm feeling better. Not good yet, but better."

"'Better' may be as good as we can do," Tom said.

FIFTY-TWO

Tom and Gwen flew out of Austin to Kansas City, with a connecting flight through Denver. "You know what will happen next, I assume," Gwen said.

"Yes," Tom answered. "Homeland Security will enter in force and commandeer the operation. We'll be thanked profusely, patted gently on the top of the head and asked to get out of their way."

"Yes," Gwen said, "but the Bureau will keep us in because we broke the case, assuming that there's a case there."

"But we won't be in charge of it."

"No, not in charge. They *did* say that they liked your ideas, however. I thought you'd want to know that."

"That's very gratifying," Tom said.

"They're also identifying likely stops along the possible entry routes—service stations, highway rest stops, that sort of thing. They've got some dogs that can smell certain explosives and they'll have agents with Geiger counters. The canines don't all look like hungry attack dogs, so they're less conspicuous. You put one in the back seat of a car and roll down the window, position them next to the gas pumps, or take them for a walk in the interstate rest areas and let them sniff to their hearts' content. The Geiger counter guys will be dressed like maintenance personnel or pump attendants."

"I just hope that if they're using Semtex it's the new stuff with the detection tag," Tom said. "Give the dogs a chance."

"Yes. It may all just be a shot in the dark, but like you said earlier, we should try anything and everything we can. We're also checking with stores that sell explosives. Presumably they already have what they need, but maybe their supplier forgot something. Maybe they want a little more det cord or something. Again, a shot in the dark, but why not try?"

"And hopefully they're intensifying the data mining. At least they've got some good key words to plug in."

"Yes, they are. The Whiteman commander is being very helpful also. He's had some ideas on how to insulate the aircraft. He's also going to protect their simulators and other training equipment. They're not like video games with joysticks. The computers that run the simulators take something like 45 minutes to boot up. We're talking *complex* and very, very expensive."

"While you were on the phone in Denver I was on my laptop," Tom said. "I was reading about dirty bombs. They're not something that you'd want set off in your living room, but neither are they as threatening as they sound. Unless you're in the immediate area, it's unlikely that the radiation would result in a significant number of deaths. Some people won't even label them WMD's. Conventional weapons could actually be *dirtier*, but radiation is like electricity. Nobody understands it and everybody fears it."

"Yes, it's a *terror* weapon more than a *weapon* weapon," Gwen said. "One of the things that we have going for us is that the population density is light. We don't have to worry about mass panic because we've got a militarily-savvy population and there isn't the problem of too many people and too few exits. We *are* preparing for mass decontamination if that becomes a necessity."

"So what do we do besides wait and pray?" Tom asked.

"Keep coming up with ideas, I suppose."

"I'd like to be in the MP box at the Main Gate."

"In uniform?"

"Yes. I'd be another set of eyes and ears and I will have had the chance to study the pictures of the likely perps."

"I can probably sell that to our people," Gwen said.

"How about you?" he asked.

"I'll try to be as close as I can to the senior agent on site."

"To influence the action."

"Yes," she said. "To 'offer input'."

"We may not need any," Tom said. "Perhaps nothing will happen at all. Maybe they're targeting Fort Hood or Fort Bliss, maybe Fort Huachuca or Fort Sam Houston. They started in San Antonio after all."

"Possibly," Gwen said. "Lot of medical personnel at Fort Sam ..."

"It could be anywhere, anyone or anything," Tom said. "All we can do is go with the best information we have. If Fox had anything to say about it (which I doubt, by the way) he might have wanted some revenge for the way he was treated in Missouri. He's already had his revenge on Len Barnes, or at least he thinks he has. And Fort Leonard Wood is less attractive as a target than Whiteman."

"Remember: they love headlines," Gwen said. "And Whiteman's much more manageable. The bigger bases are like cities, with people and equipment spread out all over the place. The bang for the buck there would be huge ... sorry about the metaphor."

"It's the one that they'll be using," Tom said, "or whatever its Arabic equivalent is."

"Yes," she said.

The Kansas City airport was basically in a large field on the far north side of the city. They picked up a rental car and began to wend their way southeast along a wide semicircle that took them to interstate 70.

Gwen drove as Tom checked his app. "I'm going to call Sally," he said. "If she had any new information she surely would have called me, but I want to touch base with her. I won't give her any of the details of our operation. I'll simply tell her that we're still trying to find Fox."

"Good," Gwen said.

When he called he got her voice mail. "Maybe she has her phone turned off," he said. "Hospitals are touchy about cell phone usage."

"She's probably on another call," Gwen said. "She'd set her phone to twitch rather than ring. She wouldn't want to miss anything."

He tried again fifteen minutes later and got the voice mail a second time."

"I don't like this," he said. "She's not the Chatty Cathy type, and certainly not when she's sitting at the side of the bed of somebody she cares about deeply."

"Maybe she's having dinner and her phone's in her purse, on the floor."

He tried again five minutes later and the call went through. "Tom," Sally said, "I've been with Len; I was just about to call you."

FIFTY-THREE

"Len's awake. He was very groggy at first and we did all that we could to make him comfortable and try to ease the way. The funny thing is that he was hungry. He opened his eyes, turned and looked at me, smiled warmly and said that he was starving. He reached out, took me by the hand and asked me if I'd like to join him for some breakfast. Then he realized that he hadn't just been taking a nap, that he had been out for a long time, that he was in a hospital, catheterized and being fed with an IV drip.

"He said he was sorry about asking for food rather than thanking me for being there with him and then he sat up and kissed me. We got an extra pillow and propped him up so that he could be comfortable. His doctor wanted to leave in all the tubes in case he went out again, but he did agree to giving him some solid food. God love him, he wanted pancakes, sausages and hash-browns."

"Sounds like serious recuperation," Tom said. He put his hand over the phone for a second and leaned toward Gwen. "Len's awake," he said.

"I told him how he got to the hospital and how long he'd been there," Sally said. "I also told him that he'd awakened on several occasions and I told him what he had said."

"It's like it happened months ago," he said. "I can remember it vividly, but it almost feels as if it had happened to someone else, like I was an observer, reading somebody else's diary or watching an old home movie in a quiet theatre. I remember the details but it's almost as if I wasn't actually there when all of it happened."

"I asked him if he was aware of anything that had been going on around him here in the hospital and he said no. He didn't remember speaking to me either, but when I told him what he had said he told me that it made perfect sense to him. We didn't know whether or not to start questioning him, to let him eat first or to let him rest for a moment. I asked him how he felt and he said that he felt fine; he was just hungry. So we started to talk and after they brought him the food he continued to talk between bites."

"I must have really been out," he said, "because this hospital food tastes wonderful."

"I told him to take his time, to talk at his own pace, that we had all the time in the world and that the primary thing was to insure his health. He smiled and said he forgot to ask for juice and coffee. 'Would you like something?' he asked."

"I told him what time it was and that I had already eaten."

"'If you change your mind, just say so,' he said, dipping the sausages in syrup as well as the pancakes."

"'Well,' he said, 'I suppose I should tell you what happened. It was very strange. I looked at a condo for us in Newport Beach. Very, very nice … and when I left the building I was met by two individuals from the government. They showed me their credentials and asked if I would accompany them.'"

"What branch of government?" I asked.

"Federal Marshals, I think. It wasn't the FBI or the Secret Service or anything like that. They were dressed in business suits, though. No Mounty hats or Stetsons."

"Ethnicity?"

"I don't know; I couldn't tell," he said. "Dark hair, dark eyes, mustaches. I figured they were Italian at first, but sometimes it's hard to tell."

"Sure," I said. "And what happened then?"

"They told me that they were there on behalf of the State Department and that a prominent foreign national required surgery. They said it was extremely sensitive, that the fact that he was sick could create instability in his country and the fact that he had come to the U.S. for the procedure could be politically embarrassing. They said that they had spoken with several major surgeons, each of whom had recommended me for the job. However, they wanted it all done on the Q-T for the reasons stated above. I asked about the illness and they told me that it was stomach cancer, that it had been detected early and that the patient hoped that the surgery could be performed laparoscopically. 'That's why everyone recommended you,' they said. I asked more questions about the illness, about the nodes, etcetera, and they said that that was above their pay grade, that I'd have to talk to the other doctors on the case. Where is the patient now? I asked and they told me that he was at the surgical site, waiting for me. I asked where the site was and they told me that they would take me there. They were evasive with regard to the location. When I asked them about the equipment I'd need, they said not to worry, that everything would be there for me when I arrived."

"And how did they transport you?"

"By private jet, from Skylark Field."

"Up at Lake Elsinore rather than from John Wayne."

"Yes," he said, "more privacy there, fewer prying eyes, they thought."

"How long was the flight?" I asked.

"A couple hours. They circled initially and the window blinds were all closed. I figured they didn't want me to know where, specifically, we were going. It was a small Gulfstream; they cruise at a little more than 450 knots once they've reached altitude, so I figure we had flown somewhere in the neighborhood of 1,000 miles from Orange County. When we landed I was whisked into a limo that was waiting on the side of the tarmac. The country was rolling hills with oak and juniper, some water, some rock formations ... when we got to the surgical site the space had just been constructed. There was a single room on the first floor of a large building. It was clean and there was modern equipment there, but nothing in support."

"You mean backup support," I said.

"Right. We weren't in a hospital. If I was being asked to extract a tooth or remove a mole, that would be one thing, but stomach cancer is something else again. Sometimes you discover things and you realize that the laparoscopic technique will be insufficient and that you need to make a large incision. They were all assuming that there would be no need for radiation or chemotherapy, but if the patient had been more seriously ill than they thought, the recovery time would have been much longer and additional therapies would have been required. At that point you wouldn't want to have to move the patient, particularly when you were in the boondocks, far from any well-equipped and well-staffed facility. They told me not to be concerned, that they were very certain about the diagnosis and that if there were any additional problems they would take full responsibility for them."

"And did you meet the other physicians?"

"Physician," Len said, "There was only one and they told me that he couldn't speak English. He worked through a translator."

"So you didn't recognize the other doctor?"

"I couldn't see him. He was wearing a surgical cap and a face mask."

"What about the translator?"

"No, I couldn't see him either. He was also in scrubs, with a cap and mask."

"Did the other doctor act as the anesthetist?"

"Yes. His translator actually briefed me. He basically repeated what the Marshals had already told me. When I did the procedure I had to talk through him to the anesthetist. It was very awkward."

"Any guesses on the translator—younger, older, shorter, taller, accent, ethnicity, physical appearance … ?"

"Dark eyes, younger than the anesthetist, shorter, medium height and weight. The anesthetist was taller and more stout."

"Fat?"

"No, not fat *per se*. What my mother would have called *husky*. Probably fifty or a little older. The translator was probably mid-twenties or so. His English was mildly British, but he spoke it fluently."

"And how did the surgery go?"

"It was fine. The diagnosis was accurate. I only had to take a part of the stomach and was able to do it laparoscopically."

"Were you able to see the patient?"

"No, not really. When I got there he was completely prepped. They had a cap on him and he was covered with feeding and breathing tubes. His body was covered with sheets except for the area around the incisions. I would guess that he was young. Mid-thirties, possibly. That's based on things like skin and muscle tone. Average height and weight, probably a little taller than the translator, a little shorter than the anesthetist."

"Facial hair?"

"No, and no sideburns to speak of. Just a little hint at the edge of the cap, but nothing out of the ordinary."

"They must have had his arm exposed, for the IV."

"Yes," Len said, "but there was no jewelry, nothing remarkable. The skin was mildly swarthy. Mediterranean, not Scandinavian, but I can't be any more specific than that."

"You said you left a mark of some kind."

"Yes, I did. I thought the whole situation was odd. Well, it would have been anyway, wouldn't it? If I were actually operating on someone of importance, someone for whom secrecy would be necessary, that in itself would be odd. What bothered me was the facility. Limos are easy, but if you can lay on a Gulfstream, that means you have access to serious cash. If the person is that important and if you have access to that kind of money, you can find a hospital or a private clinic that knows how to maintain secrecy but also provides top-of-the-line consultants and state-of-the-art technology. That foreign anesthetist bothered me as well. Maybe it was irrational on my part and maybe it was chauvinistic ... I suppose it's very possible that this was the patient's foreign doctor, who had come along for the ride, but the diagnostician would *not* have been an anesthetist. If you wanted a top surgeon, why not also go to the trouble to get a top anesthetist. I'm not saying that all of them would be English-speaking, but … anyway … it seemed odd to me."

"And your mark … ?"

"When I closed I varied the width between the sutures."

"So that he could be identified later?"

"Yes, if needs be. I thought of it as just a little bit of insurance."

"Then what happened?"

"After I finished the surgery the Marshals offered me some coffee. I noticed that the anesthetist and his translator passed, but the Marshals drank the coffee, so I figured it was OK. This was stupid of me. Truly stupid. They had put a sedative in my cup, not in the coffee. What do the teenage girls all say--duh? After a couple sips I felt sleepy and sat down. They said that I was probably just tired after performing the surgery. A few seconds later I was out. And that's all I remember."

"Does any of this sound familiar, Tom? Do any of the facts fit with your own investigation?" Sally asked.

"Yes," Tom said. "Eerily so."

"Then this would have been helpful."

"Very," Tom said. "Did you say anything to him about Nathan Fox?"

"Not initially," she said. "I wanted to get all of his memories down as clearly and specifically as possible. I was afraid that the Fox business might cloud the issue, but after he finished his breakfast, including his third cup of coffee, I raised the question with him."

FIFTY-FOUR

Before Tom could speak, Gwen's phone rang.

"Yes," she said. "I can't talk now. Lieutenant Deaton is speaking with his colleague and we'll drown each other out. I'll call you back in a few minutes."

Tom nodded in appreciation, but he had to ask Sally to repeat what she had just said.

"I was saying that I had to draw him out on the Fox stuff," she said. "It wasn't easy. Part of it is that the memories are painful, but it's also difficult for him because he's so private. I'm not sure he had ever talked to anyone about what happened between Fox and his wife."

"His wife ... you told me her name ... Karen."

"Yes, Karen. She was a Med-Surg nurse. She died of cancer."

"And something happened between her and Fox."

"Yes. It was horrible, though Fox probably didn't see it that way. He's a notorious sexual harasser; at least that's how we would describe him now. 'He was always touching people,' Len said, 'even when they didn't welcome it and often when they had told him to stop it.' It was more difficult in those days. Not that we're talking about Romans and slave girls or anything like that, but the relationships between doctors and nurses were less ... professional. There were fewer women doctors, for example, and nearly all of them were in family practice or Obstetrics. The profession has always been hierarchical and quasi-military, from the boot-camp hours of the internship to the rigid pecking orders in hospitals and medical schools ... "

"And Fox harassed Karen?"

"Yes. Len doesn't think that Fox was aware of the fact that he and Karen were married. That may just be Len's natural inclination to be generous and non-judgmental, but what Fox did was outrageous whether Karen was married or not."

"And that was … ?"

"He groped her. They were alone on an elevator together. He said something to her; Karen would never specify what he had actually said, but it was sexual in nature. She made it clear to him that she was not interested in his advances and that she found what he said deeply offensive. Just before the elevator stopped he turned to her and said, 'Well, the least you could do is give me a sample.' At that point he fondled and then squeezed her breast."

"And what did she do?"

"She didn't do anything because she was in great pain. The cancer from which she was suffering had started in that breast and she was still sore from the biopsy procedure that had recently been performed."

"She died from that cancer then."

"Yes, it spread and successive operations and other procedures finally proved inadequate. You should have heard him, Tom. You should have heard the pain in his voice and seen his eyes as he described what happened. It was as if Fox had somehow murdered her, that his touch was poisonous, that when he squeezed her it somehow released the disease throughout her body. 'I spoke to him,' Len said, in his understated way. *Spoke to him* in Len's world would be like a detective holding a criminal against a wall by the throat, with his feet dangling above the ground and his eyes beginning to pop from his head."

"He told him that if he didn't leave the city he would bring charges against him," Tom said.

"Yes," Sally said. "He also said that if he stayed he would kill him."

"Really?"

"Really. I don't think he said that at first. Fox said something to him that elicited that response. Len wouldn't tell me what he said, only that he made light of what had happened and told him that he shouldn't take it so seriously. 'He used crude terms to describe what he had done,' Len said."

"Did he say anything else?"

"Len, you mean."

"Yes."

"No, I had to work hard to extract that much from him. His wife's memory is very special to him. Whenever he speaks of her it's as if she was a saint or a martyr of some sort. Don't get me wrong; he speaks about her *realistically*, but there's a kind of aura around her name whenever he says it."

"I hope that's not difficult for you," Tom said.

"No, no, it's not. I think it's wonderful, that capacity for love, that depth of respect. It's interesting ... the one thing that he told me without any effort and without any hesitation ..."

". . . was that he told Fox that if he didn't leave he would kill him."

"Yes," Sally said. "He told me with a kind of--how would I describe it?--an *awful clarity*."

"So now it's up to us," Tom said.

"Yes, so it would appear. I'm afraid that Len overdid it a little--all of that food and all of that talk. He's resting comfortably now, but his system seemed to rise up and tell him to take it easy for a few days. He had some stomach problems and some faintness. 'It's OK,' he said, 'I had to tell you those things. This might have been my only chance.'"

"I told him to relax, that he'd be fine and that all was being done that could be done, that he had done his part and now it was up to the rest of us to find that man and make sure that he couldn't do anything to hurt anyone else."

"Is he asleep now?"

"Yes, but not comatose. It's as if he did a week's work in ten or fifteen minutes' time; he's exhausted. How are you, Tom? And how is Agent Harrison?"

"Fine. We're still investigating. We're not sure exactly what Fox is up to, but we're determined to prevent it or at least mute its effects."

"You'll keep me posted."

"Yes," Tom said, "I will. And Sally …"

"Yes?"

"Thanks. Thanks so much."

"I've got to get back to him," she said.

As soon as he clicked off, Gwen placed her call. Turning to Tom, she said, "The Kansas City Field Office SAC. He said it's important."

FIFTY-FIVE

Tom heard half of the conversation, but when Gwen was finished she filled in all of the gaps. "The visitors," she said, "this Friday. The Kansas City SAC is on site and he was filling me in on their names and numbers.

"The good news is that there were less than forty. There were a set of small groups, most of whom were identifiable. One was led by the commanding officer of the Air Force ROTC unit at the University of Kansas. He was coming in with one of his noncoms and three cadets. A second was led by the mayor of a small town in Iowa. He was bringing a couple of businessmen with him. The mayor had been a bomber pilot in World War II (he must have been very young at the time) and he was bringing a couple of Chamber of Commerce types for the briefing, the tour and the grip-and-grin. Apparently, the people at Whiteman issue certificates in leatherette folders to those who have been on their simulators, stating that they have successfully piloted the B-2 in a virtual flight."

"An attaboy for his contributors or political partners."

"Right. Same for the cadets. The ROTC honcho was rewarding them for graduating at the top of their class. Anyway, there were two other groups. The first was a set of retirees from St. Louis. Their bank runs tours for seniors, a way of cultivating and rewarding their biggest depositors. Sometimes they go to ball games, to Vermont to see the foliage, to California to taste wine ... Friday they were coming to Knob Noster to check out the stealth bomber."

"How many?"

"Fourteen. In a minibus."

"And the other group?"

"Just two people. From an engineering firm in Texas."

"Mahmud and Hakim."

"Probably. They've got all kinds of i.d., including a website for their firm. The website presents them as structural engineers. Building materials, loads, stresses and strains, that kind of thing ..."

"What names are they using?"

"Paul and Walter Harrington. Immigrants from the U.K. Been here nearly a decade."

"And the i.d. checked out?"

"Yes, though I doubt that the checks ran very deep."

"What's the SAC's plan?"

"He hasn't acted yet; he wants our advice first."

"That's a switch," Tom said.

"Spreading the responsibility around," Gwen said.

"Right," Tom said. "Anyway, I know what I'd do."

"What's that?"

"Tell everybody to stay home except for the Harrington 'brothers'. The Air Force ROTC people should be kosher and it'll be easy to check on them. Ditto the mayor and his visiting firemen. I'd be a little more hesitant with regard to the senior citizens, but it's doubtful that the bank would want to blow up Whiteman Air Force Base and their clientele are likely to be actual customers who are up in years. They could be infiltrated, I suppose, and their vehicle could be compromised, but as a group they're a long shot. I would have agents from your field offices locate all three groups, determine their departure times, check on each of their vehicles to see if they were compromised and then halt them right before they pull out of their driveways."

"And let the Harrington boys come ahead."

"Yes. I'd check further to see if they could possibly be legit. If they are, fine. My guess is, however, that their papers are going to check out but that the 'brothers' will already be in transit. We won't see them until they pull into the front gate. As I said earlier, I'd like to be there to greet them."

"So would I," Gwen said, "if somebody there can put together a uniform that will fit me."

"I'm not sure that that's a good idea," Tom said.

"Why not?" Gwen answered. There was annoyance in her voice.

"Because they may trigger their device right then and there."

"Why, Lieutenant Deaton ... I didn't know you cared."

"Of course I care, Special Agent Harrison and I don't see any need to put you in jeopardy."

"You don't think I could physically prevent them."

"I'm not sure what they'll try to do."

"Trust me," she said. "I'll be able to hold up my end."

"OK then," Tom said. "If you can sell it to the powers that be, it'll be Deaton and Harrison, together again."

"I thought it was Harrison and Deaton," Gwen responded.

"Anything but Harrison-Deaton or Deaton-Harrison," Tom said. "I'm too old-fashioned for that."

Gwen smiled. "Old-fashioned or troglodytic?"

"Hey, it was nice in those caves and rock shelters," Tom said, " ... beautiful paintings, nice jewelry, reindeer every night for dinner ..."

"So tell me about Len Barnes."

"Scary," Tom said. "He basically confirmed everything that we've assumed. Picked up by people claiming to be U.S. Marshals. Taken to a site approximately 1,000 miles away to operate on an important, but unnamed foreign national. First-floor facility—a single finished room, fitted out as an OR. The patient's identity was kept secret. He was probably in his mid-thirties, suffering from stomach cancer. Len operated laparoscopically, did some fancy, identifiable needlework on the closure sites and was offered some post-operative coffee, which knocked him out. The next thing he knew he was in Saddleback Memorial, looking into Sally's eyes."

"They took him by private jet?"

"Yes, from Lake Elsinore, not John Wayne. Then they picked him up in a limo to take him to the OR site."

"And the other people there?"

"All capped and masked. The anesthetist didn't speak English. He had a translator."

"Fox didn't want Barnes to hear his voice."

"Presumably."

"I guess they didn't want to confuse the issue while Len was operating."

"You mean, why bother with the secrecy if they were going to kill him anyway?"

"Right."

"If the patient died, so might all of them," Tom said.

"Yes. Fox had to sit tight, take his revenge without letting Len know that it was him."

"Umm-hmm. I also found out what happened between Len and Fox."

"Tell me."

"Fox groped his wife when she was suffering from breast cancer. On an elevator in a hospital. It sounds as if he hit on her, she said no thanks and he demanded what he termed a free sample. Her breast was sore from the cancer as well as from a recent biopsy procedure when he grabbed and squeezed it."

"And she was married."

"Yes."

"And he did that to her anyway?"

"Yes. I don't know whether or not he was aware that she was married or that she was married to Len."

"I would have taken him out, right then and there," Gwen said.

"What would you have done?"

"I don't know … he wouldn't have walked off of the elevator, though."

"Len threatened to kill him if he didn't resign and leave the city."

"Really?"

"That's what he told Sally."

"I knew I liked him," Gwen said, "and I haven't even had the chance to speak with him yet."

"It doesn't sound as if Fox is making the trip to Whiteman," Tom said.

"If we get past that, we'll go looking for him," Gwen said.

"Umm-hmm," Tom said.

FIFTY-SIX

"I've got their website," Tom said. "It's not very easy to read on the phone screen. Let me move things around and home in a little. OK, here we go, well … no big surprise, I guess; there's not much here. Some pretty pictures of classic buildings from hither and yon, no pictures of anything that they claim to have designed themselves or even consulted on, for that matter. Some brief bios of the two of them. English university pedigrees, red-brick, not Oxbridge. Lists of things that they're available to do; nothing on what they've actually done. No pictures of them, a couple of pages 'under construction' …"

"How about a business address?"

"A place in San Antonio. I'd bet it's a mail drop."

"But not Mahmud's old apartment address."

"No, they were more careful than that."

"They have people in their cells who build credentials over time. That's how they get Social Security numbers and tax records. They're not hacking into federal databases. Their cells can also help them with website construction and maintenance. They may want to live in the middle ages but if they ever get there they'll have their laptops and smart phones with them."

"Interesting," Tom said.

"Yes, they may be nasty and evil and intent on our destruction, but they're not stupid. Anything else there of note?"

"They have a *Frequently Asked Questions* page which is mildly amusing. It's mostly a 'no job too big or too small' bit of puffery. There's also a sop to the environmentalists with regard to their preferences for building materials."

"But nothing about their interest in *blowing up* buildings, just designing and constructing them?"

"No. For some reason or other they overlooked that."

"They probably decided to pose as engineers because Mahmud had some training in that area and they felt that they could impersonate professional engineers more easily than, what, brain surgeons?"

"It's also an international activity," Tom said. "It explains their immigration, for example. I'll bet that they've used phony passports and that the international travel there is explained by their putative profession."

"Right. 'Yes, sir, we regularly go to Yemen to consult on building materials for KFC franchises.'"

"So what about my proposal to ask the other visitors to stay home on Friday? No reason to endanger them and no reason to clutter the waiting line at the entry gate."

"I'm sure they'll buy it. It makes a lot of sense," Gwen said.

"Who will actually be there, do you think?"

"Probably the Deputy Secretary or one of the Under Secretaries from Homeland Security. My Bureau contact told me that the Secretary is testifying before the Senate on Friday. Given the degree to which that meeting has been hyped, it's very doubtful that the Secretary would cancel. It's more likely that he'll send someone he trusts into the field and tell him or her to keep him posted constantly."

"They wouldn't want to tip their hand to the al-Baradas either."

"No. All business as usual. From the Bureau there'll be the KC SAC. Possibly also the St. Louis SAC, though I doubt it. The KC person has been around longer and has a little more experience with terrorist activity. There may also be somebody there from the White House, in addition to the Homeland Security rep."

"To keep the President apprised."

"Yes. It's always a circus. Everyone wants in on the action and there are so many suits on the ground that the lines of communication get jammed. The answer is to have even more suits on the ground whose job it is to talk directly to supervisors rather than manage the situation. The managers see them as end-runners; the communicators see the managers as secretive CYAers and ... well ... the acrobats and the clowns wait in the wings trying not to step in the elephant crap."

"The CO of the base may actually be our best point of contact."

"Yes. Technically, this is the site of the 509th Bomb Wing, Mission Support Group and Medical Group. The 509th is part of the AFGSC, the Air Force Global Strike Command. The CO is a one-star, with a full bull colonel as his Vice Commander and a chief master sergeant as his Command Chief. Unfortunately, I haven't met the CO, but you're right—he's the one we should link up with. It's his command that's under threat and he knows more about it than any of the speed dialers who have flown in for the weekend."

"Then I guess we're ready," Tom said.

"At least our mission is simple," Gwen said.

"Not getting killed?"

"Bingo."

FIFTY-SEVEN

BG John Sutherland sat at a large oak desk behind a brass name plate, shallow in- and out- boxes and an oversized black coffee mug. He wore suspenders and a pin-collar shirt, the prerogatives of a general officer. Short in height and moderate in weight, he did not require glasses. A pilot. The Platonic conception thereof, Tom thought to himself.

"We owe you two a debt of gratitude," he said. "I don't have any medals or certificates at this point, but I can offer you both a decent cup of coffee. I buy it myself so I can personally attest to its quality."

When they accepted, he picked up his phone, hit a button and said, "For three." A few minutes later an airman entered with an insulated carafe, sugar, sweetener and milk on a black tray. He put it on a side table next to the CO's desk. He asked if there was anything else that the general needed and Sutherland replied, "No thanks. Looks good." He then added, "This is real milk. I don't do that whitener stuff. We all eat chemicals all day, but I like mine to be recognizable. Somehow, I don't think it's going to be necessary in your case, though. You two look like black coffee drinkers to me."

They both smiled, acknowledging the accuracy of his assumption. "It wasn't a tough one," he said.

"The coffee's excellent," Gwen said, as Tom nodded in agreement.

"I'm glad you're enjoying it," Sutherland said. "Now, let's talk business. Our job here is very, very simple. The equipment's complex, but the job isn't. We fly planes half way around the world, drop bombs on bad guys and return without being seen. It's a little more complicated than that sometimes, but not much. It's an important mission and the aircraft represent a significant comparative advantage, one that we're not anxious to lose. Whiteman is an equipment-intensive base. It's clean and it's simple and it does its job, but it's not about eyewash and parades and marching bands. It's about airplanes that do special things and cost a shitload of money. If any of them were lost, for any reason, I would have a very, very bad day. I don't *like* bad days. I'm a little jaded and as a result I don't have high hopes for a lot of unicorn-and-rainbow days, but I absolutely cannot tolerate bad ones. By now you two know that you have actually been helping me avoid them. You may not have known it at first, but you know it now. Maybe we'll get lucky and you'll be proven wrong. Maybe these two boys headed our way are going to bring us flowers, chocolates and a Valentine card from their friendly, neighborhood Imam, but I tend to doubt that.

"In about an hour we're going to be up to our eyeballs in *federales*. This base is going to be a blur of clipboards, cell phones and gray suits and when all of those cooks stick their spoons in my broth my life is going to become unnecessarily complicated. Now, I may be an aging, hemorrhoid-laden bomber pilot, but I still know how to use the telephone and who to call. From what I hear, the two of you are both prime--a small town police lieutenant who specializes in difficult-to-impossible cases and a fibbie special agent who could track Satan back to hell and turn him into a popsicle with his own pitchfork. That about right?"

"We try to do our best," Gwen said.

"And we share your concern about the Washingtonians," Tom said.

"I figure it's the three of us together on this one," Sutherland said, "and we'll just pray that the rest of them don't get in our way. Let me run it down for you, at least as I see it. Is that OK?"

"Absolutely," Tom said.

"I can hardly wait," Gwen said, smiling.

"OK. These two shitbirds are coming here to frustrate my attempts to accomplish my mission. They want to blow up my airplanes, kill my people and scare the civilians and small animals in the neighborhood. They'd probably prefer not to die in the process, but if they have to, they will. I don't know about the virgins waiting for them in heaven, but I do know that they love to get those martyrs' medals. So the trick is not moving on them too quickly or too abruptly. Whatever weapon they're bringing they're bringing in a vehicle, because we wouldn't let them walk onto my base carrying an unchecked backpack and if they're targeting an entire Air Force base they'd need much more ordnance than they could strap around their bellies or carry in a bag.

"If they're surrounded on a highway they'll just blow everybody to hell, including all of the officers who are trying to arrest them. There'll be mothers and fathers in those police cars and I'd hate to lose them. Somehow the two of them have to be tricked. We have to get to them before they can get to their cell phone or red button or toggle switch or whatever the hell it is that'll detonate that pile of plague and plastique or whatever it is that they're carrying in their trunk. We've got to separate them from their bomb. Agreed?"

"Agreed," Tom and Gwen said.

"They can't get near it. And they've got to be prevented at any cost."

"Agreed."

"At *any* cost. Of course, I'd prefer that they pay the bill rather than us."

"Agreed."

"Ever had any Norton?" Sutherland asked.

Gwen shook her head quizzically.

"Grape for red wine," Tom said. "Upscale hybrid."

"It's not going to scare any of the top cabernet growers, but with the right oak barrels and a loving hand, it does very nicely with a Kansas City strip and a largeish baked potato."

"It's what we'll have after we turn those two over to the people with the bright lights and the hard chairs," Tom said.

"But with an extra-dry martini or two to start and something with chocolate in the title after we finish," Gwen added.

"I knew I liked you two," Sutherland said, "but first we've got to separate them from their bomb. It's not going to be easy, but it's going to have to be successful, because I've got a wife, two daughters, a base full of prime airmen and aircraft to protect and no interest whatsoever in becoming a martyr."

"We've been giving it some thought, General," Tom said, "and we'd like to get your response to the outlines of our plan."

"I can't think of anything more important for me to do right now than hear it," he said, as he checked his watch. "Besides, those *federales* won't be here for another forty-three minutes or so."

FIFTY-EIGHT

The next day they did multiple run-throughs of the plan and each was fitted for a military uniform. They were dressed as airmen first class and given time to get used to their uniforms in case any alterations were necessary. They also secured the props that they would require as guards at the entry gate. When they were issued Beretta M9 sidearms Gwen commented that she would be more comfortable with her Sig. "I don't know that the al-Baradas could tell the difference," she said, "but I'm sure that we have to be dressed authentically if we're going to play the part convincingly. If I'm going to be a guard I've got to look, feel and act like one."

"Hopefully you won't need to discharge the Beretta," Tom said. "Meanwhile, think of yourself as a great method actress. You're living the part."

"I'm in the Federal Bureau of Investigation, stationed in Washington, D.C.," she said. "I'm already a great method actress."

"Then we won't have any problems," Tom said.

Later that afternoon they drove through the adjoining town to get a feel for the streets and highways, the people and the traffic patterns. They ate at a small Italian restaurant named *Luigi's*, which was operated by cooks and wait staff from Eastern Europe.

"I trust this will not be our last meal," Tom said, as he picked through the ingredients on his pasta.

"You should have gone for the simple pizza," Gwen said. "I'm sorry we passed on the wine, now. I suddenly feel like a real airline pilot, with no alcohol ingested within twenty-four hours of takeoff."

"We'll have plenty of time for some later," Tom said. "And probably a proper thirst for it as well."

"I like your plan," she said. "I didn't get a chance to talk about it with you at length, but I think it makes sense and I know that I'll be able to do my part."

"Don't hurt yourself in the process," he said, "but don't be afraid to be bold."

"That's not usually my problem," she said, smiling. "By the way, I *do* like the general."

"Yes, I do too," Tom said. "Crusty, self-assured. And he's seen real bombs. He knows what they can do. This isn't abstract to him. It's as serious as a heart attack. That's probably why he jokes about it and holds it at arm's length."

"Right," Gwen said. "I meant to tell you ... we've got a special bomb squad coming in from D.C. The airmen here know how to load them, but they don't have as much experience defusing and neutralizing them."

"Interesting, isn't it?" Tom said. "We're worried about two bozos with a big IED of some kind and our B-2's here could deliver nuclear weapons that would obliterate their countries. Still, it's their turn and we've got to make sure that they're unsuccessful."

"Yes," Gwen said. "It is. The fact that you have it doesn't mean that you can use it. We're putting all of our eggs in a tiny basket consisting of two law enforcement types armed with 9 mm automatics, a plan, some prayers and a little fairy dust."

"I was surprised that the Washingtonians would go along with it," Tom said.

"Yes, well ... they'll have nineteen snipers and three S.W.A.T. teams ready if we're not up to the task. If Mahmud and Hakim have a date with the virgins tomorrow they'll look like swiss cheese when they show up at the heavenly gates with roses and a Whitman's sampler. That's assuming that they don't get to the large button and turn us all into red vapor."

"Right," Tom said.

They finished their dinner, had some coffee and passed on dessert. "I want to call my dad tonight," Tom said.

"Afraid it could be your last call?" Gwen asked.

"I'm not fearful or apprehensive," Tom said. "It's just insurance. If something bad were to happen I'd want to know that we had talked when we had the opportunity to do so."

"I understand," she said. "I called my parents this afternoon, just before we left for dinner."

When Tom called, his dad Wayne was on his boat. "I wish you were here, Son," he said. "There's a glow across the horizon and the reflections of the lights on the marina are rippling across the water. It feels like Christmas."

"I love it when they put the lights on the sailboat masts," Tom said. "They're like abstract Christmas trees. It's a wonderful kind of beauty."

"Yes," Wayne said. "So what's up, Tom? You don't usually call when you're on assignment like this. I take it that whatever you're involved in is serious."

"Yes it is, Dad. I'm sure that everything will be fine, but on the off chance, no, on the *very remote* chance that it isn't, well, I wanted to hear your voice."

"You'll be fine, Tom," Wayne said. "Whatever it is that you have to do, just keep your wits about you, follow your plan and be ready to change it if you have to. I don't see how you can possibly fail, not with your mother watching over you and me here with a refrigerator full of cold beer waiting for your return."

"I appreciate that, Dad," Tom said. "If you happen to be saying any prayers tonight, you might add one or two for me. Toss one in for my partner as well. An FBI special agent. A young native woman. Descended from somebody who fought with Crazy Horse. Can you believe that? She never calls him that, though. She says his real name would be something like Enchanted Horse."

"I like that better," Wayne said. "She must be part of their A team."

"She is, Dad."

"I hope you haven't forgotten Sarah in all this."

"I know you're her best representative, Dad, but I think Sarah's ready to move on."

"She's a wonderful young woman."

"She is indeed," Tom said, "and I'm sure we'll always be friends, but probably not anything more."

"You're both too busy; that's your problem," Wayne said.

"I know, Dad. "Anyway, it's great to talk to you. You know I love you …"

"I love you too, Son, and if your mother were here she'd be telling you the same."

"I'll talk to you tomorrow, Dad."

"When does it all come down, Son … whatever it is that you're facing?"

"First thing in the morning."

"Thanks for telling me. Get your rest and be safe."

"I'll do my best," Tom said.

"I know you will. And Tom …"

"Yes, Dad?"

"You say a prayer or two as well. It never hurts."

"I will," Tom said.

FIFTY-NINE

"How do the gloves feel?" Tom asked.

"Not too strange," Gwen said. "They're very tight."

"That's good. Having them slip off is not an option."

"Right."

"I was amused by the response of the Homeland Security people," Tom said.

"Amused, but not surprised," Gwen said. "As soon as the general told them they were in charge but that he would handle the tactical end, they were happy."

"They can scapegoat him if the plan doesn't work," Tom said. "Meanwhile, they get to believe that they still have the biggest cell phones and clipboards."

"That's how it all works," Gwen said, "belly up to the bar for the blue ribbons but keep some space open in the dark corners if the plans go awry."

"I appreciated his help with the people in the other cars."

"Right," Gwen said. "Mostly senior officers and noncoms. Once we let them through they'll drive as far away from us as they can get, so their risk shouldn't be too great."

"No, the risk is mostly ours," Tom said. "Ours and the snipers'."

"But we get all the glory," Gwen said, smiling. "That and $7.95 will get us a carafe of the house red at *Luigi's*. And we'll probably be ready for it and a couple of refills."

"How's the uniform feel?"

"Not bad. All the straps and gloves and extras are pretty fancy. I almost feel like an airperson. And you certainly look like somebody who could brace and arrest a drunk on a Saturday night."

"Remember to look mildly robotic," Tom said. "It's all spit and polish and 'snap to' when you're the guard at the gate. You're supposed to be the first line of defense, not the guy in the booth who puts down his sweet roll and tells you how to get to Lot 17."

"Understood, Sir," Gwen said. "Are your gloves tight too?"

"Yes, really tight."

"And you're sure this is going to work?"

"If it doesn't, we'll know soon enough," Tom said.

"Here come the cars," she said. "Show time."

"Station 2, are you there?" Tom said into his mike.

"Station 2 ready," a male voice said. "No sign of anyone yet."

"Initial cars approaching," Tom said.

"Roger that. Will advise as soon as car is sighted. Station 2 out."

The three cars containing 509th personnel in civilian clothes approached the gate. They stopped, parked in line, and shut off their engines. Tom made eye contact with each of the cars' drivers and then took his place, standing next to Gwen. Nineteen minutes later the call came in.

"Station 2 here. Two men approaching in black Suburban. Please acknowledge."

"Message received," Tom said. "Thank you. Station 1 out."

He then raised his right hand and the drivers of the three cars started their engines. "Are you two ready?" he said, turning to his side.

The two men sitting on the floor behind him said, "Yes, sir."

"I'll tell you when to get in position," Tom said.

"Let's do this," Gwen said.

As the Suburban approached the queue Tom and Gwen left the box and approached the first car. Each had a clipboard and each handed the clipboard to the driver and passenger to sign. After they each signed Tom extended his hand, giving the driver directions, and the two returned to the box.

The next car in line approached and Tom spoke to the driver. He then appeared to check the Base records, to insure that the individuals were cleared for entry. Then he and Gwen left the box again, with their clipboards, and had the driver and passenger sign. Tom extended his hand, gave directions and the second car drove off.

"One more car before the bogeys," Tom whispered to the men on the floor. He then went through the same process with the third vehicle-speaking to the driver, checking his records and then going out with Gwen to secure signatures.

As the third car drove off and the Suburban approached, he whispered, "Here we go." As the Suburban got closer, Gwen whispered, "It's Mahmud driving."

Before turning to the window Tom reached down and lifted a coffee cup, taking a long drink. He then put it down and turned his attention to the final vehicle.

The Suburban stopped at the window and Tom said, "Good morning. Name please."

"Paul Harrington," the driver said, "accompanied by my brother Walter."

"One second, please," Tom said, and turned to the small computer screen on his right.

"You're here for the Spirit Tour," Tom said.

"Yes, we are. Thank you," the driver responded.

"Welcome to Whiteman," Tom said. "We'll have you sign in and then I'll direct you to the parking area for the tour. We hope that you will enjoy it."

"Thank you very much," the driver said. Both he and his passenger were wearing loose-fitting suits and each was clean-shaven.

Tom and Gwen left the box, carrying their clipboards. Each approached one of the individuals in the car and extended the clipboard and a ballpoint pen. They spoke simultaneously. "Please sign on line 12," Tom said. " … line 9," Gwen echoed.

As the men took the clipboard in one hand and the pen in the other Tom and Gwen seized their wrists, turning them over and violently crushing them against the window frame of the Suburban. They snapped them a second and third time until the wrists were clearly broken. By that time the two airmen had followed them, unlocked the doors and swung the bodies of the two men away from the vehicle. Each of them were screaming in pain and the blood from their broken wrists had reached Tom and Gwen's uniforms, the sides of their cars and the black asphalt below.

"Keep their hands away from their bodies," Gwen said, as a series of vehicles raced toward them.

"You will suffer for this," Mahmud's passenger screamed. "You will die for this!"

A few seconds later members of the bomb squad were carefully inspecting their clothing and slicing away pieces of fabric with what looked like very high-tech boxcutters. Both Mahmud and his passenger were carrying cell phones, which were removed and handed to aides who immediately returned with them to their vehicles. Two other members of the squad were inspecting the car along with two dogs. "Clear the area," the head of the team said, as another vehicle approached the gate from a distance. Heavily armored, it was attached to the Suburban by a long, heavy chain.

By now both Mahmud and his passenger were going into shock. Both were bleeding profusely; the front of Mahmud's pants were soaked with urine and his passenger's bowels had given out. They were removed, screaming, under armed guard, as the Suburban was towed away from the front gate.

"I thought the coffee cup was a lovely touch," Gwen said, as they got into a sedan and drove away.

"Gin would have been welcome," Tom said, "but I thought that might have jeopardized the mission."

"We'll have plenty of time for gin later," Gwen said.

SIXTY

"Outstanding," General Sutherland said, "outstanding. And the *federales* are gleefully peeing down their collective pantslegs. Since you're still on the case and we've got to keep the press at bay, there'll be no opportunity for you to step up on the medal stand and salute the flag. The higher-ups will issue orders; the spooks and snoopy poops will begin interrogating the jihadis; the bomb squad will check out whatever the hell it was they were carrying in the back of their SUV; the techies will try to trace their cell phone calls and all of them together will be pulling on the strings coming out of the jihadis' backsides and trying to figure out who and what they might be attached to. Meanwhile, life will go on quietly and the President and Secretary will spread some Brasso on the brownie badges they're preparing for their loyal minions. The servants of the people will all be happy not to have to share the glory with you and they'll go into *aw-shucks* mode when their bosses begin to fawn on them."

"We couldn't have done it without your running interference for us, General," Gwen said.

"I take full credit for recognizing prime personnel," the general said, "and did I happen to mention that the execution was *outstanding*?"

"You did, Sir," Tom said.

"None of that sir stuff, Lieutenant," the general said. "When you join the small club you call the other members by name. That goes for you too, Agent Gwen."

Tom and Gwen both smiled.

"I liked the plan from the get-go," Sutherland said. "You had to put them at ease. Whatever the hell it was that they were carrying, they weren't ready to set it off just yet, but they had to have been at least as nervous as we were and probably much more so. Lining up all those cars, filling out those forms, going through those motions … it made them think life was going on as usual and nobody had a clue as to their identity or intentions. The coffee cup was genius. Unadulterated genius. Sleepy sentry, propping up his eyes with toothpicks, sleepwalking through the morning exercise … those old boys didn't think that they were only minutes away from receiving some serious compound fractures. I'll say this about that: it sure as hell got their attention. Tell me some more about those gloves …"

"Tom's idea," Gwen said. "There were small pieces of gravel glued to the palms and the base of the fingers with epoxy to enhance our grip. Once we grabbed them we couldn't possibly let go or they could detonate their device."

"Wouldn't feel too good either," Sutherland said. "Helped fix their attention."

"I'm glad that Gwen recognized the driver as Mahmud al-Barada," Tom said. "The other looked like his cousin, but we couldn't be as certain as we were with Mahmud."

"It's not a mistake you would have wanted to make," Sutherland said. "A nice couple of visiting firemen … come in to see their tax dollars at work and get a little twinge in their patriotic hearts … all of a sudden their wrists are broken and they're leaking red body fluid all over their sport and utility vehicle … I'd hate to think what kind of a field day a lawyer or two or three could have had with that. But we don't have to worry about that now, do we? Only one remaining problem, though …"

"What's that?" Tom asked.

"Don't have any place to put the cuffs," Sutherland said. "All that you two vandals left us is some bloody bone and gristle and torn flesh.

I've got nineteen engineers working the problem, even as we speak. Is that too crass of me?"

"I don't think so," Gwen said. "Better to hear the two of them scream than hundreds or thousands of others."

"Exactly my thought," Sutherland said. "I love the simplicity of it. When the word gets back (and it always gets back), it'll be so, so simple. They drove on to an American air force base, planning to destroy property, kill personnel and terrorize civilians. They were met at the gate by two young airmen, one of them--get this--a woman and their wrists were broken, they emptied their bowels and were taken off to be questioned. Present whereabouts, unknown. No virgins in heaven, no martyrs' badges, no bright lights and big cameras."

"How about that bottle of Norton?" Tom asked.

"Bottle? You mean *bottles*, son. Now if I were you, I'd thank my God and then go call my parents, significant others and such. You'll also want to touch base with the powers that be back home and tell them that you both gave a damned good account of yourselves. Now, here's the deal. I've got to deal with the *federales*, pat some fannies and hand out some attaboys. At 1830 hours I'll have a car ready for us. We're going to Kansas City and eat some serious steak. By then I should have more information on what just happened and it will be my pleasure to share it with you."

'We'll see you then," Gwen and Tom both said.

SIXTY-ONE

"I'll join you for lunch in an hour and a half," Tom said. "I need to make some calls."

"As do I," Gwen said. "Just knock on my door."

"The information will come in in pieces," Gwen said. "We're supposed to share, share, share, but the individual agencies often resist those instructions and instead revert to more traditional human behavior."

"Trade, trade, trade," Tom said.

"Precisely. You show me yours and I'll show you mine. Or maybe I'll just show you part of mine, depending on what you show me of yours. I *did* learn one thing. The passenger riding with Mahmud was not his cousin Hakim. Hakim was at Heathrow Airport, boarding a flight to Abu Dhabi. His wife was with him and so were his two sons. Mahmud's passenger bore a remote resemblance to his cousin, but Hakim was positively identified at Heathrow. Actually, he was photographed more often in a single two-hour period than Paris Hilton and her dog Tinkerbell."

"Interesting that he was leaving today," Tom said.

"Actually he was in the air when our event went down. Alibi time, perhaps. Our London people commented on the fact that he made no effort to conceal his identity. He hit practically every duty-free shop in his terminal."

"Any guesses on the identity of the passenger?"

"Not yet. We should know more in a few hours. At the least, we should get that from the interrogators."

"He won't have a rank and serial number," Tom said, "so all they need to start with is his name. Of course, he'll probably have several of those along with a nickname or two."

"Yes, they're into names," Gwen said. "Pretty soon he'll just have a number."

"How about the bomb or whatever it was that they were carrying?" Tom asked.

"Bioweapon and a shitload of Semtex," Gwen said. "The former hasn't been fully identified yet, but the Semtex was untagged and odorless. That's why the dogs didn't start howling when they were sniffing the trunk. It was probably from Libya. They've always prided themselves on their collection of it."

"How much is a shitload?" Tom asked.

"A little over a hundred pounds."

"Good Lord," Tom said. "Three or four pounds will bring down a two-story building."

"Yes, they will," Gwen said. "We dodged a very large bullet. We did good, Lieutenant; as they say in Washington, we saved a lot of men and materiel."

"I talked to my chief and my dad," Tom said. "I also called Sally and was even able to talk to Len Barnes. I couldn't give them a lot of detail, but I told them that the event with which Nathan Fox was apparently connected was prevented. They asked about Fox and I had to tell them that he was not on the scene when the actions occurred."

"He couldn't have contributed anything," Gwen said. "He would have just been extra baggage, and heavy baggage, at that."

"My guess is that he'll scatter fast," Tom said, "particularly when he unglues his eyes from his favorite news channel and nothing is reported except the rise of the Dow and the Nasdaq and the growth of the national debt."

"Yes, he's a liability now," Gwen said. "They don't need him anymore and they definitely won't want him to tell the recent parts of his life story to the Federal Bureau of Investigation. He is, as they say, between a rock and a place that is very hard. Choose between your options: charges of treason or a chance to be beheaded in prime time on Al Jazeera."

"He'll wish he was back in an Urgent Care Center somewhere," Tom said, "picking dirt out of playground cuts or treating people who burned their fingers along with the Rice-a-Roni."

"What time do we need to be ready for the general," Gwen asked, "six thirty?"

"Yes," Tom said. "How about a little run in the meantime--get the cobwebs out and work up a serious appetite for tonight?"

"Works for me," Gwen said. "How about one more cup of coffee and then we meet in an hour?"

SIXTY-TWO

Sutherland was relatively quiet during the drive to Kansas City, not wanting to talk in detail in front of his driver. They ate at a restaurant just adjoining the Country Club Plaza called *L & B Steaks*.

"It doesn't stand for large and bloody," Sutherland said. "It's Lawrence and Betty. And they're both still here. They're not about to sell this certifiable landmark and goldmine to end all goldmines. I do have some bad news, however …"

"What would that be?" Gwen asked.

"Well, when I made the late reservation and informed Betty that I was bringing some serious out-of-town law enforcement personnel with me she insisted that we accept a bottle of wine as their way of thanking us for enabling them to sell expensive steaks and sleep well at night. It's not going to be a Norton. I believe she said something about a Chateau Margaux."

"We'll just have to soldier on," Tom said, "if that expression doesn't offend you."

"It doesn't offend me one little bit," Sutherland said. "I can soldier on with the best of them."

When the proprietor brought the wine she introduced herself as Elisabeth. "Some go with Liz and some with Beth," she said, "but Lawrence always calls me Betty."

"My mother's name was Elisabeth," Tom said. "It's a beautiful name."

"I bet she could cook too," Betty said.

"With the best of them," Tom said.

"We won't disappoint you here either, honey," she said.

"This is absolutely delicious," Gwen said.

"It is for a fact," Sutherland said. "You taste the hint of violets? You're supposed to, I'm told. Not that I make a habit of eating violets, but I do catch the hint of them. I'll say this too: it's got the silk and finesse of an old con beating a lie detector test."

"We should have that translated into French and sent along to the winemaker," Tom said.

Sutherland smiled. "Well, my friends," he said, "before we get too deep in our cups we should talk a little business. The news is in and it's good. It's good because it could have been way bad. Those two old boys traded in their camels for a Suburban with one hundred and ten pounds of Semtex about to deliver a godawful quantity of anthrax.

"As you no doubt know, there are nearly ninety different strains. This one was the Vollum variety, which is very, very nasty. We would have had spores everywhere, killing humans and wildlife, with the wounds resulting from the Semtex blast and the accompanying debris serving as happy breeding grounds for the spores. They would have been inhaled and ingested and spread all over the place and then carried by shoes and clothing and animals and all manner of things.

"Cleanup and containment are large, shaggy bitches under the circumstances and you can't do autopsies or embalming without a fully-equipped biohazard laboratory staffed by highly-trained personnel. What we're talking about here is death, destruction and your basic social upheaval, the kinds of things in which the jihadi-types attempt to specialize.

"And now, because of a very wise Brigadier General, with an acute ability to recognize quality in previously-unknown personnel, we have no problem whatsoever except the choice between rare and medium rare."

"Have they i.d.'d the passenger yet?" Tom asked.

"They have, for a fact," Sutherland said. "Our now limp-wristed friend is a double-threat A-lister. His name is Hakim Abbas, no relation to Hakim al-Barada, and he was an expert on both demolitions and biological warfare. I say *was* not because he has gone on to his eternal reward or punishment, but because he has now been summarily retired and will be spending the next few days, weeks and perhaps months in the gentle hands of some prime interrogators. Signor Abbas began his career building roadside bombs and then graduated to subways and hotels. He's been linked with one or two major successes and two or three failed attempts, but this was his first time out with a biological component. Thanks to us, but primarily to you, this attempt, as we say, came a cropper. Everything at this point is strictly need-to-know, but I have heard on good authority that his reaction to the events of this morning is one of profound disappointment."

"I'm happy we could disappoint him," Tom said.

"I think we should drink to that," Gwen added.

"As do I," Sutherland said. "Now how about some of Larry and Betty's best?"

SIXTY-THREE

After the wine and the steaks and the potatoes and the asparagus and the death-by-chocolate and the Armagnac, the three sat back and settled in for black coffee. "This was lovely," Gwen said.

"The best," Tom added.

"I'm very glad you enjoyed it," Sutherland said. "I hope I didn't bore you or offend you in any way and I hope I didn't get too *hired killer* on you. There is something that I didn't mention earlier when I was going on and on about the jihadis. I didn't want to throw any black crepe over the evening, but I thought I'd just mention it so that you'd know where I'm coming from.

"I had a younger sister who died on 9/11. Her name was Beth, sort of like our hostess tonight, though her name wasn't Elisabeth, just Beth. Sweet girl. Inherited all of the family brains. Lost her husband to cancer five years after they were married. Your basic tragedy. Fortunately, she was able to support their daughter. She worked as a trader for *Cantor Fitzgerald*, up on top of the first tower. Sold government bonds. Billions of dollars worth.

"The best guess is that she was overcome by smoke. She didn't have to jump off the building or anything like that. Just before she died she called home and left a message on the answering machine. Her daughter, my niece, was in school, but Beth wanted to tell her how much she loved her before she died.

"The little girl's a big girl now. The blessing was that Beth left enough money for her care and education. She's finishing medical school now at your basic Johns Hopkins. About six months before Beth died I visited her at work. Fascinating place. Old Bernie Cantor was actually a collector of Rodin statuary; I hadn't known that. The company office up there in the sky was actually in the Guinness Book of World Records as the *highest* museum in the world. It was strange ... and beautiful. That day Beth and I ate at *Windows on the World* and the next day we took Carrie, her daughter, to a Disney-on-ice thing at *Radio City*.

"Practically everybody I know either knew somebody who died on 9/11 or knew somebody who knew somebody who did. Tremendous ripple effect. Like a single crack in a large pane of glass that somehow spread and spread and just kept on spreading. It wasn't an accident. It was just what they wanted to do. It wasn't some surgical strike designed to take out a single individual or single group. It was mass murder plain and simple and the plan was to kill and maim and hurt as many people as they possibly could. They *wanted* to destroy families. They *wanted* to break hearts. They *wanted* to instill fear and terror.

"And we didn't prevent it. Now, sometimes ... most of the time ... we do. And that's a necessary and a good thing. And a couple of broken wrists? That's nothing, nothing at all. They chose the course that they pursued and they were lucky they got away with nothing more than some broken wrists. That's why I wanted the two of you there. If I had gone ... well, I was afraid that I wouldn't leave enough of them for the interrogators. What I'm saying is, that I tried to be professional rather than personal and that that turned out to be the right decision. Anyway, that's the end of the sermon. It was just something that I wanted you to know."

"Thanks for telling us," Gwen said, "and thanks for trusting us to do the job."

"Yes," Tom said. "I don't think we've had the chance to tell you the full story on our end. Gwen told her people to ask the interrogators to check out the passenger's stomach. Our guess is that he was recently operated on by a friend of mine who was coerced into the task and then poisoned and left for dead. The go-between was an old enemy of my friend, who picked him because of his surgical skills but also to take vengeance on him for things done in the past. Proper things. Good things."

"And this character is still at large," Sutherland said.

"Yes, he is," Tom said.

"Then I expect you still have some serious work to do."

"Yes," Tom said.

"Jihadi-type?"

"No. U.S. citizen. In it for the money."

"Whore."

"Yes," Tom said.

"I wish I didn't have an air force base to run; I'd much prefer to go with you and help lend a hand."

"You've done more than enough already," Gwen said.

"Thank you," Sutherland said, "but stopping the event, that's a professional obligation and something that must be done, but what you have now, that's personal. And to you, Lieutenant, it's far more serious. Be careful not to overstep but whatever you do, don't let him get away. And when you put the cuffs on …"

"Yes?" Tom said.

"Tighten them a notch or two for me."

V

ICARUS

SIXTY-FOUR

"They want us back in Kansas City," Gwen said, "for debriefing."

"I was afraid they'd want us to come to Washington," Tom said.

"No, they're sending a small team from Washington to talk to us here. They'll talk to General Sutherland and the KC SAC as part of the junket. In our case they already know the facts; they'll just reduce it all to writing. Copious writing."

"I'd rather be looking for Fox, but if they need us for a day or so we'll just have to stay here."

"Actually, Fox is going to be harder to find. He left the country the night before the attempt at Whiteman. I was just told, ten minutes ago. There was no warrant out for his arrest and he wasn't on a no-fly list, so they wouldn't have been able to stop him even if they had tried."

"You're saying that they didn't try."

"He was picked up by a surveillance camera troll, after the fact. They checked the airline records and his passport carried his official new name of Cox. He flew to Toronto."

"And from there?"

"There's no record of his leaving, but since there's nothing for him in Toronto, at least nothing that we're aware of, he probably used a different set of i.d. to leave Canada."

"Just to make it harder for us."

"He may not even be aware of the fact that we're looking for him. He wouldn't have access to the technology and human resources available to Mahmud and his people. The sum total of his knowledge right now might be coming from his iPhone. Besides, if he's not completely stupid he's aware of the fact that Mahmud's people might be after him as well."

"He wouldn't have wanted to take any chances in the U.S. Forged documents could result in arrest. Outside of the country would be different. If he's flying on an American passport and he's *leaving* Canada, and *if* he and his luggage are free of any contraband, they're more likely to say *bon voyage* than to strip search him."

"Yes, but he could have gotten the forged documents from one of Mahmud's suppliers, in which case the jihadis could trace his steps."

"Or once in contact with such a supplier," Tom said, "he could have cut a separate deal. Or he might have had his own supplier."

"Yes," Gwen said. "And since we don't have any other names than Fox and Cox, the possibilities are nearly endless. Seventy plus airlines going to over a hundred countries from Pearson International. And he could have waited awhile to leave. With eighty thousand passengers a day moving through there ... well, do the math. If you've got a calculator."

"He could be leaving the country and then returning," Tom said. "Just a little mystification ..."

"Possibly. He might also have already moved his money to one or more foreign accounts so that he could stay on the move for awhile."

"How would he have been paid by Mahmud?"

"Almost surely a step deal. Part at the time of the operation (which, by the way, *was* performed on Hakim Abbas) and part after the mission was completed. The jihadis don't pay in advance."

"So he's been stiffed."

"Unless he took steps to prevent that happening."

"But how?" Tom asked, "assuming that their policy is cash on delivery."

"Oh, I don't know," Gwen said. "Maybe he asked them to put the final installment in a safety deposit box. Mahmud would keep a key and so would he. That way he couldn't get at the money early and they couldn't abscond with it."

"Trust each other but cut the cards," Tom said. "It's probably the best deal he could get."

"Yes, but without Mahmud's key, he'd be stuck."

"Maybe Mahmud's cousin Hakim had the key. He might even have had the money for that matter. Fox left the country before the event went down. He knows now that it failed but maybe he intends to plead his case to Hakim. 'I did my part,' etc."

"And Fox wouldn't know that Hakim has already left for Abu Dhabi."

"Maybe there's another individual in London ... a banker, for example."

"Possibly," Gwen said. "Or if there's just a safety deposit box and one key there could also be a teller who might be open to a bribe."

"Fox may well have met with the whole team in London. Hakim al-Barada had a place there and Hakim Abbas came in for an initial medical screening or brought his records with him. Mahmud brought in Fox to check the test results and plan the next steps."

"It would make sense," Gwen said. "The Arab population in London is huge and it's also concentrated. Abbas could have slipped in on a forged EU passport and holed up at Hakim's place. Fox would have been far more comfortable going to London than to Yemen or Afghanistan."

"And he would have been far more comfortable if the money was changing hands there or in the U.S. There's another thing ..."

"What's that?" Gwen asked.

"We've been assuming that he's running scared, afraid of the jihadis."

"Yes."

"Maybe he's sequestered some information for insurance. The 'if anything happens to me ...' scenario."

"Possibly."

"Or maybe he's still marketing himself as their U.S. surgeon-on-call, in case they need him in the future. He didn't fail at his end, after all. He procured a first-rate surgeon who cured Abbas and got him back on his feet. Now he's available for future gigs."

"It's also possible that they could believe that he betrayed them. Why else did their attempt fail so miserably? Why were the American dogs so well prepared?"

"You know," Tom said, "we're mulling over all of these possibilities. Fox could be as well. With the jihadis in custody and under interrogation, the game has changed. A prudent person would lay low. But then … there's all that cash sitting there, saying 'take me, take me, spend me, spend me.' I'm not sure a lowlife like Fox could resist."

"Prudence has never been his long suit," Gwen said.

SIXTY-FIVE

"I called Sally last night and updated her," Tom said, as they drove to Kansas City. "I didn't give her any specifics. I just told her that we were continuing our search for Fox, who has left the country and might be anywhere."

"Did you talk to Dr. Barnes?"

"Yes, I did. He sounded just like his old self. They've actually released him from Saddleback and let him go home."

The Bureau interviewer was a woman named Janet Carlyle. Gwen mentioned to Tom in the hallway that she had once been a federal prosecutor. With them she was polite and respectful. Her questions were predictable. She wanted a timeline; she wanted every conceivable factual detail and she wanted their intuitions and impressions. She was accompanied by a secretary using a stenotype machine. Carlyle interviewed them for five and a half hours, with one brief break for coffee. She then told them that a formal statement would be prepared for their signatures and that she would be back in touch with them first thing in the morning.

"I thought she might interview us separately," Tom said.

"Professional courtesy," Gwen said. "She's telling us she trusts us. If there had been any doubt, any suspicion that we had bent the rules or lone-wolfed it in some way … we would have been interviewed separately by someone from the Bureau equivalent of Internal Affairs."

"And since we were successful …"

"Yes, that papers over a multitude of sins and indiscretions," Gwen said. "Whenever you help make other peoples' careers, they're grateful. They may not reciprocate, but at least they don't attack."

"That's why you like it in the field, away from the memos, the pen holders, the low-slung cubicles and the prying eyes," Tom said.

"That's right, Lieutenant. Once the job in the field is finished your actions are examined, but they can only examine what they're aware of and there's less of a tendency to investigate closely if you've been successful. They're willing to give you props, but they're not anxious to put a halo or a set of wings on you. That would make them look too much like desk jockies rather than 'supervisors'."

"I guess that's why I like a small Department," Tom said. "Essentially I have one boss and as long as we get along I'm free of the political games and bureaucratic maneuvering. The fringe benefit is that he has to interface with the City Council, the Mayor, the City Manager, City Attorney and local press. Sometimes I'm pulled into that web, but most of the time I'm free of it. The terms of the job are straightforward enough: just under nine square miles of space and around 25,000 residents, most of whom are financially comfortable, but with eight miles of coastline and the summer pageants and art festivals we get three million visitors a year. The visitors keep things interesting. So do the freeways and the PCH and canyon road. We sit at the crossroads; always have. Some days are quiet; many are not."

"For years they've tried to turn me into a poster child for Bureau diversity," Gwen said. "The diversity's fine, but I don't want the publicity to hamper my work and I don't want to be stereotyped, even if the stereotype is a favorable one (or one that somebody in charge considers favorable)."

"Princess Summerfall Winterspring recovers the wampum and saves the day."

"Right. I don't need that," Gwen said.

When they finished at the field office on Summit they planned on having dinner at the Plaza. "Not steak again," Gwen said. "Something a little lighter. We'll need to sleep well tonight. First thing in the morning they're going to present us with a two or three hundred page document to read and sign. And we *should* read it carefully."

They returned to their hotel to shower and change. As Tom came out of the shower he turned on the TV and checked the national news. One of the Fox blondes was standing outside Whiteman:

As we reported earlier, a terrorist attempt was made on Whiteman Air Force Base in Missouri, the home of the stealth bomber. Early indications are that an explosive device was secured by officials and that the alleged terrorists were taken into custody. Reports that the bomb included a biological weapon have not yet been confirmed. The identities of the alleged terrorists have not yet been released, but it is believed that they are part of a cell that originated in London. Homeland Security staff have assured Fox News that every step is being taken to secure the area. No damage was done to the air base or the planes there and no casualties have been reported. The current situation with regard to the alleged terrorists is unknown, but they are believed to be in federal custody undergoing interrogation at an undisclosed location.

"Wonderful," Tom said aloud. "Now everyone knows, including their friends in London and beyond." He called Gwen immediately.

"I saw it," she said. "The initial report apparently came in when we were at the field office. The information's been on the street for an hour and a half."

"I'm going to call my Dad again," Tom said, "and reassure him that everything *is* OK here. I'll also let my chief and Sally and Len know."

He talked to his Dad for ten minutes, confirming the authenticity of the report and the fact that everything was fine. "Everything was located, confined, defused and removed," he said. "The bad guys are sitting on hard chairs somewhere, answering a lot of questions."

"How close were you when it happened?" his father asked.

"We were … right there," Tom said. "I was working with a Bureau agent. We took the two terrorists into custody. That's not for public consumption, Dad."

"I wouldn't say a word," his father said. "It might tempt someone to try to take revenge on you."

"I appreciate that, Dad," Tom said.

"What's next?"

"Probably a trip to London. There's another person of interest we'd like to locate."

"Fly safely, Son."

"I will, Dad. Thanks."

He then called Chris Dietrich and briefed him.

"We have an issue," Chris said.

"What's that, Chief?"

"Sally Cornell. I just got a call from Len Barnes. She's left the city. He told her that she should stay here and let the people from law enforcement do their thing. She told him that she was afraid that they'd forget about Fox or Cox, whatever he's calling himself now, because they had blocked the terrorist attempt and taken the lead people into custody."

"Where did she go?"

"London."

"When?"

"About five minutes after the news reports came in. She already had a bag packed and ready in the trunk of her car, because she's been travelling back and forth between Laguna and San Diego. Len didn't know what airline she was on because she hadn't booked the flight yet.

She was going to drive to John Wayne and catch a connecting flight to whatever was available. I'm checking on it now."

"I'll try to find her there," Tom said. "The Bureau agent and I were just debriefed and we have to sign our statements in the morning. I'd love to leave now …"

"A terrorist event is a very big deal," Chris said. "Give them whatever they need before you go. You'll only be a day behind. I'll check with Len and see who she's likely to contact in London."

"I'd appreciate it, Chief. I don't want to have to protect her at the same time that we're chasing bad guys."

"Understood," Chris said. "I'm assuming that the Bureau agent will have contacts for you there."

"Yes, she said she would, Chief."

"Then travel safely and be on the lookout for angry anthropologists seeking revenge."

"Will do, Chief."

SIXTY-SIX

The statements prepared by the Bureau stenographer were actually 357 pages in length. "Did we really say that much?" Tom asked.

"Not really," Gwen said. "The software package puts in all of the 'he said/she saids' and there's plenty of white space for notes. It will read fairly quickly."

Tom looked at his watch. Then he looked at the stack of paper. They were booked on a late afternoon flight. When Gwen brought them two large cups of coffee Tom was checking his watch again. "Just settle in and read," she said. "We'll make our flight and not lose another day."

They were booked on the last United flight to Heathrow from O'Hare and had only fifty-five minutes between the touchdown of their Kansas City regional 50-seater and the liftoff of their London-bound 767. When they boarded the plane in Chicago they each ordered double Scotches.

"After that marathon dash we earned it," Gwen said.

"I agree," Tom said. "Sometimes I think O'Hare is in Chicago and at other times I think all of Chicago is in O'Hare."

"At least we didn't have to circle," Gwen said, "and we didn't have to clear security three or four times. So, did you enjoy reading the result of yesterday's interrogation?"

"Not really, but I was impressed by the level of accuracy. Except for a spelling slip or two, the stenographer was dead-on."

"Yes. The Bureau stenos have always been the best," Gwen said. "I admire their professionalism; it's not the job that I would look forward to doing every day."

"No," Tom said, "nor I. Now someone else gets to put on a smoking jacket, sit down by the fire, pet his red setter and read our recent autobiographies."

"Yes," Gwen said. "What a lovely prospect. Learn anything interesting from your people in California?"

"Not really. I talked to Len and to Chris. Len had no idea who Sally might have contacted in London and neither did Chris. She had to have contacted someone either before she left or soon after she landed. London is not Peoria. What are we talking about for the greater London area--3,000 square miles, 14,000,000 people or so? Chris is checking with the Met, but it's unlikely that she would have walked into New Scotland Yard and reported a missing person."

"Nor the American Embassy," Gwen said. "What would you say? Good morning. No, I don't need to replace my lost passport. I'm looking for an individual who is guilty of attempted murder and complicity in an attempt to blow up a U.S. air force base. No, I'm not a member of law enforcement; I'm just a concerned citizen. Thank you, I'll take a seat in the waiting room."

"She knows that we're on this," Tom said, "and that we'll work through channels. She's probably figuring that she could be of help if Fox somehow slips through whatever nets we can cast."

"She's trying to be helpful," Gwen said.

"Yes, but she couldn't do anything without help from local officials. Hakim's not going to have a mat outside his townhouse or flat saying, 'The al-Baradas. Welcome to our home.' She's going to have to go through official records and, I strongly suspect, police records. If he was living near Marble Arch with the bulk of the Arab community she wouldn't have much success going door to door asking questions."

"Does she have any relatives in London?" Gwen asked.

"Len said no, at least none that he was aware of. Chris sent Hector Campo to check with the people at UCSD."

"The Anthro department."

"Right. Sally's prominent internationally. She would have colleagues and friends in London and one of them would know someone who works at the Met. At the very least, she would know someone who knows someone. With the local colleague running interference she could tell her story to some DI, DCI or Detective Superintendent and try to persuade one or more of them to help her with the case."

"Of course, someone or other at the Embassy is *already* on the case," Gwen said, "but not necessarily at street level. They'll be organizing themselves and updating themselves, reading reports and making calls. Even though they may actually be CIA they'll have some Embassy title or other and there are people there with whom they would have to touch base. Sally may be thinking that she could short-circuit all of that and get to Fox before anyone else had gotten into a taxi or prowl car. If she could just locate him she wouldn't have to club him over the head or make some sort of citizen's arrest. She could stay on him until the professionals arrived."

"And that would be us," Tom said.

"Yes. I still don't like it, though," Gwen said. "She could draw attention to herself, raise suspicions, tip him off to the fact that we know of his involvement. She could also get herself hurt."

"Who's our initial contact?" Tom asked.

"The embassy has both *functions* and *issues*," Gwen said. "They do routine business with U.S. citizens and interface with the U.K. on a host of issues of mutual interest. Obviously, these include security and protection against terrorism. The individual who fronts that activity is from State, but his principal deputy is from the Bureau. He's also ex-CIA and it's a virtual certainty that he's still in close contact with his friends from the Company. His name is Ken Davis. We'll meet with him and he will already have talked to either the Commissioner or someone high up in the Commissioner's office at New Scotland Yard."

"And they should know if an American Anthropologist has been knocking on doors and asking questions."

"Yes, they should," Gwen said.

"Unless she's contacted a private investigator whose contacts inside the Met would stay mum (or what would they say—keep shtum)."

"Let's hope she hasn't done that," Gwen said.

SIXTY-SEVEN

They met with Davis and a middle-aged woman in a room in the Holiday Inn below Vauxhall Park, a short distance from the U.S. Embassy, in Wandsworth. "We use this place from time to time," Ken Davis said. "It offers some anonymity for the people with whom we work."

"This is Detective Superintendent Claire Harding," he said. "We've worked with her before. She leads an anti-terrorism task force for the Met that works closely with the Office of the Home Secretary."

"I used to be a fairly good street copper," she said. "For my sins I've been given a new title and a new role. I'm anxious to help you in any way that I can."

Tom and Gwen introduced themselves and Gwen asked the first question.

"We're looking for an American named Nathan Fox. He has changed his name, legally, to Nathaniel Cox. We believe that he has been working with Mahmud al-Barada and Hakim Abbas, who recently attempted to detonate a bioweapon at Whiteman Air Force Base."

"Yes, I've received some information on him from Ken," Harding said. "He's a surgeon and you believe that he arranged treatment for Abbas."

"Yes," Gwen said.

"We've just received a photograph," Harding said, "and we're combing through security camera images. The suspicion is that he traveled to London from Toronto. We have your timeline from the FBI and we have access to materials from Pearson International as well as from the UK."

"You've been burning the midnight oil," Tom said.

"Yes, well, what is it now on your body clock, Lieutenant—two or three in the morning? We need the coffee as much as you do."

"There's an additional issue," Gwen said. "After Fox secured a surgeon to perform a laparoscopic procedure on Abbas for stomach cancer, we believe that he attempted to murder the surgeon, a former rival of his. The surgeon was returned to California after the procedure and left by the side of the road with a significant case of alcohol poisoning. The surgeon was a teetotaler. He remained comatose for several days, but eventually emerged from it and is now well. Nathan Fox had assaulted his wife several years earlier and the surgeon forced Fox to leave the city in which he was then practicing. Fox chose him to do the surgery on Abbas because of his skill, but he then, we believe, poisoned him in order to secure revenge for the surgeon's earlier actions against him. The surgeon's wife died; he remained single for many years and he now has a girlfriend who sat with him while he was comatose. She knows of his relationship with Fox and has now come to London to find him. She left the day before we did."

"That complicates things a bit," Harding said. "You *will* give me the information concerning her …"

"Of course," Gwen said. "Her name is Sally Cornell; she's an anthropologist at the University of California, San Diego."

"The surgeon emailed me a picture," Tom said. "If you'll give me your email address, I'll forward it to you."

"Thanks," Harding said. "I wonder if she's contacted the Yard. She could hardly find this man Fox on her own in greater London."

"We don't know," Tom said. "Our best guess is that she might have contacted a colleague at one of the London universities and asked that person to put her in contact with someone in law enforcement. She has no known relatives in the UK, but she doubtless has multiple colleagues in its social science departments."

"Good idea," Harding said. "I'll check to see if there have been any enquiries. Do we know what flight she took?"

"Actually, I just received an email on that from the Bureau," Gwen said. "She took a United shuttle to San Francisco and then a United flight to Heathrow from there. I'll jot down the information for you."

"Thanks," Harding said. "I don't like having civilians in the way. They can be hurt. They can also be *used*. They complicate things unnecessarily." She paused before resuming. "There's something else that I haven't told you about yet ..."

"I'm already aware of what Claire is about to tell you," Ken Davis said, as he pushed back from the table and stood up. "I'll let her continue. I have to get back to the Embassy and deal with other things. If we can help in any way, please contact us. In the meantime, you can work with Claire directly and she'll keep us apprised of any developments. Good luck." He took his coffee cup with him as he left.

"Yes ..." Harding continued. "We have picked up some information, part of it through internet sweeps, part of it through a confidential informant ... there is evidence to support the belief that we are about to be subjected to an attack. It is likely but by no means definite that the attack will come in London. It is also likely that the attack will come soon."

"*Soon* as in days, weeks or months?" Tom asked.

"*Soon* as in days or hours," Harding answered.

"As part of a coordinated scheme?" Gwen asked. "Something linked with the attack on Whiteman?"

"It sounds more like reprisals for the failure of the attempt on Whiteman," Harding said.

"So there are members of the Abbas group alive and well and operating in London," Gwen said.

"Oh yes. And my guess is that they'll be interested in your Dr. Fox."

"Thinking that he betrayed them in Missouri," Tom said.

"Yes. Of course, they couldn't be sure, but as I said, they'll be interested in discussing the matter with him. At length."

"And he'll be interested in talking with them because it's unlikely that he's received full payment for his services," Tom said.

"I think he must be a fool," Harding said. "If I were him I'd be hiding under a rock somewhere."

"That would be his native habitat," Tom said. "The problem is that fools can be dangerous."

"Very," Harding added.

SIXTY-EIGHT

"The traffic has been intense for the last eight hours," Harding said. "Most of it involves code, but we caught references here and there to your B-2 bombers and al-Barada, who has been elevated to the rank of martyr even though he remains very much alive by all accounts. There is talk of reprisal, but it is generally couched in metaphor. 'They' will feel the sting of the scorpion's tail; 'they' will be bathed in blood and taste death … the usual rants."

"What form do you expect the reprisal to take?" Tom asked.

"Very difficult to say," Harding responded. "Last time they attacked ground transportation systems. It's not enough for them to simply inflict pain and cause death; they want to instill terror. They want people to feel helpless and trapped. We stood up well that time. We caught them almost instantly and carried on as if little had happened."

"The trick is to take away their headlines and deprive them of anything approaching fame or glory," Gwen said.

"Quite," Harding said. "The afternoon press helps by running the bank of blank-stare pictures. Mouths gaping, unkempt beards, dead eyes. A moment of notice for an afternoon or two and then a very long stay in a small prison cell."

"The problem is that there are so many possible targets," Tom said. "The city is vast in both size and scope. With relatively few large buildings the population density is reduced but it's spread across a broad landscape and that landscape is filled with signature structures of historic and cultural value. At any moment there are groups of individuals in theatres, museums and other tourist venues. You have a monarchy which could be struck as well as a parliament and weapons could be brought in by boat as well as by aircraft, trains or automobiles. The cameras certainly help and the fact that driving in the inner-city requires a toll and, usually, a prior internet registration creates a nice obstacle, but the challenges remain enormous."

"Yes," Harding said, "and one cannot become comfortable because of the fact that communities concentrate in specific locations. There may be a large number of Middle Easterners, for example, in certain sections of London, but all are free to come and go as they please. Weapons can be disassembled and divided among a group of individuals, all of whom converge on one or more points from multiple directions. For those reasons, we rely upon informants, many of whom have been quite helpful, and not just moles within the cells. We also hear from British citizens, from pensioners and walkers, individuals exercising dogs or pushing prams. Local PC's know their neighborhoods and talk to their residents. We're not at all defenseless, though it's fair to say that we are often stretched."

"But they've also positioned members of a specific terrorist group hundreds of miles from the target and then assembled them at the last moment," Gwen said.

"That's true," Harding said.

"Have any specific targets been identified in the last few hours?" Tom asked.

"There has been talk about striking the wealthy and powerful, but London is an expensive city, as I'm sure you're aware. The wealthy and powerful can be found nearly everywhere, from the flats of Chelsea to the boxes in the Palladium or the Opera House, the balconies in the Royal Albert Hall and the dining rooms in Park Lane Hotels. The shops in Old Bond Street, in Jermyn Street, Sloane Square, Savile Row, the Burlington Arcade, Selfridge's, Harrod's, Fortnum & Mason's, Harvey Nichols ... it goes on and on: the Tower, the Greenwich Observatory, Canary Wharf,

Covent Garden, the Tate, the B.M., the National Gallery, the Pall Mall clubs, Leicester Square, St. Paul's, the Abbey, Somerset House, the Cabinet War Rooms, the Banqueting House, the RSC and the Barbican; Victoria, Waterloo, Paddington, Charing Cross, King's Cross … there is *not* a dearth of targets."

"Not to mention millions of people," Tom said.

Before Harding could respond her cell phone twitched. "Excuse me," she said, clicked to accept the call, identified herself and then listened for the message. After she clicked off she put her phone on the table beside her coffee cup.

"That's not terribly helpful," she said. "Fox (calling himself Cox) came in on an Air Canada flight and was filmed at Heathrow. He was seen heading for a taxi queue, but has not been identified since. Dr. Cornell was filmed as well, after arriving on her United flight. She was also seen at her terminal Assembly Point, but she simply passed through it; she was not meeting anyone. She was then identified heading for a taxi queue, but there have been no further sightings since her arrival. What do you yanks say—the gang's all here? *Here*, unfortunately, is somewhere on our island, probably somewhere in our capital city.

"We are not, however, without a little joy. We *have* identified the approximate location of Hakim al-Barada's new property in London and we hope to identify the specific location presently."

"Near Marble Arch?" Gwen asked.

"No," Harding said, "a tad more upscale, close to your former embassy building."

"In Mayfair," Tom said.

"Yes. We have him on camera on at least six occasions, all within a block or two of Berkeley Square. His wife is with him in three of the pictures and in two they're carrying shopping bags, so it's very likely that they were living nearby. We're analyzing the pictures and studying the directions in which they're walking in an effort to narrow down the location of their house or flat, most likely a flat. We'll then look at specific locations and distinguish between residential properties and commercial properties and see which properties have been let and which are occupied by permanent residents. We'll find the specific property; I have no doubt of that."

"And it's quite possible that Fox would have met with Abbas there," Tom said.

"More likely than not," Harding said. "There would have been no reason to meet anywhere else. A more public location would have involved a greater risk of exposure. I have to say that I'm somewhat surprised by this particular location, but on second thought it may have been a good one for them, given their purposes."

"Could you expand on that?" Gwen asked.

"Of course. This is very expensive property with expensive commercial establishments. There is pedestrian traffic, to be sure, but not the hordes of individuals that one would find on Oxford Street or, to a lesser degree, Piccadilly. There are, to put it simply, fewer places in which one might hide or pass unnoticed. On the other hand, it is a rather unlikely place to locate if one were a Middle Eastern terrorist or the cousin of such an individual ..."

"So that one could hide there in plain sight," Tom said.

"Yes, or dress as a wealthy businessman on the one hand or a deliveryman on the other and pass unnoticed," Harding said.

"How is he dressed in the photographs?" Gwen asked.

"I haven't seen them yet. They're emailing them to me," she said.

"On the other hand, he would only be a short walking distance from Marble Arch and the residential properties in that area," Tom said.

"Twenty minutes, perhaps," Harding said.

"With shops and restaurants and hotels in between."

"Yes," Harding said. "A Berkeley Square location would separate him from the rest of the community but not isolate him from it. And with all of the shopping venues on Oxford Street there would be a nearly limitless set of locations for quick meetings or the exchange of documents."

"So that once we have identified the location of Hakim's property we can place it under surveillance," Tom said.

"Yes."

"And if it is unoccupied, search it and install listening devices?"

"Of course," Harding said.

SIXTY-NINE

"Mount Street?" Tom said. "Between the old embassy site and Berkeley Square?"

"Yes," Harding said. "It makes a great deal of sense, when one thinks about it. The street is filled with posh shops: art galleries, antique dealerships, restaurants , even a nice butcher's shop, if you're interested … on Berkeley Square book dealers and private clubs, automobile dealerships, small casinos, florists, small grocers' shops … during the day it's bustling, with steady pedestrian traffic and heavy vehicular traffic from shoppers' and deliverymens' vehicles. At night, things quiet down, particularly on Mount Street. The shops all close and the restaurant patron traffic is predictable, 'cyclic' if you will. It's safe and quiet … you'll see the occasional couple walking after dinner and, of course, the local residents, though they are relatively few in number. The flats are smallish and very expensive …"

"*Pieds à terre,*" Gwen said.

"Yes, in many cases," Harding said. "The larger places are on Farm Street and Hill Street … many more permanent residents there. On Mount Street you can slip in and out during the day and hardly be noticed. In the evening, any surveillance vehicles would be obvious because of the nature of the neighborhood."

"And if Hakim's wife took off her hijab and substituted a Hermès or Gucci scarf, she could pass unnoticed," Tom said.

"Have you been intercepting my email?" Harding asked. "Here …" She put some photographs on the table of the tea room in which they were meeting. Most of them were of Hakim al-Barada. He was dressed in a smart business suit. His facial hair had been shaved and he was wearing a soft fedora.

"Just another member of the idle rich," Tom said.

"Yes, quite," Harding said. "Look at Munirah. That purse would cost at least £2,000 in a New Bond Street shop and the scarf looks like Hermès to me."

"And if this makes any sense ..." Tom said, "she's relating to him in western fashion. Look at her eyes. Look at the positioning of her hands. This is your average rich couple, off for a day of shopping and a lunch with expensive wine."

"How long did they occupy the flat?" Gwen asked.

"Three months. It let by the month but there was a mandatory six-month minimum. They paid in advance and then abruptly abandoned the property along with the rent for the remaining three."

"Has it been rented again?" Tom asked.

"No. One of my DS's spoke with the estate agent who handles the property. He said that the owner is considering occupying it for a month or two, so there've been no adverts on it; it's currently vacant."

"Can we see it?" Tom asked.

"In an hour," she said. "The estate agent is showing one of his other properties. As soon as he's finished he'll give the key to the flat on Mount Street to my DS and we'll meet him there."

"Any word on Sally Cornell?" Tom asked.

"Not a great deal," Harding said. "We've checked with the local universities as well as with the people at the Yard. No one has seen her or heard from her. We *have* located her hotel, however. She's staying at Bailey's in Gloucester Road. She registered there with a VISA card. Unfortunately, she's out now. She did take breakfast there this morning, but then she left. I have a WPC there, waiting for her when she returns. She'll call me the minute she makes contact with her."

"Remind me of that location," Tom said.

"Kensington. Just across the street from the Gloucester Road underground station."

"Piccadilly line?"

"Yes. Four stops to Green Park. She's ten or fifteen minutes away. Or could be. We've no idea where she actually is now."

"Any word from the people at the hotel concerning her comings and goings?" Gwen asked. "Local or long distance phone calls?"

"No, unfortunately no one saw her leave. And there were no phone records beyond a routine call to housekeeping," Harding said. "Very few use hotel phones these days; they all use mobiles. She ate breakfast early. She was finished and had left the dining room by 8:30. My WPC did a quick inspection of her room. Nothing remarkable there. No notes on the hotel notepad, for example."

"All done electronically now," Tom said.

"Yes, I'm afraid so," Harding said. "But there were no weapons, no blood, no sign of violent activity or anything like that."

"Camera images from the area?"

"No, not yet," Harding said.

The flat on Mount Street was two floors above the street level, the 'second' in British parlance rather than the 'third' in American. It was small—no more than 1,200 square feet—but very nicely 'fitted' as Harding commented: expensive drapes and bedclothes, antique furniture, marble, granite and imported stone in the mini-foyer, kitchen and bathroom. The rent was £12,000 per calendar month.

The drawers were all empty, as was the medicine chest in the bathroom and the cabinetry in the kitchenette. "We can do a forensic sweep," Harding whispered. "I'm not sure what we would learn, but it would be useful to have a record of fingerprints in case we need to prove that certain individuals were here."

"This is interesting," Tom mouthed.

"What?" Gwen gestured.

"Here," he waved. He was on the floor, looking at the lower frame of a table next to the 'lounge' (or living room) couch. He wasn't touching anything, even though he was wearing clear plastic gloves.

"Listening device?" Harding gestured.

Tom nodded, Yes. He used his index finger to indicate the location and then positioned his thumb and index finger to indicate how small the device was. The three of them moved to a tiny porch off of the kitchenette.

"It would appear that someone did not trust the al-Baradas or, at the least, thought it might be useful to check on them from time to time," Tom said.

"This is interesting as well," Harding said, indicating a kind of polish running the length of the door frame. "I doubt that the forensics team will find much here."

"Furniture polish of some sort?" Gwen asked.

"Yes, all along the door frame and around the knob. There's a slight citrus scent. When the flat was vacated it was wiped down, very carefully."

"They had things to hide," Tom said. "We already knew that. Now we need to know the specifics and it doesn't look as if they've made it easy for us."

SEVENTY

"How powerful do you think that transmitter is?" Tom asked.

"Maybe good for a couple hundred yards," Gwen said. "It would have been monitored from the street, in all likelihood, unless, of course, there was someone in a nearby apartment."

"We'll check," Harding said. "There's no one on our current watch list who lives in this immediate area, but someone new could have moved in, either permanently or temporarily."

"Clarify the cell relationships for me," Tom said.

"You mean who was a member of what," Harding said.

"Yes."

"The Abbas cell is the key group. Mahmud al-Barada appears to have been an active member. Hakim al-Barada's relationship is more shadowy. We have proceeded on the assumption that he was a collaborator, an *enabler*, if you wish, but not an active terrorist. The al-Barada family has some oil wealth, but most of their wealth was earned by their father, who was a contractor. Mahmud is now a putative student, but actually an active terrorist. Hakim is older. He looks after the family money and spends time in London. Some of the Arabs come to London to play. They dress in Italian couture, go to local dance clubs and do things that they can't do at home.

"Hakim was here, we believe, to oversee investments. Not that he doesn't enjoy London night life, but he *is* married and is seen frequently in his wife Munirah's company. There appears to be real affection between them. So he's here, by and large, to work and sometimes to play.

When Mahmud needs him, or his flat, he makes himself available. He is supportive of their activities, but he does not participate directly in them."

"And they're keeping tabs on him with the transmitter, just to make certain that he doesn't stray from the plantation," Tom said.

"Stray from the plantation? I like that," Harding said, "and yes, that's what they seem to be doing."

"How many other men in the Abbas cell?" Gwen asked.

"We're really not certain," Harding said. "From the level of email and cell phone traffic we think it's a relatively small group, perhaps no more than five, but individuals come and go. They have different specialties and different assignments. We have photographs of him in the company of at least four different individuals, but photographs are very limited ..."

"Unless the cameras are monitored constantly, you only know what *happened*," Tom said, "not what *is* happening."

"Yes, unfortunately. The images are found, but the individuals have since moved on. The system is very efficient *after the fact*. If a crime occurs we can quickly reconstruct the scene and determine who was in the area, but terrorist crimes are separated by months and, usually, years. Meanwhile, we observe the presence of individuals, but without an actual crime we can't prosecute them and we're hesitant to question them because they would then know that we're aware of their presence. Basically, we seek to contain them—to identify their presence, to find their physical locations, to trace their associations, to intercept their communications.

"Abbas was most frequently seen in the Bayswater area, two underground stops from Marble Arch on the central line. A *straight shot*, you yanks would say."

"Lots of international restaurants in Bayswater," Tom said. "Convenient for meetings."

"Yes," Harding said. There are restaurants around Marble Arch as well, of course, but our guess is that he moved along the north side of the park, through the Lancaster Gate area ..."

As she spoke her cell phone twitched. "Excuse me," she said. The call was from one of her assistants. As she spoke Gwen left the porch and continued to search Hakim's flat while Tom stood at the side of the window in the lounge, looking out onto Mount Street and checking lines of sight.

"Well, we have something," Harding whispered, taking them back to the porch. "I'm not quite sure what it is, but it doesn't sound good."

"What is it?" Tom asked.

"A name for their operation; at least that's what we think it is. It was obtained by an informant, whose Arabic is better than his English. Phonetically he came up with something roughly approximating *Ickaruse*."

"Icarus," Gwen said.

"So we believe," Harding said.

"The son of Daedalus, escaping Crete using wings fashioned by his father," Tom said. "He was told not to fly too close to the sun or to the sea. He had such a good time flying that he forgot his father's warning. The wax holding the feathers and wings together melted from the heat of the sun and he fell into the sea ... well, *that's* clear enough."

"What do you mean?" Harding asked.

"Fliers enjoying themselves, not paying attention to threats or warnings. Suddenly they fall out of the sky."

"They weren't happy when we foiled their 2006 plot," Harding said, "liquid explosives on trans-Atlantic flights to America. This could be a form of revenge for our success then as well as for the Americans' success now."

"Smuggling explosives aboard a plane ... that's a lot to plan," Gwen said. "If the action being contemplated now is in reaction to the failure at Whiteman, it must have been in the works for a long time. It's not something that you could throw together in a matter of days. Then again, it could be something simpler but just as nasty."

"Like a surface-to-air missile," Tom said.

"Yes, I don't even like to think about that," Gwen said.

"It's not as if we haven't anticipated the use of such a weapon," Harding said. "The area around Houndslow is under constant observation, but it's impossible to keep every possible flight path covered. The MANPADS are particularly difficult."

"Man-portables," Tom said.

"Yes. And sometimes carried by vehicles. Soviet versions are still common in their client states," Harding said.

"Perhaps Mahmud and Abbas can help us with this," Gwen said. "I'll put in a word. We can add it to the list of questions for their interrogators."

"Good idea," Harding said.

"Well, this *is* interesting," Tom whispered, as he returned to the window."

"What's that?" Gwen gestured with her hands.

"Sally Cornell," he whispered. "She's standing in the alleyway across the street."

SEVENTY-ONE

Tom hurried across Mount Street, with Gwen and Claire Harding following. When he reached Sally she acknowledged him verbally but didn't move.

"Hello, Tom," she said. "You should move back into the shadows. I don't want to be seen speaking with you or with Special Agent Harrison."

"By whom, Sally—Fox?"

"Of course. He came by yesterday at about this time, but I was unable to get to him. I was just coming up the street when his taxi arrived. He jumped out, rang the bell, waited, rang it again and then began pounding on the door. He was very agitated. By the time I got to where I'm standing now he had gotten back into the taxi and left. He was gesturing wildly inside the car, giving orders to the driver."

"How long have you been watching this place?" Tom asked.

"From the moment I arrived in London. I can't observe all day because it would be too obvious. I try not to be away for more than a few minutes. There's an office building in Berkeley Square with a public toilet and I can get water and baguette sandwiches from the mini-market on the south side of the square."

"But how did you know about this place?"

"This is the flat rented by someone related to the terrorists. He's just abandoned his lease and gone."

"I understand that," Tom said, "but how did you find out about it?"

"I just called Clifford Gates and he gave me the location."

"Clifford Gates?"

"The rental agent. He handles apartment rentals all over London. When we come here for conferences or to work at the British Library, he finds us inexpensive places to stay. Inexpensive by London standards, at least. He knows all of the estate agents. They trade information and share fees. We've used him for years."

"So you told him about the events in America."

"Yes. I gave him the general information and it was easy for him to do the rest. It would have been much more difficult if the man—al-Barada-- had owned the property or was borrowing it from someone else, but when you limit the search to an upscale area in or near Marble Arch and you're sensitive to the fact that the apartment might have been recently vacated … well … it was easy. I called Cliff before I left California and he had the information for me when I arrived. Actually, he had two possibilities, but the estate agent for the first described the tenant as being in his seventies or eighties and the agent for this property described his renter as being in his late thirties or early forties."

"Hakim is 37," Tom said.

"Well, there you have it. And Cliff was obviously right, because this is where Fox came, hoping to meet with him. He doesn't know that he's left, apparently, and his relative couldn't tell him because he's being kept incommunicado. At least I hope that he is."

"Yes, he is," Tom said. He then acknowledged Gwen, who nodded to Sally and shook her hand.

"We didn't expect to see you here," Gwen said.

"So it would appear," Sally said.

Tom then introduced Sally to Claire Harding and explained to her Sally's relationship with the case.

"So you've been waiting for Fox to come by this flat?" Harding said.

"Yes, I have."

"What were you going to do if you saw him here?"

"Follow him if I could. I thought about confronting him, but I realized that he could become entangled with other terrorists here in

London and that it would be better if I simply found out where he was staying and then contacted the authorities so that they could follow him and see what he was trying to do and who he made contact with. When they learned all that they could, they would then arrest him and send him back to America."

"That was wise," Harding said. "And did I hear you say to Lieutenant Deaton that you actually observed him here yesterday?"

"Yes."

"And you're certain that it was him."

"Oh yes. Len described him perfectly, even down to the chronic impatience and the swagger. I assume that he's here to be paid … ?"

"That's our assumption," Tom said. "He might have received something in advance, but they would not have made full payment until after the operation was successfully completed. It's been completed, but not successfully …"

"I saw the report on the web … on my iPhone, actually," Sally said. "They tried to do something at an air force base in Missouri … the one where they keep the stealth bombers."

"Yes," Tom said.

"Well," Sally said, "it was pretty obvious to me that if Fox was in charge of securing Len to perform a surgical procedure in the U.S., there must have been some preliminary meeting to check the patient. If he had something that was inoperable and immediately life-threatening, there would be no need to take the next step. Similarly, if the patient simply had indigestion or food poisoning or something there was no need for an operation at all. Either way, they'd want to check first. If they had already been able to come and go in London, London would be the logical place to do the initial check. I mean … there was no reason to go to the trouble of getting the person into the states if they weren't going to do the operation anyway."

"I understand that you're an anthropologist," Harding said.

"I was," Sally said. "Lately I've been an intensive care nurse and an amateur investigator."

"And not a bad one as far as I can see," Harding said.

"Thanks. I'd rather be playing the role of an anthropologist," Sally said, "but there is absolutely no way in hell that I can let this bastard get away with what he did to Len. He came very close to killing him and as it was, Len could have remained comatose or fallen into a vegetative state. Len and Fox ... they have a history. I don't know if you're aware of the details ..."

"I'm not, but I understand the outlines of the situation. You're very brave to come here like this."

"Thank you. Can you help me?"

"I can," Harding said. "I have a PC who was a lorry driver before he joined the Met ..."

"A police constable?"

"Yes," Harding said. "His name is Ken Johns. I'll put him in plain clothes and give him one of the Met's taxis. They're actual London taxis, but with enhanced computer setups and communication devices. He can park in the area and you can observe the building with him. If Fox appears again the two of you can follow him. You will, of course, immediately notify us if and when that occurs."

"Thank you," Sally said.

"And Dr. Cornell ..."

"Yes?"

"Please don't attempt to confront him in any way."

"I don't want him to escape," Sally said.

"I understand that," Harding said. "None of us want him to escape, but there are many dangerous individuals in London, some of whom may be aware of his presence here. Since his work for them is now finished and they know that he has personal knowledge of their operatives, they're not very likely to sit down for tea with him if all he has to offer them is a bill for previous services that led to a failed operation."

"You're saying that they would simply kill him."

"Yes."

"I wouldn't necessarily consider that an unfavorable outcome," Sally said. "I'd prefer to see him arrested, tried, publicly humiliated and executed for treason, but it's unlikely that that would happen …"

"Dr. Cornell …"

"Yes?"

"They would also murder anyone in his presence and if they used some form of explosive they could damage property and kill innocent bystanders. Even if we caught them at it, they would still have accomplished a terrorist incident."

"I understand," Sally said. "We'll call you when we see him."

SEVENTY-TWO

"They'll do everything that we can't do," Johns said. "They'll check for credit card transactions, using several possible names. They'll check hotel and B&B registrations. By now the pictures of him from the states will be available to the Met. They'll be routed to all street coppers. They'll check CCTV images. Since they know that he was here on Mount Street yesterday, they'll see if they can track his taxi's direction as it left Mayfair ... basically all of the tech functions and labor-intensive activities."

"They should keep an eye out for him at Heathrow and Gatwick," Sally said. "If he figures that he's not going to be paid and that, in fact, he might even be in danger here, he'll leave. At least if he has any brains, he will. What's the origination point for the train to Paris now?"

"St Pancras station."

"They should cover that as well."

"I'll suggest that to the Superintendent. It's very difficult, however ..."

"I understand. I do a lot of European travel and I realize that there are many airports in the UK. You can take the train to one of them or drive to one of them. I suppose you can even take a boat across the channel, even now with the chunnel."

"Yes. They keep selling or reincorporating the service, but it's certainly available and it's cheaper. If money is no problem, you can take a cruise ship from Southampton or Harwich," Johns said. "It's an island, after all. If I were him and I thought that an international terrorist network was after me, I'd probably avoid all of the obvious points for ingress and egress. If we can cover them, so can they. I'd find a mountain or cave or maybe another island somewhere and make myself as inconspicuous as possible."

"Strangers in small towns are easily noticed," Sally said, "but I suppose you're right; there aren't too many jihadis or jihadi sympathizers in the Hebrides or Orkneys."

"No, at least not yet," Johns said.

"How long have you been with the Met?" Sally asked.

"Four years," he said. "Six years with the police. I began in Birmingham."

"You're from there?"

"No, I'm from Manchester originally, but Birmingham had vacancies when I was looking for a job."

"Harding said you were a lorry driver before that."

"Yes, chiefly in the Thames valley but in the west country as well."

"Which is more stressful, driving a lorry in English traffic or being a police constable?"

"It's often the same thing for me; they always want me to do the driving. You're a college don, I understand."

"Yes, I'm an anthropologist. I teach at the University of California at San Diego."

"I've never been there," Johns said. "I've been to Florida and I've been to Las Vegas, but not to California."

"British tourists always come to Florida," Sally said.

"Cheap fares," Johns said. "The traffic *there* can be stressful."

"You should try California," Sally said.

"They say that this Fox or Cox fellow was from Texas."

"Not originally. For years he was based in Philadelphia."

"That's in Pennsylvania."

"Yes."

"I haven't been there either. I was going to go to New York once, but the dates for my holiday were changed and I had to cancel the trip."

"Tell me about Harding," Sally said.

"Street copper. A good one. She came up through the ranks. One of her major cases involved a London rapist. She personally apprehended him. He didn't go quietly and she had to ... disable him. He was in hospital for six weeks afterwards. The afternoon papers covered the case for a week and a half. Two years ago they assigned her to the anti-terrorism group. I don't think she cares for it particularly, but she does the job well."

"Why doesn't she care for it?"

"I think because so much of it is administrative. Surveillance systems, data mining, CCTV image checks ... the systems are very important. She has individuals who do that work for her, but she has to supervise them and it's an endless process. Most of the work is preventative. She prefers problem solving. Not that she would ever say that, but I think that's the case. She likes to deal with individual crimes and individual criminals. She likes to outsmart them and track them and she particularly likes to arrest them ... look into their eyes ... warn them concerning their right to silence ... it's very dramatic sometimes. She likes that. We *all* like that. Anti-terrorism is a process rather than a story. If we do our jobs properly, there *is* no story. Everything *stays as it is*. Every crime and every arrest, on the other hand, is a small bit of drama. It's like a play, with the conflict and suspense and climax ... except that it's real."

"Headlines are difficult," Sally said. "In most cases we try to avoid them, but if we're successful and we draw the attention of the press it can be addictive. Once we've experienced the high ... the rush ... we want to do it again. I can understand her situation, particularly if she was involved in a high-profile case. Did you meet Special Agent Harrison?"

"The yank? Just in passing."

"She broke a major terrorism case in America. Her personal story is interesting also. She's a Native American."

"Like a red Indian?"

"Yes, though we wouldn't say it that way. She's a descendant of someone who fought with Crazy Horse. She doesn't refer to him in that way, though. She says that it's a mistranslation and that his name was actually more like 'Enchanted Horse'."

"The American press must love that."

"They do, but she doesn't like the attention. It keeps her from doing her job. The FBI wants to make her a celebrity, put her picture on recruiting posters ..."

"She and Harding would make a good team then. Harding likes to work the streets, look down the alleys and search the dustbins, frighten the rats and watch them run ..."

"Tom Deaton's a southern California police lieutenant. He works in a resort community, but he somehow manages to become involved in major crimes."

"Money attracts thieves," Johns said, "and drug dealers ... and gangs ... and organized crime."

"Yes," Sally said. "He's very intelligent and very well educated. He can do the physical things as well, but most of his work is mental."

"Interesting," Johns said. "The three of them working together ... it should be *very* interesting. Wait a sec. Look to your right there ... the man walking east on the opposite side of the street ... look familiar?"

"Where?"

"Just there, at two o'clock ..."

SEVENTY-THREE

"His name is Amraziri," Harding said, handing Gwen and Tom the photographs. "We haven't linked him to Abbas with absolute certainty, but the circumstantial evidence is considerable. They've both been seen in the same neighborhood on the same day. We have picked up cell phone traffic between each of them and a third man, presumably an interlocutor."

"Do you know the identity of the third man?" Gwen asked.

"No, but we've voice-printed his speech and we can link him with each of them."

"Middle East accent?" Tom asked.

"The conversations have all been in Arabic," Harding said.

"Tell us about Amraziri," Gwen said.

"We don't have grounds for an arrest," Harding said, "but we suspect him of involvement in multiple terrorist events. He presents himself as an investment counselor. That provides cover for his international travel, so he moves around the Middle East, through the former Soviet republics and major financial capitals …"

"Telling people to buy low and sell high, but probably also checking on weapons availability, funneling money to local cells, carrying messages back and forth and generally making sure that operations are on track …" Tom said.

"Yes, exactly," Harding said.

"And he's in London now?" Gwen asked.

"He came through Heathrow last evening," Harding said. "He wouldn't have anything in his possession when he entered the country, but he could have information on the importation of a weapon."

"Everything done by word of mouth," Tom said. "Brought in on a fishing boat … perhaps transferred from one fishing boat or pleasure craft to another, then picked up somewhere on the coast, driven to London by private vehicle--no electronic communications. Unless someone's bugged his pinstripes or is following him around with a parabolic microphone, it's a shrewd plan."

"Yes, unfortunately. He can't do it alone, however. The more who are involved, the greater the likelihood that we can locate one of them," Harding said. "If we can locate one or more, the greater the likelihood that we can prevent whatever it is that they're trying to accomplish."

"Anyone else in the mix?" Gwen asked.

"One other that we know of. A man named al-Gazri. He works out of a rug store in Audley Street, just below Oxford Street."

"Close to the former site of the American Embassy," Tom said.

"Yes, but that's probably incidental. He's presenting himself as a simple sales clerk's assistant. When you're looking at a large pile of rugs …"

"Yes?" Gwen said.

"He's the one who helps flip them so that you can see the rugs below the top rugs on the stack."

"Wouldn't tax the gray matter too much," Tom said. "Leave lots of room for other planning and plotting."

"Yes," Harding said. "The thing is, the store is a family-run business. The other rug flipper is a brother-in-law of the owner. All of the other employees are members of the family. Why invite al-Gazri inside the tent?"

"Does he have terrorist ties?" Tom asked.

"Not that we can act on. He's been in interesting places at interesting times and he has university training in chemistry and law."

"He didn't major in rug flipping," Tom said.

"No. Of course, there's no crime attached to—what do you yanks call it—underemployment?"

"Just a large, stinking pile of suspicion," Tom said.

"We have al-Gazri under multiple forms of surveillance," Harding said, "and we're continuing to look for Amraziri and Fox. We have several very good grasses (sorry; you would say *informants*) that we're pressing as well."

"Any more email or cell phone traffic with regard to Icarus?" Tom asked.

"Nothing recent," Harding said. "We've alerted officers at all of the airports as well as members of the RAF. If they failed at attacking your planes, perhaps they'll have a go at ours."

"Where would most of the planes in the UK be?" Tom asked.

"The principal station is near High Wycombe, in Buckinghamshire."

"Close to London," Tom said.

"About thirty miles," Harding said. "The station was used by the yanks during World War II. It's the sort of place they'd enjoy destroying."

"So what can we do to help?" Gwen asked.

"That's the problem," Harding said. "Most of the tasks are technical. I have a small army of police constables combing through data sets and photographs. It's what I most dislike about this job ... I'm always managing and directing when what I really want to do is get out on the streets with handcuffs and truncheons. The problem is that the bloody terrorists have gone high tech, so that's how we must find them, at least for the most part."

"It's a very important job," Gwen said. "I'm sure that's why they picked you to do it."

"Thanks. I tell myself that as well. Most of the time, I'm sorry to say, I find it difficult to believe."

"Where is their rallying point?" Tom asked. "Where have they been most frequently seen?"

"That's a long shot," Harding said, "and I hate to see you waste your time. However, if I had to pick an intersection point it would be in the general neighborhood of Bayswater Road and Queensway. There are restaurants along Queensway. Any one of them would be a possible meeting place."

"But probably not a bar or a restaurant that specializes in pork," Tom said.

"No. You would think that they might use such a place for misdirection, but that's not the way that they think."

"A kebab restaurant possibly?" Tom asked.

"Yes, particularly if it is *halal*. I can ask a member of my staff to check and see if any restaurants there advertise themselves as such. I can also show you the word in Arabic."

"And you can give us pictures of the major players," Gwen said.

"Yes, those that we know of," Harding said.

"The least that we can do is walk through the area and keep an eye out. Maybe we'll get lucky," Tom said.

"It would be better than just sitting here," Gwen said.

"Yes. I know how you feel," Harding said. "I wish I could join you. In the meantime I'll be in touch with Ken Davis. If he's learned anything I'll let you know immediately."

"Good. Thanks," Tom said. "How should we dress?"

"Smart, casual," Harding said. "Business people eating ethnic. At night, no coat or tie. A leather jacket perhaps …"

"I wish I could add a 9 mm automatic," Tom said.

"Not at this point, I'm afraid," Harding said, "even though *they* might have them."

SEVENTY-FOUR

"Is that him?" Ken asked.

"It's him," Sally said. "Big as life and twice as fat and ugly and angry. And there he goes again, ringing the bell and pounding on the door."

"He's upset … almost desperate."

"He's been stiffed for his end of the deal," Sally said. "He's not used to people telling him no."

"Now he's going to get himself killed," Ken said, as he watched Fox walk backwards into the center of Mount Street. "He's trying to see into the second floor window, but the draperies are closed."

As Fox looked at the adjoining windows a taxi swerved past him, a red taxi in this case. He stared at it as it receded in the distance. He appeared to be even more perturbed. Then he walked back and tried the bell and door again, pounding first and then pulling angrily on the polished brass knob.

"Wait a sec," Sally said. "What have we here?"

"In the doorway … to the west?" Ken said.

"Yes."

"A young man."

"He looks as if he's following Fox," Sally said. "Did you see him peek out and then go back in?"

"Yes."

"I can get a picture of him with my cell phone," Sally said. "Your colleagues should be able to blow up the image."

"Not necessary," Ken said. Sally heard a succession of clicks. "I have a digital camera built into the binocular."

"Fox is leaving," Sally said. He had his hand up as a taxi came around quickly from Berkeley Square.

"Now the boy is running toward Berkeley Square to find a taxi," Ken said. "Wait, here he comes. He told the driver to leave before he had the door fully closed."

"Follow them," Sally said.

"Don't worry, I will," Ken said.

"Where is he headed?"

"Toward the Connaught, but he wouldn't take a taxi there; it's just down the street ... turning on Carlos Place ... heading north on Duke Street, stopping, paying the driver ... he's going into the Marriott Hotel."

"Right by the old American Embassy site."

"Yes. Here's the boy now, following him in. Let me find a place to park that's out of the way ... "

"I'm going in," Sally said.

"I'm not sure that that's a good idea," Ken said. "What if he comes right back out?"

"You can call me on my cell phone."

"I could lose you. If he gets by you and comes back out I'll have to either leave you here or let him go. We're too close to Oxford Street and Marble Arch. The traffic and the buildings are too dense. He can take side streets and back streets and disappear into hundreds of different shops or flats in a moment."

"OK, we've got him for now. Let's stay here for a few minutes at least," Sally said. "I'm afraid that he may be aware that he's being followed and that he'll take some side or rear exit from the hotel. Just a minute ... here comes the boy; he's walking toward us."

As he approached the car Ken lowered the passenger window. "Are you available?" the boy asked. "I thought you might have just pulled up and your passenger was leaving."

"I'm waiting for an additional person," Ken said. "Sorry."

The boy said, "Sorry" and hurried up the street, looking for another taxi.

"He's thinking that Fox will come out and get in a taxi from the hotel queue. If he comes in right behind him he's afraid that Fox will notice him."

"I think you're right," Ken said. "Wait a sec; here comes Fox and he *is* getting into a taxi."

"They're headed north," Sally said. "Where's the boy?"

"Running there, along the side of the street … about two car lengths behind. I don't think Fox sees him. He's hoping he can find a taxi at Oxford Street."

"That'll be congested, won't it?" Sally asked.

"Probably, but there are traffic restrictions. We'll see buses and cabs. Perhaps someone will be dropped off at one of the shops or department stores. Damn!"

"What?" Sally said.

"He caught the light and crossed Oxford Street as that bus cut in front of me. OK … steady again … now George Street … Baker Street … I can't lose him now …"

"I don't see the boy any longer," Sally said. "He must have gotten caught up in the pedestrian traffic on the north side of Oxford Street."

"He's lost him," Ken said, "and we may well do so next. If he hops out and starts working his way through alleys and commercial buildings, we're stuck. He could get to Marylebone Station, to the Baker Street Underground station, to bloody Madame Tussauds or even into Regent's Park."

"Do you think he's aware of the fact that we're following him?"

"I hope not, but it's always a possibility. He seems angry, as if he's preoccupied or concerned about something. It's as if he's casting around, flailing …"

Suddenly Ken hit the brake hard and Sally slid forward in her seat, hanging on to the hand strap as well as she could. The car in front of him had stopped for a red light and he was now boxed in on all sides. "Damn. Damn, damn, damn," he said.

SEVENTY-FIVE

"Well, this is interesting," Harding said.

"What's that, Guv?" her assistant asked.

"An emailed photo from Ken Johns. A young man following Nathan Fox …"

"Yes?"

"He's the son of a carpet shop owner in Audley Street. His name is Aamir."

"The shop in which al-Gazri works?"

"Yes, the very one," Harding said.

"There's an Afghani rug in their window," her assistant said. "It's an odd color, purplish brown I think … it's filled with images of weapons."

"They like weapons, Jamey," Harding said. "They use them to defeat the infidels."

"That would be *us*," her assistant said.

"Yes, I'm afraid it would," she answered.

"Lieutenant … Claire Harding … just for your information … the anthropologist has seen the surgeon; he was being followed by the son of the rug shop owner."

"And he wasn't aware of it?"

"Apparently not, though one can never be certain."

"So they have their doubts about him."

"Yes. That would be the conclusion that I would draw."

"Perhaps we're on the right track then," Tom said.

"Perhaps."

"The question is—will they ignore him, eliminate him, or use him?"

"Yes, *that's* the question," Harding said.

"Where did the surgeon go?"

"From Mount Street to the Marriott at Grosvenor Square, then north toward the general area of Baker Street and Regent's Park and then, unfortunately, into the mist."

"He'll be back," Tom said.

"We're counting on that," Harding said.

"What?" Gwen asked. "What's happened?" She was buzzing in his other ear.

Tom clicked off from Harding and told Gwen what they had learned.

"He's staying at the Marriott at Grosvenor Square?"

"They don't know that for sure," Tom said. "Maybe he was meeting someone there. It's a major tourist venue and it's close to the rug dealer's shop and the Middle East community near Marble Arch. Perhaps they've used it for meetings in the past. Perhaps someone left something there for him."

"Maybe," Gwen said.

"What we do know is that he's unaware of the fact that Hakim al-Barada has flown the Mount Street coop. He probably believes that al-Barada is avoiding him. He's welching on their deal and that's making Fox very angry. His next step would be to find some of Hakim's other London contacts …"

"But would he know any of them?" Gwen asked.

"I don't know," Tom answered, "but the rug dealer is aware of his presence (or the terrorist suspect, al-Gazri, is and feels free to order the rug dealer's son around)."

"The rug dealer may be an unwilling participant," Gwen said. "Either way, somebody in the shop knows who Fox is. He (or they) also know who Fox was involved with and what happened as a result of their conspiracy. At this point they're simply keeping an eye on him. And as you told Harding … at least I think that's what you told Harding … they have to decide whether to simply ignore him, to clip him or to try to use him in some way. I hate this."

"What?"

"Standing around here, looking at other people eat, while there are sightings and car chases throughout central London. A *kid* is following our perp and we're walking around like beat cops."

"But it's largely a matter of luck and happenstance," Tom said. "This is the likeliest neighborhood in which the jihadis might be expected to meet; at least that's what Harding believes. So if they *do* meet here, we'll have first crack at them. In the meantime we soldier on, trying to look inconspicuous while we basically waste our time. On the other hand … we don't have to simply suck our thumbs and sit on our hands … what if we took a break and went to have a look at the rug shop?"

"Why don't you go? I'll stay here," Gwen said. "Harding expects us to be here. You can always taxi back in a matter of minutes and we'll be in cell phone contact all the while that you're gone."

"OK. I'll check it out and you can take a turn the next time."

"Deal," Gwen said.

The store was called *Oasis*, but in the lower right corner of the front window was a name in gold lettering: Azhar Karsh, Ltd. Presumably this was either Aamir's father or the name of some parent company of which *Oasis* was a branch or franchise. An antique Persian carpet hung on one side of the window. Very nice and very pricey, well above the level of quality that the mullahs allowed to be shipped to the U.S. these days. On the shelf below the front window were several small prayer rugs and just beyond the front door was a 6' x 9' Afghan war carpet. The shop was narrow, but deep. Tom found his way to the alleyway behind and made some eyeball measurements, calculating that there was an enclosed space behind the showroom that was equal to it in size, more than adequate to hold a bathroom, accounting area and additional storage space for multiple stacks of rugs. Or living space. Or a significant cache of weapons.

There was a window approximately seven feet above ground level in the space at the rear of the shop, but Tom was unable to hear any voices inside or the sound of any work being done. When he returned to the front of the shop he saw a single individual standing in the shadows behind the carpet displays, a Middle Eastern male at least forty years of age. The proprietor, Tom assumed.

He found a tearoom with a decent line of sight to the shop, where he scanned a newspaper and nursed a cup of black coffee for the better part of an hour. Only one client came to *Oasis*, a smartly-dressed woman with an expensive hairdo, accompanied by a driver in a business suit. The two went into the shop and the driver emerged first, carrying a rolled carpet that Tom estimated to be four to four and a half feet in width. The roll was very large. Possibly a hallway runner of some sort, Tom thought. The man he assumed was the proprietor walked the woman to the door. Each was holding some paperwork and the man was bowing politely, thanking the woman for her business. When she left, Tom got another cup of coffee and the man in *Oasis* returned to the shadows at the rear of the showroom.

SEVENTY-SIX

"It almost seems pointless to return to Mount Street," Sally said.

"I know," Ken answered, "but it's where Harding will expect us to be. Even if Fox doesn't return until tonight or tomorrow, someone else might show up, the way the carpet dealer's son did."

"Aamir ... what is it--Karsh?"

"Yes."

"Good legs. Good stamina. He may need it if he has to get away from that al-Gazri character. Of course, they may all be members of the same extended family."

"Hard to say," Ken said. "Sometimes the locals are complicit in the terrorist activities; sometimes they go along with them because they're afraid of what might happen to their relatives back in the home country if they don't. At this point we don't know enough about any of them to say. All that we know is that al-Gazri's presence is very suspicious and that there is some connection between Hakim al-Barada, Nathan Fox and someone in the carpet shop."

"Fox is here for the money," Sally said. "He's a creep, a slug. He's not interested in international terrorism; that would require him to show allegiance to something beyond himself. He was willing to seek revenge against Len because Len humiliated him and hurt him in his pocketbook, but that's as far as he would go. Everything with him is either ego or money. He keeps turning up at al-Barada's door to collect his cash. He might even demand interest. The idiot doesn't know that al-Barada's already left the building, but he continues to fume and flail."

"Loudly," Ken said.

"Yes, always," Sally said. "He's a blowhard, a bully. When he attacked Len he had help. He would never have done it alone. Len would have put him right on his ass and slapped him until he cried."

"Is Dr. Barnes that violent?"

"Oh no, he's not violent at all, but in the case of someone like Fox he would make an exception. He'd begin with words, but if words were inadequate, he'd move on from there. And if he were attacked first he would retaliate instantly."

"As would you?" Ken asked, smiling.

"I wouldn't waste too much time on the words," Sally said, "particularly not with a coward like Fox."

Before he could ask another question, Ken's cell phone twitched.

"Johns," he answered.

"Ken … Claire Harding … we've picked up Fox on a CCTV camera."

"Where, Guv?" he asked.

"Shepherd Market. He may just be having a late lunch or he may be meeting someone."

"Which restaurant, Guv?"

"He was photographed just outside the Kings Arms pub, but he could be in any one of a number of places."

"We're on our way, Guv."

"Fox?" Sally said.

"Yes, in Shepherd Market, just a few blocks away. We'll drive, park and then walk. It's the original site of the fair from which Mayfair takes its name. They closed it in the eighteenth century and the area was developed by a man named Shepherd. It's now known for its shops and restaurants."

"Oh yes, I ate there several years ago," Sally said. "At a place called *Tiddy Doll's*. It was named for the Frenchman who sold gingerbread at public executions."

"Closed now, I'm afraid," Ken said.

"The food wasn't anything special, but there was a man there who sang Gilbert and Sullivan and played music hall songs on the piano. It was fun."

"There it is," Ken said. "The Kings Arms Public House. Very nice."

"Someone should stay outside, in case he's not in there," Sally said. "Why don't you go in and order a drink. You'll draw less attention than I would."

"Oh? I'm sorry to hear that."

"You know what I mean."

"Of course," Ken said.

He came back out ten minutes later, the slight scent of beer on his breath.

"No orange juice?" she asked.

"Implausible," he said. "I just had a half pint."

"Is he there?"

"He is. Working his cell phone with his left hand and his fork with his right."

"So he's alone."

"Yes, for the moment."

"What is he eating?"

"It looked like chili con carne on rice."

"With a drink?"

"Yes, a pint."

"He's stressed and needs comfort food," Sally said. "This time we won't let him get away from us."

SEVENTY-SEVEN

"Was he talking on his cell phone?" Sally asked. "I couldn't see from my angle. He may have been listening to someone at the other end or perhaps just surfing."

"He may just be calling al-Barada's number. We should get closer ... see if we can overhear him talking. I'm going in."

"He's hitting the numbers as if he's poking a subordinate in the chest," Sally said, on her own cell phone. "He's angry and frustrated. Now he's stabbing at his food as if it's trying to escape."

"He's still trying to reach al-Barada," Ken said. "Wait ... just a sec ..."

"What is it?" Sally asked.

"The boy who was following Fox earlier ..."

"Yes?"

"He's coming down the street, toward the pub. See if you can get closer to Fox."

Sally carried her glass of orange juice to a table adjoining Fox's. She set it down and began rooting around in her purse, as if she was preoccupied and had other things to do than pay attention to him. She then removed a pocket calculator and began to enter numbers in random order. She punched function keys and stared at the calculator as if it was a genie that could answer all of her wishes and solve all of her problems.

Aamir entered the Kings Arms, looked around and then joined Fox at his table. Fox asked him if he wanted something to drink and Aamir said no. "I received your call," he said. "What do you need from me?"

"I wanted to speak with your father," Fox said. "His friend told me that he could help me with my problem."

"Your problem?"

"His friend and I had an agreement," Fox said.

Sally continued to work at her calculator, pausing momentarily to take a sip of her orange juice.

"That is between you and my father's friend," Aamir said.

"The friend is no longer available to help me," Fox said. "His responsibility is now your father's responsibility."

"I don't know what you mean by the word *responsibility*," Aamir said.

"Your father does," Fox said. "That is why I need to speak to him."

"You can meet with him tomorrow," Aamir said. "He is not available today."

"What time?" Fox asked.

"It will be in the evening," Aamir said. "He will have to call you with an exact time."

"Where?" Fox said.

"He will tell you that. He keeps his own schedule. I cannot speak for him."

"Do you have my number?" Fox said.

"Yes, from when you called me earlier."

"I was calling your father," Fox said.

"Well, I have it," Aamir said, "and I will give it to my father so that he can call you. He will do so. You must be patient. And you should not eat food such as that and drink that alcohol. It is not good for you. It will not keep you healthy and strong."

"Thanks for the advice," Fox said. "Now make certain that your father calls me. I'm becoming very impatient."

"I can see that," Aamir said. "You need to relax and take care of yourself. All will be well. My father will see to that. You need to trust him."

"Just make sure that he calls," Fox said.

Aamir got up from his seat, replaced it under the table and walked quietly to the door. He walked out onto the street and hurried away, reaching for his cell phone as he turned the corner.

Sally sipped her orange juice and put her calculator back in her purse. She could see Fox with her peripheral vision. There were droplets of sweat along his hairline. He gulped his beer and slammed the glass down on the table, pushing away the remainder of his meal with his other hand.

He then got up and walked toward the sign for the toilets. Sally got up and walked outside.

"I can fill you in on what they said," she told Ken Johns. "He just went to the toilet. Unless there's a rear exit he'll be coming out soon. We should be ready to follow him."

"Did he get a good look at you?"

"No, I was sitting to the side and behind him. Aamir may have seen me, but I don't believe that Fox did."

"There he is," Sally said. "He's looking for a taxi. This time we have to stay with him."

SEVENTY-EIGHT

"He's closing the shop," Tom said. "It's not one of those 'back in 10 minutes' cards. It's a large ***Closed*** sign. He's talking on his cell phone with his left hand as he's pulling down the sign with his right."

"Just a second," Gwen said. "I've got a call coming in from Harding. I'll call you back in a few minutes."

Tom had moved to a small table outside the teashop. Shaded by a cloth awning he remained inconspicuous, but he had a better view of the carpet store. A few minutes later a van pulled up outside the door. A single man got out, locked and checked all of the doors on the van, and walked to the door of *Oasis*. He ignored the sign and knocked on the door. Tom could hear his hand strike the door frame, even through the noise of the street traffic.

The proprietor came to the door, saw who it was and opened it immediately. The two of them then walked to the rear of the shop as Tom's cell phone twitched.

"Me again," Gwen said. "Harding just heard from Sally and her driver, Ken Johns. Fox was eating a late lunch in a pub in Shepherd Market, Mayfair. The carpet dealer's son met with him there. His name is Aamir."

"The son?"

"Yes. Sally overheard their conversation and she's pieced together what she thinks has happened. Fox either met Aamir's father earlier or was given his name by the al-Baradas. He believes that the rug dealer is a potential contact for him. Either the rug dealer is one of the al-Baradas' partners or he is positioned to represent them. It sounds as if Fox is trying to collect his money and expects the rug dealer to hold up the al-Baradas' end of the deal …"

"And the boy is the go-between?"

"Fox told the boy that he was trying to reach his father, but the boy responded on his father's behalf. Fox wants to deal directly with the father, but the father's unavailable today. He told Fox that his father would speak with him, but not until tomorrow evening."

"That's interesting," Tom said. "Most of the time he just stands around in his shop, waiting for somebody to come in. He had one customer all the while I was here."

"Maybe Karsh (assuming that's the father's name) doesn't want to see him at the shop. He's setting up a meeting on his own terms."

"In darkness?" Tom asked.

"So it would seem," Gwen said.

"Anything else?"

"Not really. Apparently the boy was lecturing Fox on his eating and drinking habits. He told him to change his diet and to relax, that everything would be fine."

"And the Jews were told that the Nazis were going to let them shower," Tom said.

"Yes. Sally said that the boy was very cool. He didn't let Fox bully or intimidate him."

"Possibly because he knows what his father has in store for him," Tom said.

"What's happening at your end?"

"A guy just pulled up in a van. Even though the rug store was closed and the dealer wasn't standing by the door, the man from the van pounded on the door and the dealer appeared immediately. He let the van driver in, locked the door behind them and the two of them walked to the rear of the shop. I can't see them now because the van is blocking my view."

"Did the driver remove anything from the van?"

"No, but he checked the doors very carefully to make certain that they were locked securely."

"I wonder what's inside," Gwen said.

"Exactly my thought," Tom said. "Maybe we'll find out tomorrow night, if not before."

"I'll call Harding for backup and join you there," Gwen said.

"Not enough time. They're leaving now," Tom said. "I've got to find a taxi and follow them."

SEVENTY-NINE

Ken Johns put down his cell phone as they followed Fox from Shepherd Market. "Ready for some comic relief?" he asked.

"Always," Sally said.

"They've been able to track Fox's movements in the Marriott at Grosvenor Square."

"And?"

"He wasn't there to pick up something from his room or to meet with the members of a terrorist cell."

"He went in to use the men's room."

"How did you know that?"

"My second guess was going to be that he went to the bar for a quick drink."

"Anyway, the cameras also tracked Aamir's movements. It's clear that he was following Fox. In case we ever need it, that evidence is there."

"He's headed toward the park," Sally said. "No, wait, he's stopping at the hotel there ... the Hilton."

"He could have just walked. The traffic gridlocks because of the one-way streets and the convergence of traffic at Hyde Park Corner. It's taken him longer to drive there than to walk there. He must be very lazy."

"Yes," Sally said, "unless he thought he was being watched and he could lose whoever was following him in the traffic."

"Maybe he's got indigestion from that chili."

"I certainly hope so," Sally said. "I'm sure he didn't get a look at me in that pub. I'll follow him into the Hilton."

Two minutes later she called Ken on her cell phone. "He's in residence here," she said. "He stopped at the front desk to check for messages and then got on an elevator that stopped on the 19th floor. He wasn't going to a restaurant or bar; there are twenty-eight floors, at least."

"Find a comfortable seat," Ken said. "I'll work this through Harding. If I go in and present my identification card we'll spend fifteen minutes wending our way through their command structure, trying to find someone who will talk to us. Harding can call the hotel manager and save us all of that time."

Eight minutes later he and Sally were in the office of an assistant manager. Her name was Charlotte Downs. She addressed Ken as *Police Constable Johns* and Sally as *Dr. Cornell*.

"Mr. Hampton asked me to speak with you concerning one of our guests," she said, "a Dr. Cox."

"Yes," Ken said.

"He's been in residence now for several days. He was scheduled to leave in a week, but he's just called down to inform us that this evening will be his last night with us."

"Is it common for business people to book a room for a long period of time and then leave early?" Sally asked.

"Yes, quite common. They don't know how long their business will take, so they book for an extended period, then cancel when they're finished."

"And he's definitely leaving tomorrow?"

"I'm not certain when he's leaving London, Dr. Cornell," Downs said. "This is the last evening that he'll be staying with us. He's asked the concierge if he can check out tomorrow but leave his luggage here and pick it up later."

"Did he say when he'd pick it up?"

"No, Dr. Cornell, he did not."

"We'd be very grateful for any other information you could provide us," Ken said.

"Such as?" Downs asked.

"Anything in the record at all."

"Yes, well, his room rate is £312. It includes breakfast. He's taken his breakfast every morning that he's been with us. He's been paying for his room in cash. Rare for an American, but acceptable, of course. His room has a single king-size bed and a partial view of the park. He has not made any telephone calls except to the Concierge. He did not come in by private automobile (or at least he has not asked us to park an automobile for him). There have been no special requests made of the housekeeping staff. That's all I have, I'm afraid."

"Is there a room open on either side of him?" Ken asked.

"Just a moment," Downs said and turned to her computer. "Yes," she said a few moments later, "the room between him and the elevator. I assume that that would suit your needs."

"Yes," Ken said. "That would be perfect."

"We would appreciate it if you would refrain from drilling through the wall, Police Constable Johns."

"I understand," Ken said. "I don't believe that that will be necessary."

"I'll ask my assistant to get you two keys. And you may keep your vehicle in its current location. We would, of course, appreciate your removing it as soon as you are able to do so."

Ken nodded approvingly.

"One other question," Sally said.

"Yes, Dr. Cornell?"

"Do you know what time he usually presents himself for breakfast?"

"Just one second ... " She checked her computer screen. "Between 7:15 and 7:45."

"Thank you," Sally said.

"You've been very helpful," Ken said.

Downs just cocked her head to the side, as if to say, 'I'm happy to have been of service, now please leave.'

"I'll call Harding," Ken said, as they walked to the elevator. "We have miniature cameras that we can install opposite his door and highly-sensitive listening devices for the wall. We can take turns sleeping and observing."

"Yes," Sally said. "When he leaves tomorrow, we'll be right behind him."

EIGHTY

Ten minutes after they had positioned themselves in the room next to Fox's they heard mumbling through the wall. "He's walking back and forth as he talks," Sally whispered. "His voice goes in and out."

"He's mostly listening," Ken said. "Did you hear his phone ring?"

"No, he may have it on *silent*," Sally said.

"Keep listening," Ken said, as he tightened his shoelaces. "He may be receiving directions of some sort and we'll have to be ready to follow him."

She held the open end of a glass against the wall, with her ear pressed against the base. "This isn't really working," she said.

"I'm going downstairs and get the car ready," Ken said. "If he leaves, call me and come down on a different elevator."

Five minutes later she heard Fox's door close; through the peephole she saw him hurry past her door toward the bank of elevators. Pausing a second, she called Ken. "He's on his way down," she said. "I'm right behind him."

When she got downstairs Ken was waiting for her in the police taxi. "He just left," Ken said. "If the traffic's light we'll be able to find him."

"There," he said, "he's going north on Park. Possibly toward the rug store on Audley Street … no … he's not stopping there … he's going to Oxford Street … to Selfridge's for a little shopping. You'll have to follow him. It's a maze inside, not as bad as Harrods, but vast. I'll stay nearby outside. As soon as you can tell where he's exiting, call me and I'll meet you there."

"Will do," Sally said.

"Hurry, there he goes," Ken said.

"I've got him," Sally said. "He's asking a sales clerk for information ... now he's walking ... he's ... no, he was just stopping to look at something in a showcase ... he's walking again ... he's looking around ... I don't think he knows I'm following him ... it's just compulsive behavior ... probably has something to do with feelings of guilt ... he's walking again ... he's going toward the designer section ... he's in women's accessories ... Prada purses ... Vuitton scarves ... no, wait ... he's in the Gucci section now ... he's talking to a sales clerk; she's showing him a briefbag of some sort. It's not like a hardshell briefcase. It's made of cloth, not leather. It's black ... something between a briefcase and a carry-on bag ... he's nodding approval. He's buying it. Forgive my curiosity, but I'm going to walk by and look at the display ... £1,950 ... whoa ... that's a lot to pay for a bag."

"Don't let him see you," Ken said.

"Don't worry. He's rooting around in his pocket for his wallet and credit card. She's wrapping it for him, with tissue and ribbon ... now she's putting little gold stickies on the edges of the tissue ... now into a shopping bag ... get ready, Ken. Unless he's going to buy a lot of other things he'll be leaving quickly.

"He's on the way out now ... he's heading to the west exit, near Oxford Street."

"I'll pick you up outside," Ken said. "He'll walk up to Oxford Street for a taxi ... unless he's going to walk back to his hotel ... there, I see him ... yes, he's walking south toward Oxford Street ... OK, I see you ... just wait by the door ... I'll be there in a second."

"We've got to talk to that Downs woman," Ken said, as they followed Fox back to the Hilton. "I want to make sure that no one was in his room while we were gone. I also want to know when he orders food and what he orders."

"And what kind of wine he orders," Sally said. "He may be worried that these could be his last meals."

"No," Charlotte Downs said. "No one asked for a key for his room. I'll call you if and when he orders any meals from our in-room dining service."

"Whoever called told him to buy a bag," Sally said. "They may have specified a designer bag … something that a contact could recognize rather than something generic. The Gucci bag reeks class, but it's subdued in its design. It's not recognizable from a distance unless one is using special optics and it's plausible that a well-dressed man might carry it through central London."

"From what you said, it would hold enough explosives to do very serious damage," Ken said.

"Yes, but it would also hold a great deal of money," Sally said. "He may be thinking money and they may be thinking plastic explosives. Either way, he's the bag man. That's his role. That's what they want him to be. And he's comfortable with that, probably because he thinks they're going to fill it with something *he* wants rather than something that they want."

"It wouldn't call attention to itself in the dark," Ken said, "not like those fashionable vinyl bags with the logos and designs in bright colors."

"That's right," Sally said.

The phone rang. Ken answered, "Yes?" He then began jotting notes on the tiny pad of paper next to the phone.

"He's dining in," he said. "Tenderloin of beef, medium rare, with asparagus and roasted potatoes. A small green salad with bleu cheese dressing; chocolate mousse for dessert. Very manly."

"How about the wine?" Sally asked.

"I'm not sure I spelled it right. *Calon Ségur?*"

"Good stuff. A whole bottle or a split?"

"Whole bottle, £325."

"He's worried this may be his last."

EIGHTY-ONE

"Very interesting," Harding said. "And we'll get those audio materials over to you right away. I'm still waiting to hear from Deaton. He's trying to follow the people from the rug shop. I've sent backup to Harrison at Queensway and I'll reinforce Deaton if I need to. This could all just be normal runaround, but we can't afford to take that chance."

Five minutes later Tom called Harding. "I'm afraid I'm going to need some more sterling," he said.

"Long ride?" Harding asked.

"Yes, and the driver shows no sign of a willingness to stop."

"How many are there?"

"Two. The shop owner and the driver. I couldn't get a good enough look at the driver's face and he moved too quickly to allow me to take his picture, even in profile."

"Was he broad in the shoulders with a small hump in the center of his back?"

"Yes, as a matter of fact."

"Al-Gazri. The presumed terrorist."

"I have to give him credit," Tom said. "He's driving very ably, piloting a large van through narrow streets, on the left side of the road. Probably also using his left hand to manipulate a standard transmission with multiple gears."

"Where are you now?"

"I actually knew for awhile," Tom said. "We were driving along the King's Road, past all the antique and art shops in Chelsea. We passed the Royal Hospital there and then crossed the bridge. Is it the Albert Bridge?"

"Yes, the wobbly one. Troops are told to break step while crossing it."

"It's beautiful at night though, isn't it?"

"Yes, it is."

"Anyway, we crossed the bridge, were on the south side of the river and we drove by a signed entrance to Battersea Park. We then turned right. We're now driving through a light industrial area, with some homes and downscale businesses."

"The taxi driver will know exactly where you are," Harding said. "They're actually heading toward Wimbledon. At least, that's the most fashionable section in that general area. They could also be taking that route to get onto the A3, which would take them to the M25 and beyond."

"Then I'll definitely be needing some more British currency," Tom said.

"Don't worry about that," Harding said. "The government may be bankrupt but it can always eke out a few quid for a helpful taxi driver."

"Just a second, I think we may be stopping. We're in an industrial area. Let me ask the driver … we're in Wandsworth. I'm going to pass my phone to him so that he can give you our precise location."

"Just stay there in the taxi, in case they decide to leave quickly," Harding said. "I'm on my way."

She was there eighteen minutes later. "That didn't take long," Tom said.

"We left as soon as we knew your general route and we're not in the habit of obeying all of the traffic laws," Harding said. "One of the benefits of London street noise is that we can use the siren without drawing any particular attention." She then paid the taxi driver with some form of scrip, told him that he could leave and invited Tom into the back seat of their unmarked police vehicle. Harding then returned to the passenger seat, next to her driver, a police constable dressed in plain clothes.

"Anything happen since they entered the warehouse area? You *do* know that we're in the area of the American Embassy."

"No. So far they're staying put. Unfortunately they went through the gate, which was locked behind them. They then drove around to the side of the building and into the structure itself. I haven't seen them since they drove inside. There's a glow of light in the upper windows, but it was there before they entered."

"Did the gate open electronically?"

"No. A man came out as they approached and opened it for them. They must have been in cell-phone contact."

"The warehouse is no longer in formal operation," Harding said. "I had someone check on it when the driver gave us your exact location. It was in service until about six months ago. It was used to store auto parts for mechanics' service centers in south London. Then the renters moved to Clapham. It's been available for sale or lease since then, but so far there have been no takers. It could have been leased temporarily, however. It's basically just a large vacant space with some shelving surrounded by a brick structure. We can get more details tomorrow. Right now I'm interested in what's going on inside. Is it the *Oasis* delivery van that they're using?"

"I don't think so," Tom said. "I don't know the British nomenclature, but it's not the kind of van that Americans use for small loads. I'm thinking of businesses like florists or plumbers. This was more like what we would call a moving van."

"For removals."

"Yes," Tom said. "For moving household furniture."

"That's interesting," Harding said. "They wouldn't need a lorry like that for oriental carpets. Perhaps when they were originally establishing the business, but not for routine pickups and deliveries."

"No," Tom said. "The question is, are they picking something up here or dropping something off?"

"Or just diverting us from their real operation," Harding said. "If their purpose is to bring down a passenger plane they wouldn't need a van or lorry at all. A hand-held surface-to-air missile could be transported in a golf bag. That's the problem with the bloody things."

"And we don't know what else they have inside the building," Tom said. "They could have multiple vehicles of multiple sizes and have all of them leave at the same time."

"You're right, of course," Harding said. "We'll need several teams here so that we can follow all of them, if that's their plan."

"How many airports are in the area?" Tom asked, "four or more?"

"We generally say five," Harding answered, "Heathrow, Gatwick, London City, Stansted and Luton."

Tom didn't respond.

"And there are further complications," Harding said. "Ken Johns and Dr. Cornell are following Fox …"

"Yes … ?"

"He just returned from a shopping trip to Selfridge's, where he bought a cloth briefbag. A Gucci—£1,950. It's black and it would be difficult to see in darkness but it would be recognizable by a confederate because of its quality."

"And he's hoping that they'll be filling it with money."

"Probably, but it's more likely that they would want to fill it with plastic explosive, then dress him up in his best chalk-stripes and have him stroll into Harrods or Victoria Station or, well … you get the idea."

"When is this likely to happen?"

"Fox is checking out of his hotel in the morning. He just had a very expensive dinner."

"His last supper?"

"Quite possibly, though he may not know that."

EIGHTY-TWO

"Hi, Chief; it's Tom again. I was sorry to wake you up, but now that I've been given access to a secure line I wanted to bring you up to speed on where we are. Things are moving quickly and I may not be able to get back to you until after this is resolved."

"That's OK," Chris Dietrich said. "Run it down for me."

"Fox is staying at the Park Lane Hilton. Sally is in an adjoining room with a constable from the Met named Ken Johns. He's a driver ... professional-level. Fox is checking out early, this morning actually; late yesterday afternoon he was on the phone with someone; immediately thereafter he went to one of the major department stores and bought an expensive briefbag. He probably thinks it's for money, but his handlers may have something else in mind. Sally and Ken have Met backup, so if and when Fox makes his move someone will be able to follow him."

"I'm not sure that that's a good idea, having a civilian in the middle of an operation," Chris said.

"I understand, but she was able to find him in London as quickly as the Met could."

"Well, she's anything but stupid and she's as committed as anyone could be. It's also possible that whatever Fox does will be more of a sideshow than a main event."

"That's what we figured, Chief. Yesterday, Harrison, the FBI agent and I were watching two locations. The first was a likely gathering point for cell members, in a neighborhood just north of Hyde Park. The second was a commercial storefront near the former site of the American embassy, where one employee and possibly the owner have links to the al-Baradas, their intermediaries and probably their superiors.

"Harrison didn't see anyone suspicious, but I followed two of the individuals from the storefront to a warehouse in an industrial district south of the river, near the current site of our Embassy. They were driving a large moving van. No one has left that location as yet, but the area is now filled with Met officers in unmarkeds, ready to follow them. Harrison and I are at New Scotland Yard with Superintendent Claire Harding. She's the Met's point person for the operation."

"I've heard of her," Chris said. "Don't ask me where, but I have. She's very, very good."

"Yes. We just met with her a few minutes ago. She informed us that a man named Amraziri has left London. He had just arrived a few days earlier and now, suddenly, he's gone. He presents himself as some sort of international economic consultant, but he's believed to be a weapons broker and a communications link."

"The job makes it plausible that he should travel hither and yon. What he's *actually* doing is anybody's guess."

"Precisely. Anyway, he left this morning for Paris on the Eurostar train. One of the Met constables spotted him in St. Pancras Station. We're not sure what he was doing here--providing the information on the delivery of a weapon, greenlighting a project, delivering some cash … possibly all of the above. Whatever he was here to do he's done. He's now on his way to the Gare du Nord."

"So it sounds as if everything is coming together, with the countdown clock ticking."

"Yes, exactly."

"But Fox is there, believing he's about to collect his fee."

"So it would appear. He turned up regularly at al-Barada's cousin's flat, pounding on the door and pulling and jabbing at the doorbell. Sally identified him before the Met got there. Then suddenly he stopped ringing and pounding and went shopping for a briefbag."

"He made contact finally."

"Yes."

"He's out of his depth. At least from everything I've heard about him ... he's *way* out of his depth. To them he'd be a *useful idiot.*"

"At best," Tom said.

"The last time we talked, you mentioned that there was chatter concerning a specific operation ..."

"*Icarus.* No new information on that, specifically, but no information that would contradict it either."

"Falling out of the sky because of distraction and arrogance ... that sounds pretty specific to me," Chris said.

"All of the U.K. airports have increased security," Tom said, "and the police forces are reinforcing the security personnel wherever and whenever possible. They're afraid that they may be dealing with a surface-to-air missile."

"Hand-held."

"Yes. It could have come in in parts over time. It wouldn't be hard to smuggle. There was also the fear that a weapon could have been stolen, internally. The Brits actually purchased some from the Russians--to study them so that they could combat them--but it appears that the stockpiles here are secure. There are other ways to bring down an airplane, of course."

"Like a briefbag with a little plastic explosive, leaning against the bulkhead, below the window."

"Yes. We don't figure Fox for a suicide bomber, but he could be an unwilling dupe. They hand him some 'packets of cash' with an odorless plastic surprise instead. Tell him they've sewn the money into the walls or bottom of the bag, so that Customs officials won't confiscate it ..."

"And he won't root around suspiciously, because he wants to protect the cash."

"Yes. I think that's a long shot though. They would usually plan their operations more carefully. They would never count on somebody lumbering into their cell meeting at the last minute, presenting them with a different opportunity."

"It could be a sideshow though."

"Yes. A two-fer of some kind. That's why the Met is keeping close tabs on him."

"I really appreciate the update, Tom. Anything else?"

"Not at the moment, Chief. Just a second; one of Superintendent Harding's constables is signaling me. I've got to run."

EIGHTY-THREE

PC Johns at the Park Lane Hilton: "He's eating breakfast, Guv. And then some. Juice, eggs, Cumberland sausages, a small breakfast steak, fried tomato, toast, butter, marmalade, and a pot of coffee with cream. He's reading the *Guardian*."

PC Hastings at the Diggs Buildings, Wandsworth: "No movement, Guv. No one has left or entered. The lights remained on all night. No chimney smoke. No deliveries."

PC Hubbard at the *Oasis* in Audley Street: "They're closed, Guv. The son, Aamir was in the back of the shop. No one saw him enter; he must have a flat of some sort on the premises. He came out about ten minutes ago and put the ***Closed*** sign in the window. Then he walked toward the back of the shop and into the shadows. We haven't seen him since."

Inspecteur Delacroix, Interpol: "The individual of interest—Amraziri—arrived in Paris, took breakfast at a hotel and then taxied to Roissy/ Charles de Gaulle. He boarded a plane to Dubai and is now en route. To our knowledge there were no contacts with individuals in Paris."

"Why didn't he just fly out of Heathrow?" Tom asked. "Did he expect there to be heightened security? Delays? A terrorist incident?"

"Perhaps he made contact with someone in the hotel toilet," Gwen said, "or on the Eurostar for that matter. Or with the putative taxi driver. Or at the airport ..."

"Perhaps he wants everything done face-to-face," Tom said. "He doesn't want to risk anyone cracking a cell phone communication or an email."

"He's a very elusive man," Harding said. "We've never been able to develop the evidence that would support an arrest or conviction. He takes great pains to make that difficult for us. I think it's fair to say that whatever it is that they've planned is now imminent and they're taking every precaution to maintain silence and security."

PC Hubbard at the *Oasis* in Audley Street: "Hubbard again, Guv. Aamir has left the shop by the back door and is walking south on Audley Street. PC Gaines is following on foot and PC Dillard is following in a Met vehicle."

"PC Gaines here, Guv. The subject turned left on Brook Street and right on Duke Street ..."

Harding, Deaton, Harrison and Harding's assistant, DS Ford, were following on Harding's computer screen.

"The subject is now turning right on Grosvenor Street ... and walking south again on Audley Street. He is turning from time to time to check and see if he is being followed ... he is now entering the Grosvenor House Hotel ... he is in the lobby lavatory ... now exiting the lavatory and looking around again to determine if he is being followed ... he is exiting the hotel on the west and making his way to the park ... he is now walking due west in the park ... now northwest ... he is sitting at a bench and making a phone call ..."

"Are you close enough to hear him?" Harding asked.

"No, Guv. He's on a single bench in an open area. If I approach it will be obvious."

"PC Johns, Guv. Fox is receiving a telephone call. He is covering the phone with his free hand in case he needs to muffle the sound of his voice. He is listening, Guv … still listening … he terminated the call and returned his mobile to his jacket pocket … he is signalling to the waiter … getting more coffee …"

"Gaines again, Guv. Aamir finished his call and clicked off his mobile. He spoke for about thirty seconds … no more than a few sentences … he is turning around … getting up … walking west.

"He's at the shop at the Serpentine, Guv … sitting alone … sipping coffee … I'll continue to observe and call in as soon as conditions change."

"So," Harding said, "Fox now has his marching orders, but he appears to be in no hurry to implement them."

"The fact that he has to check out at midday is no guarantee that their operation will occur then," Tom said. "I would think that they would wait for darkness, particularly given the number of cameras that can observe their actions."

"It depends on the target though," Gwen said. "They can hit an airplane in darkness or light. If they want to hit a large civilian population in central London, you would think that they would strike when the greatest numbers are there."

"Unless they're hitting an entertainment venue," Harding said.

"I didn't check the paper this morning," Tom said. "Where are the royal family today?"

"The Queen is in York," Harding said, "dedicating a new hospital. Prince Charles is in Bristol, speaking at a youth center which was made possible by a gift of funds from the Prince's Trust. The rest are either at Windsor or in the country. Andrew was playing golf this morning at Sunningdale--in Berkshire, near the Ascot Racecourse."

"Distance?" Gwen asked.

"Thirty miles or so from central London, ten miles southwest of Heathrow. He often plays early. He'll be finished before Fox has to leave the Hilton."

"And no one is likely to hold up his foursome," Tom said.

"No one else may even be playing," Harding said. "It's one of the most exclusive clubs in the world, with a small handful of members."

"Just another reason for them to hate you and us," Tom said.

"Yes," Harding said, "they're never short of reasons to hate."

"Gaines, Guv. Aamir walked up to Bayswater Road, took the tube west from Lancaster Gate to Queensway."

("That's the Bayswater area," Harding said.)

". . . he's walked off of Queensway, into an adjoining street on the west ... he's entering a building using a key. He stopped looking around when he left the Queensway tube station."

"He's probably home," Harding said. "Give the precise address to DS Ford. He'll check on it." She then handed the phone to Ford and turned to Tom and Gwen. "He's back in his comfort zone, listening to the clock tick down."

EIGHTY-FOUR

"The building is owned by a bank with strong Middle Eastern ties," Ford said. "There are no records of individual flats being let."

"They may launder money, but I doubt that they sponsor terrorism directly," Harding said. "The flat may be a *quid pro quo* for services rendered. It could also be very, very small, a simple *pied à terre*."

"And probably not a bomb factory," Tom said.

"No, they have plenty of other space for that," Harding said.

A few minutes later a uniformed constable entered the room with a tray of sandwiches. "Better that we stay together here, rather than scatter for lunch," Harding said.

Pure English fare: crustless sandwiches with an assortment of fillings—slivers of cucumber, cheddar cheese that had been grated into tiny tubes rather than served in slices, thin, faintly-pink pieces of ham and some smoked salmon. The English officers reached for the salmon, the Americans for the cheese and ham. The cucumber went last. There was also a tray with small, refrigerated bottles of still and sparkling water and small cans of cola and the carbonated lemon/lime drink which the Brits term *lemonade*. There were glasses but no ice.

"There's also fresh coffee, Guv," the constable said. She returned with it a few minutes later, setting it next to the tray of drinks. Harding nodded to Ford that she'd like coffee as she hit the lit button on her landline. A minute and a half later she replaced the phone in its cradle and took a drink of her coffee.

"Interesting development," she said. "That was Ken Johns. Fox has checked out of the Hilton, but he's left his luggage with the porter. One of our PC's was watching him carefully. He opened the briefbag which he purchased yesterday, put the newspaper in it that he was reading during breakfast and took it with him."

"So the bag was empty, or largely so," Tom said.

"So it appeared," Harding said. "Johns said that he's carrying it as if it's weightless."

"And no one was seen making contact with him?" Gwen asked.

"No, not in his room and not in the hotel dining room. The only phone call that was observed or overheard was the one in the dining room, presumably from Aamir."

"And where is he going now?" Tom asked.

"He was just leaving the hotel; I'll check back with Johns in a few moments."

"He's going into the park," Harding said. "What is it with these people—an overweening desire to feed the bloody pigeons? Johns says he selected a bench, wiped it off with a tissue, opened his briefbag and is now reading the bloody *Guardian* again."

"But he's not making phone calls," Tom said.

"No, no phone calls. He's killing time."

"Whatever their operation … it can't be scheduled for too late in the evening," Tom said, "assuming that it's scheduled for the evening at all."

"Because if he waits too long he'll have trouble obtaining transportation out of London," Gwen said. "If the operation was scheduled for the late evening or early morning he would have kept his reservation for another night at the Hilton."

"Yes," Tom said, "but he's obligated himself to return to the Hilton after the operation, unless he's prepared to abandon his luggage. Of course, he may not be aware of any operation at all. He believes he's going to collect his money, taxi back to the Hilton and then leave for one of the airports."

"Or one of the train stations," Harding said. "He may simply wish to disappear quickly, rather than give the Arabs a chance to change their minds. He could deposit the money in any bank or wire it to an account elsewhere, but it would be very difficult to do that before business hours tomorrow. If he travels by train he wouldn't need to go through the security checkpoints that he'd face at the airports."

"I wonder if he's booked a flight," Tom said, "or, for that matter, space on a train."

"I'm checking on that now," Harding said. The WPC who brought us our sandwiches is looking into it."

The WPC, whose name was Ellen Liddle, came back into the situation room a few minutes later. "Nothing yet, Guv," she said, "but we'll continue to check."

Harding thanked her. After she left, Harding turned to Tom, Gwen and DS Ford. "I hate to have to wait like this. Particularly here, inside. There's nothing else that we can do, of course, but it's still not to my taste. Hastings and Hubbard will be checking in in a few minutes …"

They checked in on alternating quarter-hours. Nothing was happening at *Oasis* and nothing was happening at the Diggs buildings in Wandsworth. Harding called Gaines at the Bayswater apartment. "No sign of movement, Guv," he said. "I have a man on the rear door as well as the front. We had a visual a few minutes ago; he appeared to be going from his lounge to the loo."

Harding thanked him and hung up the phone. "Great progress," she said. "Aamir has stood up, walked across the flat and relieved himself. I hope the experience was an unpleasant one."

Johns called back fifteen minutes later. "He's found a vendor and purchased some coffee, Guv. We're not sure where he's putting it. By our count that's his seventh cup."

"And you'll tell me when he decides to rid himself of it," Harding said.

"We'll watch him closely, Guv, in case he attempts to meet with someone along the way or in one of the public toilets."

"Good," she said, "thanks." She hung up and said, "Not exactly the sort of thing I'm anxious to recount to the Chief Constable if he asks for an interim report …"

"I'm sure we could hurry the process …" Tom said.

"How?" Harding asked.

"By telling him what the Arabs actually have in mind for him."

"Yes, if we only knew it," Harding said.

Ten minutes later a plainclothes officer came to the door and summoned DS Ford. Five minutes after that, Ford returned. "Mobile phone chatter," he said to Harding. "It could be important."

EIGHTY-FIVE

"It's basically gibberish," Ford said. "An email and a mobile phone conversation. Both in Arabic. A lot of disconnected words and expressions, probably designed to distract more than anything else. Unless it's part of a code, most is simply white noise. There were, however, three identifiable words: *Cox, south* and *Hungerford*."

"Hungerford ... the town?" Tom said.

"Possibly," Harding responded, "but there's also the bridge. You yanks may think of it as the Charing Cross Bridge (it's still called that, from time to time). The bridge between Westminster Bridge to the west and Waterloo Bridge to the east. Exclusively a railroad bridge originally. There are now pedestrian bridges on either side, the so-called *Golden Jubilee Bridges*. The name refers to the 50th anniversary of the Queen's accession, in 2002. From an engineering point of view (and, hence, a security point of view) it's a dodgy area, because the Bakerloo tube line tunnels are there as well—just a few feet under the river bed."

"Sounds like an excellent terrorist target," Tom said. "Pedestrians, tube riders, individuals on the trains in and out of Charing Cross ... particularly if the incidents could be coordinated."

"It could be coordinated if you were using a suicide bomber," Gwen said. "At least you could wait for the train on the railway bridge in the center of the structure. The tube train would be trickier, but the effects could be ... *incremental*."

"The tunnel could be weakened," Harding said, "and then implode later. The explosives would pose the primary threat, but then the collapsing bridge (particularly with a full train on its rails) would pose the secondary threat. Even if the tunnels appeared to survive we would have to suspend service on that line. That would gridlock tube traffic, disrupt train and pedestrian traffic and generally give the civilian population reason to doubt the integrity of our transportation systems. It would certainly give the jihadists what they're seeking: human slaughter, economic disruption and generalized terror."

"And in a central, high-visibility location," Tom said. "Everyone taking Thames boat tours, everyone going to the Royal Festival Hall or the London Eye, everyone walking along the embankment ... they would all see the devastation."

"Yes," Harding said, her tone very sober now. She had put down her coffee cup and held her expression of resolve.

"And *Icarus* could be a train plunging into the river instead of a man plunging into the Icarian Sea," Tom said, "although there would be other men as well. Men, women, children, pets ... everyone on the pedestrian bridges as well as on the train or *trains* above them. And if the ends of the pedestrian bridges survived the explosion there would still be people clinging to them, running toward them, screaming, trampling one another. The very definition of terror."

"Of course it could be the town to which they're referring," Harding said, "but I don't think so. Not with the word *south* in the communications. A suicide bomber would have to choose whether to cross the bridge in a southern or northern direction. The word makes much less sense in the context of a village or town. Besides, the original bridge reference was not to the town but to the Hungerford Market, which was the site of the initial station building. It *could* refer to the town now, but that's a long shot."

"Or he or she would have to be *directed* to cross along the north or along the south," Tom said.

"There is, however, the issue of Fox's willingness," Gwen said. "I have a great deal of difficulty imagining him as a suicide bomber. A fool, perhaps. A dupe … but not a willing participant."

"And there's nothing that we know of that they could threaten him with. There's no family back in Yemen or a spouse being held hostage somewhere," Tom said. "They would have to trick him in some way."

"Give him something to carry and tell him it can be exchanged for money," Harding said, "or give him the first installment of what he thinks is cash and direct him to another destination for the remaining installments. They've directed him to purchase that black bag. Now they'll tell him where to carry it."

"And rush hour might be the most opportune time," Tom said, "at least from their point of view."

"Yes," Harding said. "There are trains between Charing Cross and London Bridge, trains to Dartford, Gravesend, Sevenoaks, Tunbridge Wells, Hastings, Margate, Ramsgate … it's one of the busiest stations in London and the Northern line runs through the tube station as well as the Bakerloo, with the District, Circle and Jubilee lines nearby."

"Could you get me an unmarked motorcycle?" Tom asked.

"A motorcycle?" Harding said.

"Yes. I assume that we'll stake out the site. If we can prevent the incident, Fox and any of his handlers in the area will start to scatter. I don't want to be trapped in bus and car traffic, particularly if this all happens during rush hour. The motorcycle would give me much more flexibility to chase one or more of them through busy city streets."

"We have very nice motorcycles," Harding said, "BMW's, but we'll have to remove the police signage or they'll be identified immediately."

"It wouldn't be uncommon for someone to stop along the river," Tom said. "I could be a messenger, relaxing for a few moments after a long day's work. I could even dress the part."

"I'd like one as well," Gwen said. "We could be on either side of the river."

Tom looked at her with an expression that suggested he was suppressing the urge to ask a question.

"I can ride a motorcycle," Gwen said. "The faster the better."

"I'll see what I can do," Harding said.

EIGHTY-SIX

The late morning dragged on into the late afternoon. Aamir was still in his Bayswater flat; Karsh and al-Gazri were still at the Wandsworth warehouse and Fox had walked back into Mayfair for a late lunch at Richoux. Breakfast had tided him over nicely; he had a Welsh rarebit, a small green salad and a glass of white wine. He passed on dessert when it was offered. When he finished he walked to Berkeley Square, purchased an afternoon paper from a newsman's stall, found an open bench under the Square's plane trees and proceeded to read it. He still carried his black briefbag. He made no calls and did not pause to meet with anyone. There were only two significant details concerning his behavior: he was moving south, toward the river and when he left his lunch table to visit the men's toilet he had left his briefbag on the floor beneath his chair.

"No one touched it, Guv," Ken Johns said, "no one at all. We watched very closely. We're assuming that there's nothing in it worth stealing and nothing that Fox would feel compelled to protect."

"Richoux is expensive," Harding told Gwen and Tom. "Not astronomically expensive, but it's not the sort of place where you'd worry about a bag being stolen. Particularly in their Mayfair restaurant—most of the customers there already have expensive purses and briefbags. Several."

By 4:00 they were positioned at Hungerford Bridge. Both Tom and Gwen were in leather, messenger's suits. Their helmets were locked on their motorcycles' handlebars. They ate packaged sandwiches and drank from plastic bottles of still mineral water.

Harding had positioned two teams of officers from the Specialist Firearms Command, half on foot and half in unmarked vehicles. The officers on foot carried concealed Glock 17's, while those in vehicles had both Glocks and Heckler & Koch MP5 semi-automatic carbines. Eight of the CO19 officers were equipped with sniper rifles and positioned in nearby buildings with clear lines of sight to the bridge.

At mid-afternoon a decision was made to permit railroad traffic to proceed across Hungerford Bridge and to continue service on the Bakerloo Underground line. Security was increased in both the railroad and tube stations and contingency plans were made in the event that the terrorists achieved some degree of success.

"If we halt service, they'll know that we're onto their game," Harding argued. "I don't like to jeopardize civilians, but we need to arrest these individuals and we won't be able to do that if we announce to them in advance that we're aware of their plan. We'll all simply have to be as vigilant as we possibly can and take them down as swiftly as we can once we've identified them. So far there is no indication that they are aware of the nature and degree of our surveillance efforts, so that if we maintain those efforts we should be able to anticipate their actions."

One of Harding's superiors asked if it was wise to permit the American officers and the American civilian to participate in the operation.

"The civilian is unarmed, Sir," she said, "and she understands that she is operating at her own risk. She is an intelligent person and she has demonstrated an ability to successfully locate and observe one of the individuals on the other side. That individual is also an American and, to a degree, we believe, a 'civilian'."

"But the American on our side is personally involved, is she not?" the Assistant Commissioner asked.

"She is, Sir, but it has not impaired her ability to function effectively," Harding said.

"It might actually motivate her," the Assistant Commissioner interjected.

"Yes, Sir," Harding said.

"But I suppose you've thought of that, haven't you, Superintendent?" the Assistant Commissioner said.

"Yes, Sir," Harding answered. "The thought did not escape me."

"It would not disappoint you to see her have a go at him, would it?" he responded.

"No, Sir. I must confess to a desire for justice in this regard and as you know I have had great difficulty in attempting to reduce my own regrettable reputation for responses of that nature."

"We know of your reputation, Superintendent," the Assistant Commissioner said, "and be assured that we do not consider it *regrettable*."

"Thank you, Sir," Harding said, as they all smiled.

"And you've armed the yank lieutenant and FBI officer."

"Yes, Sir, with Glock automatics."

"I dare say they'll know how to use them," the Assistant Commissioner said. "With most of their countrymen carrying such weapons, they'd better be able to."

"Yes, Sir," Harding said.

"Well then, you'd better get to it," the Assistant Commissioner said. "You *will* let us know if we can offer any further help ..."

"Yes, Sir," Harding said.

"Good luck then ... and good hunting."

Rush hour came and went and everyone remained in place but Fox, who had finished his paper, picked up another and walked into Green Park. An hour later he was on his feet, walking in the direction of Whitehall. "He may be later than we expected but at least he's not headed in the opposite direction," Harding said to Johns.

"No, Guv," Johns said, "and there's still been no contact with any of his possible confederates, either in person or through the use of his mobile. At this point he's only exhibited three things: strength of bladder, an inclination to walk in a southerly direction and an uncommon curiosity for the afternoon news."

"He doesn't expect to find himself in their headlines," Harding said. "He may well be surprised ..."

EIGHTY-SEVEN

"Hastings, here, Guv. The two principals have left the Diggs Buildings and are driving north."

"To Putney Bridge or Wandsworth?"

"Neither, Guv. They're driving in between the two bridges, straight to the river."

"In the large van?"

"No, Guv. They're in a Ford Mondeo."

"Just the two—Karsh and al-Gazri?"

"As far as we can see, Guv. No one is visible in the back seat and the boot does not appear to be weighted down to any degree."

"Stay in close touch," Harding said.

"Hubbard, Guv. Aamir just walked past the window again. He was wearing a robe of some sort and eating from a small tray."

"No indication that he plans to go out?"

"None, Guv."

"Let me know if that changes."

"Johns, Guv. Fox walked through St James Park, along the Mall, and into Trafalgar Square. He's in the Strand now, walking east."

"He's really getting his bloody constitutional, isn't he?"

"Yes, Guv. There's still been no contact with anyone and he's made no calls on his mobile. He *has* checked his watch several times."

"Are your vehicles close by? I don't want him to suddenly take a taxi and do a runner."

"Yes, Guv. Dr. Cornell and I are on foot. The vehicles are behind him as well as beyond him."

"Good."

"Where is he now, Ken?"

"On Northumberland Avenue, walking toward the river."

"He's going to the bridge," Harding said.

"It's five minutes 'til eight, Guv."

"He's missed his dinner, hasn't he? He must have other things on his mind. Stay with him Ken."

"We're on him, Guv."

"You're certain that no one has contacted him and that his bag has not been out of your sight."

"Dead certain, Guv. I'd stake my life on it."

"Let's hope that that won't be necessary," Harding said.

At 7:59 the call came in from the Assistant Commissioner. "Superintendent ..."

"Yes, Sir?"

"We've just received an anonymous call, unfortunately from an untraceable mobile. The caller said that a bomb will be detonated on one of the Golden Jubilee Bridges in five minutes."

"Could you trace the caller's location, Sir?"

"It came from somewhere above Hyde Park."

"In the Queensway area, Sir?"

"Yes, approximately."

"Thank you, Sir."

"What do you intend to do, Superintendent?"

"Hold our positions, Sir. They're calling because they wish to provoke a reaction."

"You think they want to create chaos, with officers and vehicles converging on the scene with lights and sirens and disrupted traffic."

"Yes, Sir. It would increase the size of their target. Alternatively, they could set off a small blast and then a larger one when the crowd converged to watch."

"It is often *their* way," the Assistant Commissioner said. "But you told me that this Fox fellow is carrying what you believe to be an empty bag."

"Yes, Sir."

"Then why would they draw all of this attention?"

"I don't know yet, Sir," Harding said.

"Well, that's very awkward."

"Yes, it is, Sir. Hopefully the reason for the call will become clearer soon."

"It bloody well will, Superintendent. You have about two minutes."

"Hastings, Guv. I've been trying to reach you."

"I've been on with the Assistant Commissioner, Jim. What is it?"

"Karsh and al-Gazri, Guv. They're on the river."

"On the river?"

"The tide is out, as you know, and they were walking in the gravel above the sand. They were picked up by an inflatable boat."

"An *inflatable* boat?"

"Yes, Guv."

"Did it come from above or below Wandsworth?"

"Above, Guv. They're headed toward you at a high rate of speed."

"Who else is in the boat, Jim?"

"Two men in dark suits, Guv."

"How are Karsh and al-Gazri dressed?"

"In dark suits as well, Guv."

"Then that's it," Harding said. "That's bloody it."

EIGHTY-EIGHT

Harding put down her mobile and got on the police net. "I've just heard from Hastings. Karsh, al-Gazri and two other men are approaching us in an inflatable boat. An anonymous caller, almost surely Aamir, has notified the Met that a bomb is to be detonated on the Golden Jubilee Bridge. They're expecting us to react. The boat is the key to it …"

"Superintendent," Tom said, "you're saying that they want us to believe that the inflatable is a police boat."

"Yes, from the Marine Policing Unit. They use inflatables for several purposes, among them surveillance against terrorism. Fine irony, what? The unit is responsible for fourteen miles of river, from Hampton Court to Dartford Creek. Above the Court is the responsibility of Surrey Police, below it the responsibility of Essex and Kent police."

"And where is the Marine Policing Unit based?" Gwen asked.

"At Wapping," Harding said.

"But they could be on patrol anywhere within their jurisdiction," Tom said.

"Yes, and if there's confusion and a host of people and vehicles converging on Hungerford Bridge, they could largely go unnoticed—just another team in the crowd."

"So Hungerford Bridge might not be the target at all."

"More than likely, it's not," Harding said, "and if they're successful they would have a nearly unimpeded means of escape. They could speed away from the scene, ahead of all the snarled street traffic and escape into the city from some dark corner on the edge of the river."

"I'm taking my bike down to the river," Tom said. "With the tide out I can ride on the sand or gravel."

"I am as well," Gwen said.

"Don't shoot one another," Harding said.

"There are good targets everywhere," Gwen said. "The Houses of Parliament, Big Ben, Westminster Bridge ..."

"I don't think so," Tom said. "Remember: *Icarus.*"

The sound of the boat could be heard in the distance.

"The London Eye," Tom said. "It's lit up like a Christmas tree. There are as many as 800 people, looking out over the city ..."

As the sound of the boat diminished Tom rode quickly in its direction along the south bank, as Gwen made her way to the north side.

The boat slowed to a crawl under Westminster Bridge, emerging slowly from under the second northerly arch. They're positioning themselves, Tom thought to himself. Then the facts all flashed before him ... compulsive reading of the pamphlet in his hotel room: the largest Ferris wheel in Europe, for a time the largest in the world, 32 sealed passenger capsules, each weighing 10 tons, each capsule representing one of the London Boroughs, each containing as many as 25 people--a landmark, a symbolic site ... the perfect target.

Then the crucial fact: the London Eye is still the tallest *cantilevered* wheel in the world, all supported by a single A-frame on its southern side. That's the target, he thought, not the individual capsules--shatter the A-frame and the entire structure falls from the sky; they're not coming to place explosives at the base or frighten the passengers with sprays of machine gun fire; they're coming to shoot at the point of greatest structural vulnerability and then quickly turn around and escape. We fixate on Hungerford Bridge while they come in under the radar. They're seen as reinforcements, not as the enemy. He looked at the boat more closely as it emerged from beneath the arch; he could see the simulated police uniforms. No weapon yet in sight. No matter. It won't take them long. They'll score their one significant shot, turn abruptly and leave; the rigid inflatable boat will fly across the water, slapping like a hovercraft and they'll disappear into the darkness.

"Gwen, they're going to shoot at the Eye," he said. "We'll have them in a crossfire, but we don't want to shoot each other." He positioned his bike as the boat came into full view.

"Get behind your bike," he said. "They're likely to return fire and they'll be heavily armed."

"I'm already there," she said, from the darkness.

As the boat slowed to a stop, opposite the Eye, one of the men in the boat stood up, a tubular weapon positioned on his right shoulder.

"Now," Tom said, as both he and Gwen opened fire. It was a tough pistol shot to the center of the river, but they filled the air with rounds. They saw his body jerk back and forth and heard Harding's voice over the police net, focusing the attention of the snipers.

A second man took the first one's place, lifting the weapon to his shoulder and beginning to take aim as his head exploded from the simultaneous sniper fire. Tom reloaded and began shooting at the boat itself in an attempt to disable it and prevent its escape. Suddenly the gravel to his right was riddled with shot and the fragments pinged against his bike, one of the pieces striking him in the cheek.

"The last two men," Gwen said, "with machine guns now ..." Then the side of the boat to the south exploded in a large fireball, hurling the body of the shooter into the air and covering the river with fragments of wood, metal and rubber. A weapon Harding hadn't previously mentioned ...

"The last man made it overboard," Tom said. "He's coming toward me."

Tom remained behind his bike, waiting for the man to emerge from the water. Flailing against the current and partially masked by the dark water, Tom could still see the strap of his automatic weapon slung over his shoulder. "I've got him," Tom said to Harding. "Hold off the snipers."

A full minute later the man made it to the shore, his chest heaving, his mouth gulping for air.

"Take off the weapon and throw it to the side," Tom said. The man was no more than twenty yards away, his eyes now visible. He crawled to his feet and began to grab at the weapon's strap, hoping to aim it at Tom. By now he was in full view of all of the snipers' night-vision scopes. They watched as his body jerked violently to the side, Tom filling his shoulder with 9mm rounds.

"I can hit your head as easily as your shoulder," Tom said, as the man snarled and whimpered at the same time. Then he rolled over on his back, away from his weapon and Tom was on him, kicking the machine gun to the side and searching him with his left hand as his right aimed the Glock at the center of his temple.

The man's eyes were flashing in the moonlight and the glow from the London Eye. "Calm down," Tom said. "You're going to live. We have a few questions to ask you. It shouldn't take more than five or six weeks to ask them …"

"Is everyone all right?" Harding asked.

"Yes," Gwen said, "I'm coming over to the other side of the river."

"Tom?"

"Yes, I'm fine. My friend here will need some medical help, but he should live. He's lost some blood."

"Ken?"

"Ken?" Harding repeated.

"I'm fine, Guv, but when I tried to get down to the river to back up Agent Harrison, Fox got past me."

"Where is he?"

"He was heading toward the Strand. I'm in pursuit."

"Where is Dr. Cornell?"

"She's gone after him, Guv."

EIGHTY-NINE

"She had a pair of trainers in her purse, Guv. She slipped off her street shoes and put them on while we were observing Fox on the bridge."

"Hopefully that will give her something of an advantage," Harding said. "Try to catch up with them."

"I will, Guv," Johns said and clicked off.

Harding called the Met next. "This is Superintendent Harding," she said. "We have a man in the general area of the Strand. He is being pursued by a Police Constable and a yank woman. Please do the following: block off Bedford Street and Southampton Street with marked police cars. I want to see a great deal of police presence there. Also, ask the theatres and shops in the area to lock their doors and ask the staff at the Savoy to stand in front of the hotel, in their uniforms, blocking his entrance. I want to keep him on the Strand or in the immediate vicinity. I do not want him to make his way to Covent Garden and get lost in the Market or get on the tube. I also want security forces to stand at the entrance to Charing Cross Station. The man is approximately 52 years of age, tall, stout and well-dressed in a business suit. When last seen he was carrying a black briefbag. Understood?"

"Yes, Guv," the dispatcher said.

"Tom?"

"Yes. I'm on my way on my motorcycle."

"I am as well," Gwen said.

Harding turned to DS Ford. "We'll get his attention at least. It will take Deaton and Harrison awhile to get to the Embankment and up to the Strand, but once there they'll make a great deal of noise and outrun him at every turn."

"Yes, Guv, and it's not as if he was a central part of the plot. We've taken all of the individuals who were."

"So far as we know," Harding said. "I want him as well and I'm certain that Dr. Cornell wants him even more than I do. I must tell you, Ford, it's bloody good to be back on the street …"

Sally had adjusted the strap on her purse and slipped it over her head like a messenger's pouch. The vehicular traffic on the Strand had slowed to a near stop as the police cars converged on the area, blocking points of ingress and egress. She saw shopkeepers and theatre staff locking their front doors. Pedestrian traffic had apparently stopped with the sound of the gunfire on the river, with gawkers moving south toward the Embankment in an attempt to see what had happened.

When she first saw him, Fox was attempting to gain entrance to a discount clothing store on the south side of the Strand but he had looked in her direction first, saw her running toward him and decided to continue running east. He didn't know who she was; he probably believed her to be a WPC in plain clothes.

He paused several times, looking left and right, but she was closing with him as he approached Savoy Court. He turned the corner, approaching the hotel, but then returned to the Strand and ran across the street, through traffic. He looked up Southampton Street and then turned to the left, watching a man in a white apron locking the door to the *Kimchee* restaurant. By then Sally was within fifty yards of him and he turned and ran east, slaloming through the cars gridlocked on the Strand.

Seeing police vehicles on the Aldwych he continued to run east, running past St. Mary's Church, toward St. Clement Danes. By now his chest was heaving, his mouth gulping air, his side pierced with pain. He turned and saw Sally within thirty yards of him. Then twenty-five. Then twenty.

Trying to summon the strength for a final burst of speed, he saw the line of uniformed officers approaching him from the east. Standing at the entrance to St. Clement's, below the statue of Sir Arthur Harris, he saw Sally running toward him. Thinking he might take her hostage or use her in some way to gain his release he stepped toward her, but she continued running. Suddenly, she leapt into the air, driving her right fist into the center of his face and slamming his body to the pavement.

He tried to move his legs and lift his body with his hands and elbows, but she struck him a second time and then a third, crushing his nose against his cheeks and loosening his teeth. She raised her fist to strike him again, but someone held her right arm. She turned and saw a uniformed constable. "I believe you've stopped him very nicely," he said.

"He can't be allowed to leave," Sally said, the words coming out between deep breaths.

"We have no intention of permitting him to leave," the constable said.

Just then Gwen skidded to a stop beside her, with Tom a few yards behind.

"I don't want them to let him go," Sally said.

"I don't think there's much chance of that," Tom said. "Are you OK?"

"I'm fine, just fine," Sally said, getting to her feet. "Never better."

NINETY

With Fox and the remaining terrorist, al-Gazri, in custody, Harding made initial reports to the Assistant Commissioner and Commissioner and promised the required paperwork early the next morning. An hour and a half later she joined the Americans in the Waldorf Hilton hotel bar in the Aldwych.

"What's on offer?" she asked.

"Anything you want," Tom said. "We're having Scotch."

"And Dr. Cornell?"

"A double," Sally said.

"Well, you all deserve doubles," Harding said. "By the way, there will be no problem in extraditing Fox. He won't be riding in the front of the plane this time. He'll be cuffed in the back, listening to the noisy children. No Scotch for him. Ever again, perhaps. A nice irony, don't you think? A man who tries to kill using alcohol is then deprived of it, himself. And I dare say there will be moments in his future life when he would dearly love a taste or two of it."

"Thank you for all of your help," Sally said.

"No need to mention it," Harding said. "Have you called your colleagues in the states?"

"I called the Director," Gwen said. "He's very pleased. He'll be talking with his counterparts here tomorrow."

"I called my Chief," Tom said. "He's authorized me to buy another round of drinks for all and cautioned me to avoid speaking with the press."

"They'll praise us politely tomorrow," Harding said, "just as they write about how close we came to disaster and how many individuals were inconvenienced by our road blocks. There will be letters complaining of our use of force ..."

"But not from the people on the London Eye," Tom said.

"No, not from them," Harding said.

"I called Len," Sally said, and left it at that.

"How is he?" Gwen asked.

"He's fine," Sally said.

"Was he pleased that you had caught Fox?"

"Yes. He asked if I was all right. I told him that I was fine."

"One matter has not yet been revealed to the press ..." Harding said. "The hand-held missile ... there were three found in what was left of the boat. We'll check the river bottom tomorrow, though I doubt that we'll find anything there."

"Backups in case the first one missed?" Tom asked, "or backups for subsidiary targets."

"We'll see what al-Gazri has to tell us," Harding said. "The point is that it might have been much worse than we originally thought."

"How about Aamir?" Gwen asked.

"Resting comfortably at what is commonly termed *a remote location*," Harding said. "We'll be talking to him at length. It's always so much better when we have two and they don't know what the other is saying."

A few minutes later the bartender came around from the side of the bar with a bottle in his hand. He removed the cap and placed it on the table. It was 25 year-old Macallan. "Courtesy of the hotel manager," he said.

"Please give him our thanks and regards," Harding said.

"Her," the bartender said. "Her husband and son were on the London Eye this evening. She's just learned that you were here."

"You were right, Lieutenant," Harding said. "Our work *is* appreciated."

NINETY-ONE

"I don't know why, I just felt like shrimp," Len said. "I've never been in a coma before, but it seems to have had an effect on my tastes."

"Chilled shrimp and Grgich Hills Chardonnay are no indication of illness," Tom said. "It shows that your mind and imagination have never been more healthy."

"I felt like shrimp too," Sally said, "especially with that cocktail sauce that Len makes—a little more horseradish than usual and with fresh lemon juice, not the stuff from the round plastic bottle."

"A loaf of bread, a jug of wine, thou and shrimp cocktail. How can you beat that?" Gwen said.

"The bread's from LaBrea Bakery," Len said. "They distribute it throughout the country now."

"Next to the old *Campanile*," Tom said. "Some thought it was the best Italian in L.A. In Charlie Chaplin's old offices."

Gwen nodded and she and Tom took a few steps closer to the living room window, looking out over the Pacific. The sun was golden, but it somehow turned to bright silver as it reflected off the water.

"Your new home is beautiful," Gwen said.

"I wanted to surprise Sally," Len said. "This unit was available and all I had to do was sign the papers and have someone move my things."

"A *unit* is the way Len describes a 4,000 square foot penthouse," Sally said. "That's why I love him; there's no pretense about him, none whatsoever."

"It was fun," Len said, "and I was at the point where I needed some fun. Here I was, looking for a new condo and all of a sudden these two strong-arm types interrupt my househunt. The next thing I know is I don't know anything … I'm comatose in Saddleback Memorial being fed through a tube. I didn't even get a chance to sample the rust-colored jello."

"And you still haven't," Tom said, "what with the napoleons, the tiramisu and the gelato …"

"Sally loves the gelato," Len said. "You know the difference between gelato and ice cream, Tom? Besides the reduced butterfat? It's dense. *Dense*, Tom. Ice cream has cream, milk and sugar, but it also has air. Gelato's served a little warmer too, but it doesn't have all that air. It's concentrated … it's intense."

"I love the wine," Gwen said.

"Mike Grgich was the winemaker at Chateau Montelena … when the Americans beat the French in the blind tasting," Len said. "There are no Grgich Hills. Hills is the coffee guy, Grgich's partner."

"You've really become an expert," Sally said.

"What else was I to do?" Len asked. "I'm here looking at the walls, waiting for the paint to dry and you three are running around England, chasing terrorists and Nathan Fox."

"It's not 'you three'," Gwen said, "it's 'you lot'."

"You lot," Len said, "to whom and for which, as I should have said, I am profoundly grateful."

"Len reverts to this quasi-Yiddish when he's feeling sentimental," Sally said.

"And would you rather I sounded like Yoda?" Len asked. "So, seriously now, you were chasing Fox through the streets of London … in tennis shoes …"

"Trainers," Sally said, "and I had a lot of help. The police actually surrounded him and kept him from getting away."

"And then you knocked him to the ground and struck him …"

"*Pummeled* is a little closer," Gwen said.

"Or maybe *mauled*," Tom said, "or *hammered*. Or *beat the crap out of*."

"Right at the base of Sir Arthur Harris' statue," Len said. "Bomber Harris."

"Yes, as a matter of fact," Sally said. "St. Clement Danes is an R.A.F. church. It was an IRA target for a long time."

"Dr. Johnson worshipped there," Len said. "There's a statue of him behind the church."

All three of them just stared at him.

"What? What did I say? I told you; I'm sitting here looking at four walls. I wanted to feel closer to you lot, so I went on the internet …"

"Fox is being questioned now," Tom said. "They're trying to figure out the jurisdictions. He could be prosecuted federally as well as in California, Texas and Missouri. Sally's too modest to mention the fact, but she's received a citation from the British Home Secretary as well as from the FBI."

Len put his arm around her and hugged her as Sally turned and kissed him on the cheek.

"I felt bad about all this," Len said. "I wanted Sally to help me pick the place. On the other hand, I wanted to surprise her. We needed more space and … I just thought that … if the place was ready when she returned … that … well … that maybe she'd stay a little longer … you know … if it was nice and comfortable …"

She kissed him again.

"You really like it?"

"I love it," she said, "how could I not love it and how could I not love you?"

"The name of the building is a little pretentious," he said. "They call it *Sur la Mer*, but it actually *is*, so the name is fair enough. Everybody seems to think that it's the nicest place in Newport Beach, so I figured you'd approve."

"I approve," she said. "It's a wonderful surprise. And … what? You look skeptical. Why are you looking at me like that? I'm not going to leave."

"I was just afraid that after all that adventure you might think about changing your life; maybe you'd want to join the force … taking bad guys down … hearing the cuffs snap … it could become addictive."

"It *could*," Sally said, but I'm not really interested."

"That's good; I'm glad," Len said.

"For me," Sally said, "it was never business; it was always personal."

"You did it for me."

"And for your wife," Sally said. "Don't ask me to explain that part, since I didn't know her, but … I don't know … somebody had to do this and you couldn't, so it was up to me."

"I'm glad that you did," Len said.

"I know you are," Sally said, kissing him again. "Now, about that gelato … I hope you got some coconut."

෨෨෨

www.ingramcontent.com/pod-product-compliance
Lightning Source LLC
Chambersburg PA
CBHW032048020426

42335CB00011B/233